Subversive Women

WOMEN'S MOVEMENTS IN AFRICA, ASIA, LATIN AMERICA AND THE CARIBBEAN

edited by

SASKIA WIERINGA

Zed Books Ltd
London and New Jersey

*Subversive Women: Women's Movements
in Africa, Asia, Latin America and the Caribbean*
was published in 1995 in South Asia
by
KALI FOR WOMEN
B 1/8 Hauz Khas
New Delhi 110 016
and
in the rest of the world by
ZED BOOKS LTD
7 Cynthia Street
London N1 9JF, UK
and
175 Fifth Avenue
New York, NY 10010, USA

Second Impression 1997

A catalogue record for this book is available from
the British Library
US CIP data is available from the Library of Congress
ISBN 1-85649-317-2 hb
ISBN 1-85649-318-0 pb

Distributed in the USA exclusively by
St.Martin's Press Inc.,
175 Fifth Avenue
New York, NY 10010, USA

Editing and Design by Shampa Banerjee

Printed in India by Raj Press, R-3 Inderpuri
New Delhi 110 012

Contents

Preface

Almost ten years have passed between the inception of the research project on 'Women's Movements and Organizations in Historical Perspective' and the writing of this preface. During this decade the 'progress' promised by national governments and international agencies has not materialized. Instead, there has been growing misery, with economic deterioration, devastating wars, and increasing numbers of suffering humanity.

The Somali women who speak to us in this volume with so much courage and hope are hit by the most vicious war their country has seen in recorded history. One of the authors of the chapter has taken refuge abroad, the fate of the others is unknown to me while I write these lines. Of the poems recorded by the Somali researchers, Kaha Ahmed Sara'a's *Let Alone Rewards*, composed over 25 years ago, articulates the deep sense of betrayal felt by women who had participated in the national revolution and her own fears of national disintegration. The betrayal is a bitter reality even today, and her land is indeed being torn asunder.

> My skin hangs loose on my bones
> My eyes are veiled with clouds
> Those I have led I now must allow
> To go forward without me.
>
> LET ALONE THANKS, I'VE BEEN FORGOTTEN!
>
> In the new scramble
> The people dispersed
> Grasping and shouting,
> Satisfying greed.
> And I waited.
>
> LET ALONE GIFTS, I'VE BEEN IGNORED!

Protested under the shade of our flag
My comrades shamed it,
Ignored me, did not receive me.
I was sent away empty from their homes.

LET ALONE REWARDS, I'VE BEEN THREATENED!

And I had dreamed
Somalia as one.
But no longer is Somalia one home,
Now each keep to his own.
I had filled a large *hamo** with dreams
And shouted 'Do not loosen the ropes!',
Hoping for one great feast.
But I have been cast aside,
So easily thrown over a cliff.

LET ALONE REWARDS, I'VE BEEN THREATENED!

Sudan is in the stranglehold of the fundamentalist Muslim Brothers. In the war in the southern part of the country and the raging economic crisis, women and children are again the hardest hit.

Peru, another country in which this project was carried out, is confronted by a murderous terrorist movement which has recently started killing feminist leaders.

Indonesia's military leaders have still not released their hold over the country. The small independent women's, labour and ecology groups in the country are faced with strong repression.

India is struggling with a severe economic crisis.

The economies of the Caribbean are so strongly tied to the US that life for the poor is becoming harder.

In almost all of the countries represented here, at the time when work on this volume started, the authors could hope for a better life, which seems even further away today.

This book is dedicated first of all to the Somali women who see their land daily being destroyed, whose children are dying and who are themselves faced with starvation. Let us hope that

---

*Vessel in which milk or water is stored.

after this nightmare is over they will have enough strength left to speak out their views on the reconstruction of their country. And that this time their voices will not be ignored.

This volume is also dedicated to all women in Peru, the Sudan and elsewhere in the world, who are struggling for a better future for themselves and their children.

Many people and institutions have been involved in this project. The Directorate General of International Cooperation of the Ministry of Foreign Affairs of The Netherlands provided the funds. In the beginning of the 1980s, this was a pioneering act for such a body. Our thanks to all the officials who supported us in this struggle. The Institute of Social Studies provided academic, logistic and administrative support in all phases of the project. Special thanks are due to all the colleagues of the Women and Development programme, Maria Mies, Kumari Jayawardena, Mia Berden, Geertje Lycklama, Rhoda Reddock, Thanhdam Truong, Amrita Chhachhi, Loes Keysers, Jyotsna Gupta and Renée Pittin.

Others at the ISS, who supported this project to an extent far exceeding their duties include Els Mulder, Ros Payne, Marianne van den Berg, Selma Noort and Lise Sylla.

The participants of the Women's Movements course were exposed to many of the ideas which helped shape this volume, and provided many insightful and critical remarks and observations.

During the last phase of working on this book I had the great pleasure of teaching this course together with Virginia Vargas. Her friendship, political commitment and academic brilliance provided invaluable support.

There are several others who contributed in different ways in the many years of the project and the shaping of this book. My partner Fineke van der Veen, my friends Anky Brouwer, Vera Goedhart, Marion den Uyl, Britt Fontaine, Marijke Mossink, and Lenie Brouwer, all got drawn into this project more than they may have originally envisioned.

Above all, it was the commitment of all the researchers in the various country teams, our growing friendship and our increasing belief that the histories of the movements in our individual countries can help shape the future of the entire world, which made this project such a rich and wonderful experience.

Finally, this volume should be seen as based on the collective efforts of Chhaya Datar and Nandita Gandhi from India; Julia Suryakusuma, Lies Marcoes, Dida Pattipilohi and Pamela Pattynama from Indonesia; Maritza Villavicencio, Cecilia Olea and Virginia Vargas from Peru; Raquia Haji Dualeh, Faduma Ahmed Alim, Dahabo Farah Hassan, Amina Mohamoud Warsame, Maryam Farah Warsame and Amina Haji Adan from Somalia; Zeinab Bashir el Bakri, Fahima Zahir, Belghis Badri, Tomadur Ahmed Khalid and Madiha al Sanusi from the Sudan; and Rhoda Reddock, Beryl Carasco, Wendy Rodney, Joan French and Honor Ford-Smith from the Caribbean.

SASKIA WIERINGA

1
Introduction: Subversive Women and Their Movements

Saskia Wieringa

The Institute of Social Studies (ISS) research project, 'Women's Movements and Organizations in Historical Perspective', brought together researchers from five countries (India, Indonesia, Peru, Somalia, Sudan) and one region, the Caribbean. The project was conceived to promote better understanding, through historical analyses, of experiences of women involved in women's movements in their own countries, with the aim of strengthening these and other women's organizations and movements.

No single question motivated the research process. The research teams sought separate paths on the basis of their own interests, informed by the concerns of the feminist institutions they were linked to. The findings reflect the complexity and diversity of the various movements in their different contexts. Only a part of all the richness of the data collected is presented in this volume.

The project attempted to uncover ways in which women have been stretching the boundaries of social conventions within which they are confined, empowering themselves and acting in defence of what they perceive as their interests.

The most striking finding was that women have been subverting the codes determining the spaces in which they move in many more creative and devious ways than we have ever imagined. We also discovered that the history of this subversion was continually being distorted and destroyed.

Women's acts of resistance, of self-affirmation, as social actors in their different historical and political contexts, are already in themselves subversive to existing power relations; but women have been 'sub-versive' also in another sense: in circumventing, uncoding and denying the various, distinct and multi-layered verses in which their subjugation is inscribed.

and in replacing them with their own verses. Sometimes literally, as the oral poetry of Somali women testifies, at other times by creating their own cultures of resistance, re-shaping and transforming their surroundings.

The present collection records both successes and failures in such cases of subversion and resistance. Several case studies document defeats, and the destruction of women's organizations. Clearly, not all women's movements or organizations aspire to transforming power relations within which women live out their subordination—a creation of intersecting relations of gender, race and class; nor are they equally successful in their attempts to transform their surroundings. Nevertheless, it is important to document and understand women's history, the changing face of feminism and the myths that surround women's movements.

Women's history

Feminist historians such as Kelly[1] and Lerner[2] have clearly demonstrated that the writing of history is an essentially biased process, a selective recording of events influenced by the historian's individual interests and perceptions. It is also accepted that women's collective actions have tended to remain invisible to historians and social scientists. Where women's movements have been recorded, they have often been interpreted, even by feminist social scientists, in a biased way, as I will demonstrate in the case of the Chinese sisterhoods.

All this has given rise to the many myths surrounding the history of women's movements. For several reasons I feel it is vital that these myths are exploded: first, because knowledge of women's historical involvement in resistance movements can have an empowering effect on present-day feminists; and second, because a partial and distorted view of women's history hampers the creation of international links between women and the growth of solidarity between black and white feminists.

Feminism, a contested concept

Feminism has always been a contested concept. I prefer to use the terms 'women's movements' and 'women's organizations', except where women belonging to those movements or organizations specifically call themselves feminist. In this introduction I will only deal with two aspects of feminism, its political and analytical dimensions.

The researchers involved in the project are all self-declared feminists and many belong to feminist organizations. The working definition of feminism most of them could agree on was quite straightforward: an awareness of women's oppression on domestic, social, economic and political levels, accompanied by a willingness to struggle against such oppression. It was understood that women's oppression was compounded by class and race relations, and that struggles surrounding these issues could at times have greater weight than solely women's struggles. It was also understood that in their struggles for national liberation, against imperialism, in labour movements and in race or food riots, women participated in a gendered way.

However, not all women's groups would call their organization feminist. In other cases, a hard battle had to be waged before some organizations could 'come out' as feminists. See Vargas[3] for an account of the painful struggle Peruvian women waged before they would call themselves 'feminist'. In such cases the word 'feminist' denotes more or less a *rite de passage.* By calling these organizations feminist before their 'coming out', we would deny the enormity of their struggles.

Recognizing the political dimension of the word 'feminist' offers some scope to locate the concept within its historical context. What may be called 'feminist' in one historical period or in one particular political setting, need not be called 'feminist' in another. The issues taken up by a specific organization are not in themselves the criteria to decide whether an organization can be called feminist or not. An issue like education for women, which many women's organizations in both North and South took up in the first decades of this century, could be very subversive where it was linked with women's social and political empowerment. It could also have a conservative ring to it if the value of 'educated mothers' in male-dominated nuclear family surroundings was stressed.

Most contemporary feminists would agree that feminism is not a one-dimensional social critique, but a multi-layered, transformational, political practice and ethics. The transformation is towards feminization and democratization on domestic, social and political levels, as well as towards economic levelling and an end to racial discrimination. But in different social and historical contexts, feminists may have other issues to fight for.

Jayawardena has demonstrated that the concept of 'feminism' was widely used in many Third World women's movements in the beginning of this century: 'Early feminism in the Third World was one of the important forces for social change in the late 19th and early 20th centuries....'[4]

Villavicencio's contribution to the present collection also clearly indicates that Peruvian women used the term 'feminist' to describe themselves and their aspirations. Yet many people in those countries, especially those belonging to 'progressive', leftist organizations, see feminism as a western concept which is only applicable to struggles of western, white, middle-class women.

Similar problems crop up with organizations fighting for women's issues in countries with a socialist movement. Although the rhetoric used there may not be as radically feminist as that used by western feminists, yet the issues being fought for are in many cases those taken up by feminists in other environments. And as women in the socialist environment usually have the full support of the entire state apparatus, their issues are taken up generally in a massive and successful way. Women's education, basic health facilities and other welfare related issues are dealt with in a highly effective manner. Yet women's organizations under those circumstances are usually organized in a democratic centralist way, as the cases of APRM, Gerwani, and SWDO amply demonstrate in this volume.

Women in such organizations are not engaged in a process of feminist consciousness raising: at best they are participating in programmes with which they agree, at worst they are fulfilling targets set by people at the top of the organization. As such, their methods of operation may not fall within our earlier definition of feminism, even if their activities will.

There is another reason why feminism and Marxist-Leninism do not easily converge. There are historical reasons why women operating within a Marxist context conflate feminism with the bourgeois and the reactionary. They will not easily call themselves feminists.

From an analytical view, feminism is tied up with such issues as transformative processes, the shifting and unstable concept of 'woman' itself and women's identity and consciousness. Feminist theoreticians such as de Lauretis,[5] Haraway,[6] Nicholson[7] and Trinh[8] have produced a vast body of literature on these topics which I cannot even begin to review in the space of this introduction. I will just hint at some of their critical insights which are relevant for this discussion.

As de Lauretis writes, feminism has enabled us to rethink the materiality of the ideological, and the way the political operates in everyday life: 'Feminism defines itself as a political instance, not merely a sexual politics, but a politics of experience, of everyday life, which later then in turn enters the public sphere of expression and creative practice...', and '...feminism has located [epistemological priority] in the personal, the subjective, the body, the symptomatic, the quotidian, as the very site of material inscription of the ideological.'[9]

Feminism is thus also a discursive process, a process of producing meaning, of subverting representations of gender and of re-creating new representations of gender, of womanhood, of identity and the collective self. As such, feminism carries multiple meanings, limited neither to recent movements, nor to western contexts. Feminism is located both in public outbursts and in struggles in the private domain, for these private struggles are always expressions of the external collective processes. In this volume, the *zar* ceremonies in the Sudan and Somalia and the oral poetry of Somali women demonstrate the ways women can manipulate their private domains in response to collectively felt pains.

Several critical themes run through the development of feminist theories. One is the debate on equality versus difference which has long been seen as a binary opposition.[10] Scott[11] has suggested that it is much more fruitful to point out their interdependence; that it is an illusion to stick to this opposition. It is more relevant, she writes, to look very critically at the way these concepts are being deployed. Feminist philosophers such as Braidotti[12] and Haraway[13] denounce the construction of binary oppositions as examples of male-dominated science. The case of Jamaica in this volume demonstrates clearly how the manipulation of this opposition resulted in the domestication

of women, their exclusion from the labour force and the promotion of nuclear families and monogamous marriages (among
others through mass weddings organized by a women's organization).

A related theme is the deployment of the category 'woman'.
At least since Mary Wollstonecraft, feminists have denounced
biological determinism. If 'woman' is seen to be a historically
contingent construction, what is the ground upon which feminist politics can be built? Will we not, by de-constructing and
de-essentializing the very definition of the central concept of
feminism, ultimately denounce feminism itself as an illusion?

Various positions have been taken around this dilemma.
Kristeva[14] has taken this line of thinking to its ultimate point
by claiming that feminist practice can only be negative: 'a
woman cannot be'. Feminists like Daly,[15] Rich[16] and Irigaray[17]
have countered this argument by challenging male definitions
of womanhood. Their work has been geared towards decoding
those definitions and inscribing 'woman' from a female-centred
position.

Recent post-structuralist writers such as Haraway,[18] Alcoff[19]
and Flax[20] take 'difference' as the starting ground of their politics and writing. However, they focus on the plurality of
women's experiences themselves. 'Difference' is thus no longer
an essential quality, but a location of politics. De Lauretis theo-
rized this position most lucidly when she pointed out that a
gendered identity is never a simple given: subjectivity is always constructed through a continuous process in which we
are not just passive recipients, but also active creators of
gendered power relations. Through a process of reflective practice, agency can be restored to individuals. According to de
Lauretis the identity of a woman is the product of her own
interpretation and reconstruction of her history, as mediated
through the cultural discursive context to which she has access.[21]

Several essays in this volume point to the painstaking process of simultaneously decoding the meaning given to 'woman'
in a specific context and re-inscribing a different meaning.
Vargas presents the gradual discovery of the political importance of heterogeneity, plurality and ambiguity as feminist practice in Peru, and the creation of a feminist consciousness. Ford-

Smith in her account of an experiment in popular theatre describes the resistance embedded in popular theatre, and the elements of gender subversion it has traditionally harboured.

Defining women's movements

Women's movements have never spoken with a single voice. A comprehensive definition is thus difficult to arrive at. In my view, a women's movement can be seen as the whole spectrum of conscious and unconscious individual or collective acts, activities, groups or organizations concerned with diminishing gender subordination, which is understood as intersecting with race and class oppression. Sections within this movement may disagree with each other, but different demands will continue to crop up at different times, challenging the dominant system in specific ways.

Movements are not static, they should be seen as processes which are modified as they come in contact with everyday life, confronting politics and generally (but not always) the state, in a constant process of reflection, communication and negotiation. They generate certain social processes as they define and redefine themselves. They are composed of social actors who, in engaging themselves in these movements, assert their agency in reflecting upon their experiences of oppression and constructing their identities. Not all aspects of their identities will be constituted by elements of the movement; other power relations will intersect with the collective will, sometimes causing ambiguities and contradictions, at other times strengthening each other.

Melucci has pointed to an important aspect of social movements: they may consist of invisible networks of small groups submerged in everyday life. Within these 'invisible laboratories', Melucci writes, movements may question and challenge the codes of everyday life.[22] Thus social movements may appear in waves of visibility and latency.

This is clearly the case with women's movements. After a period of visible mobilization in large parts of the world at the turn of the century, the women's movement receded from view: take the cases of Peru and the Caribbean. Yet it did not totally disappear.

Taylor and Rupp refute the general assumption that the American women's movement died in the 1920s and was not resurrected until the mid-1960s. According to them, this period was ignored in historiography because only formal male activism was seen as constituting a movement. 'Women have been less likely to be aggressive and to use disruptive and confrontational tactics in pursuit of their aims'.[23] The 'invisible' periods in the women's movement were not the same in all socio-political contexts. When the movement lay dormant in Europe and the United States, in Indonesia and the Sudan it went through its most vigorous and subversive stages.

In many cases the criteria used to describe women's acts of rebellion are modelled on formal, leftist male activism. In pre-twentieth century movements, women's defiance is often analysed by using the yardstick of present-day social activism. Their resistance is not put in the socio-historical context in which it originated. This is demonstrated in the case of the anti-marriage sisterhoods which existed in Guangdong, southern China, for over a century. Croll, who devotes only one page in her book 'Feminism and Socialism in China' to these sisterhoods, writes: 'The anti-marriage associations were expressions of opposition to the traditional forms of "fate", but they remained at the level of fate and furnished a form of escapism rather than a significant force for change.' She concedes that 'the rebellious spirit and the alternative life-style of these primitive feminist associations constituted a consciously deviant form of behaviour,' but concludes that not until the twentieth century did a women's movement start which began to 'widely and collectively protest against the traditional role and status assigned to them in family and society.'[24]

Topley, whose pioneering work in the fifties on these sisterhoods is still the major source of information, dismisses their political relevance in the following way: 'The anti-marriage movement in Kwangtung cannot be regarded as any positive progressive movement; the women merely refused to accept sexual relationships with men.'[25] Chafetz and Dworkin classify these 'communal sisterhoods' among the 'precursors' to a Chinese women's movement.[26]

Escapism? Deviant behaviour? No positive progressive movement? Precursors? Let us consider for a moment what these sisterhoods actually stood for. For over a hundred years thousands of women silk-workers made vows never to wed, preceded by hairdressing rituals resembling the ones at marriage. They swore friendship to each other and lived in pairs or groups in 'vegetarian' halls or monasteries devoted to the cult of the goddess Guan Yin. As Topley indicates,[27] these women liked to be free to move about, detested to 'become the slave of a man' or a 'human machine of propagation', and abhorred the loneliness of marriage and its lack of economic independence. Some of them expressed a distaste for heterosexual relations altogether.

According to Topley, their culture allowed them to live these independent lives, as unmarried women were able to earn an income in the silk industry. Also, it was not considered morally wrong not to marry in that region. An added factor was the tradition of religious insistence on purity and chastity.

Life in one of the Golden Orchid Associations, as the sisterhoods were also called, offered the members the possibility of a career in religious affairs and political status not open to married women. Modern commentators note that the movement (which disappeared after the victory of Mao's Red Army, when it was seen as a feudal and backward practice) left a legacy of chastity in the region, which has made the introduction of family planning more successful there than in other regions of China. Also, there is still a strong tradition of female labour. Remnants of the movement can be found in Hong Kong[28] and Singapore.[29]

In modern terminology, the movement can be seen as sustained subversion of compulsory heterosexuality, which was targeted as one of the primary factors causing women's subordination. Their resistance was collective, involved the construction of a female counter-culture, stimulated women's economic independence and extended their private concerns into the public domain; they 'did not escape to private chambers,' but made public commitments.

In my view, the sisterhoods, operating in their own sociohistorical context, should be regarded as a full-fledged women's movement. The parameters of women's subordination are historically specific; so are the expressions of women's resistance. Feminism has not been formulated by one or more founding-mothers, as socialism has. Women's movements thus do not start from a certain period in time. There have probably been many more women's movements than we are aware of. The example of the anti-marriage sisterhoods is just one case in point.

These earlier movements have not always fought for issues women of this century are interested in. Criteria developed to assess present-day expressions of women's resistance and of social activism cannot be applied uniformly in different historical contexts. Our own research has uncovered various forms of women's rebellion which had not been documented so far. Whether these should be seen as women's movements can only be decided by locating them firmly in their socio-historical contexts.

Most attempts to categorize women's movements date from the mid-1980s, when apparently the need for labelling was strong. Focusing on present-day white American feminism, Eisenstein distinguishes three periods with their corresponding theoretical perspectives.[30]

In the first phase, visionary and utopian feminist writers called for equality and sisterhood. The second phase is characterized by an insistence on difference which, in Eisenstein's view, led to essentialism and the metaphysics of Daly. In the last instance then feminism should recognize diversity, put more emphasis on socio-economic issues (which in the United States were neglected) and reclaim its radicalism.

Young takes a different approach and distinguishes between humanist and gynocentric feminism. In her view humanist feminism 'defines gender as accidental to humanity' and urges both women and men to 'pursue self-development in those creative and intellectual activities that distinguish human beings from the rest of nature'.[31] Gynocentric feminism on the other hand is based on the recognition of the superiority of values embodied in the traditionally female experience and rejects the values of violence and individualism embodied in traditionally male-dominated institutions.

According to Fraser, Kristeva identifies three types of feminism. Her first two categories overlap with Young's typology, an egalitarian, reform-oriented humanist feminism, versus a culturally-oriented gynocentric version of feminism. Under this last category she comprises the *écriture féminine* of French writers such as Cixous and Irigaray who aim to foster the expression of a feminine sexual and symbolic specificity. The last category Kristeva distinguishes, consists of those feminists who claim that the category 'women' does not exist, and that collective identities are dangerous fictions.[32]

Jaggar[33] distributes four nametags among various feminist streams: liberal, Marxist, socialist and radical. For several reasons I am wary of this labelling exercise. In the first place, because I am struck by the complexity of views expressed by authors commonly classified in one of the above mentioned categories. Upon closer reading I often found that although the focus of the writing would differ, many authors would express their anger and visions circling around similar themes. Secondly, because I am afraid that such a neat exercise might lead to distorted and simplistic views of the movement, and to fragmentation and divisiveness. I would like to stress that to me the transformational power of the women's movement lies in its varied approaches to women's subordination and in the recognition that this diversity is a source of its strength, as it enables women to challenge patterns of domination from various sides and from several levels simultaneously.

To me feminism is not a canonized body of theories, but rather a widely divergent, sometimes contradictory amalgam of positions. Likewise, women's movements are not uniform social constructions. What does seem relevant to me, though, is exposing various popularly held myths about western and non-western women's movements which hamper the growth of international solidarity.

Myths about women's movements

The relationship between Third World and western women is coloured by the existence of various popular myths about their respective movements. However incongruous they may be in reality, the myths are pervasive in both western and Third World cultures. Mohanty, for instance, casually dismisses the difference between 'white, western, middle class liberal feminism' (which is the only form of western feminism she refers to, implying if it is not the only one, at least it is the most important

branch of present-day white feminism) and the feminist politics of women of colour in the United States as the contrast between 'a singular focus on gender as a basis for equal rights,
and a focus on gender in relation to race and/or class as part of
a broader liberation struggle.'[34]

Also, Johnson-Odim refers to a 'widely accepted perception'
among Third World women that feminism emerging from
white, middle-class western women 'narrowly confines itself
to a struggle against gender discrimination.'[35] She herself is
aware of a history of broader feminist struggle in the United
States which makes her accept the possibility of an international
feminist movement. Western women reinforce this stereotype
of their own feminism where they indeed confine themselves
to a singular focus on gender, limiting their politics to discourse
analysis, and ignoring western feminism's history of concern
with anti-racist and anti-imperialist struggles.

I will distinguish here four myths which give rise to many
misunderstandings between western and Third World women's
movements. These four popularly held notions inform many
current misconceptions, although three of them are grounded
in the histories of pre-World War II and colonial women's movements, while the fourth relates more directly to present-day
women's movements. They are the so-called division between
bourgeois and socialist women's movements, the notion that
first-wave western feminism was primarily concerned with
equal rights and the vote, the perception that early Third World
feminism was mainly devoted to anti-colonialist struggles and
the assumption that Third World feminism is primarily concerned with issues of food and labour, while western feminism
concentrates on body politics.

The idea that the women's movement in the late nineteenth
and early twentieth centuries was divided into two discrete
sections—the bourgeois women's movement concerned solely
with the vote, and the socialist or proletarian women's movement attempting to alleviate the burdens of working women—
was politically motivated; historically it is hardly justifiable.
Yet this myth continues into the present day, giving rise to accusations and counter accusations, dividing women by class
and issue.

Historically, women in Europe, Latin America and the United

States, being a 'legally inferior caste',[36] were severely hampered by their lack of any rights. Nor surprisingly, the attainment of equal rights was a serious concern for them. But that was not all, and the early women's movements were much richer in their ideas, debates and practices, much more radical and subtle than we give them credit for today.

Equal rights were thus an important, but not the sole concern of western women. And not only of western women. As the chapters on Peru, the Caribbean and Indonesia in this volume demonstrate, struggles for the vote and equal rights (for instance in the marriage law) were important concerns for women in those countries too.

The 'modern' western women's movement arose in the wake of struggles for equality and emancipation which followed the American (1776) and French (1789) revolutions. While the white male leaders of these revolutions fought hard (and mostly successfully) to limit the newly-won rights to their own group, Parisian working women with Olympe de Gouges as one of their leaders fought on the barricades for their rights. In her famous pamphlet, 'The Rights of the Woman and the Female Citizen' (*Les Droits de la Femme et de la Citoyenne*, published in 1791), she demanded women's access to social and political rights. She paid dearly for her courage: she was beheaded in November 1793. Her political defeat preceded her death—already in October of that year all women's clubs and associations had been prohibited.

The first women's collective political action was also triggered by attempts of men to exclude women from their revolutionary activities. While women were in the majority among those fighting for the abolition of slavery in the United States, they were denied a seat in the World Anti-Slavery Convention which was held in London in 1840. Elisabeth Cady Stanton was so infuriated by this refusal that she was among those writing the Declaration of Sentiments at the first women's rights convention held in Seneca Falls, in 1848. This Declaration of Sentiments still stands as a passionate and powerful denunciation of the various ways in which men have acquired power over women. It strongly opposes such views in society which attributed women's problems to their 'natural' condition of passivity and docility.

Thus, from the start, women's fight for political rights grew out of the struggles for emancipation and freedom by workers and slaves.[37] In France,[38] England[39] and the United States[40] it has been documented over and over again that women workers were among the first to demand political rights, and that women from the middle classes struggled courageously to support them.

Flora Tristan (1803–1844), of Peruvian-French, middle-class descent, opposed slavery and fought for the emancipation of both male and female workers. Even before Marx, she called for an international conference of workers in which equal rights of women and men would be seen as an indispensable condition to bring about 'the human unity'.[41]

Thus the roots of the women's movement are to be found wherever women were denied their rights, exploited as workers and forced to be emotionally and economically dependent on men. A look at the Seneca Falls Declaration of Sentiments of 1848 will illustrate this position:[42]

He has taken from her all right in property....
He has monopolized nearly all the profitable employments....
He has denied her the facilities for obtaining a thorough education....
He has endeavoured in every way he could, to destroy her confidence in her own powers, to lessen her self-respect and to make her willing to lead a dependent and abject life....

Not only did bourgeois women see the vote as something worth striving for; women workers too realized that without political rights and education no improvements in their working conditions would be possible. A weaver from Glasgow stated in 1838:[43]

You cannot expect me to be grammatical in my expressions, as I did not get an education, like many of my other fellow women that I ought to have got, and which is the right of every human being.... It is the right of every woman to have a vote in the legislation of her country....

Coming from different backgrounds and with a different set

of emphases, western women activists have been putting forward the following demands from the late seventeenth to the beginning of the twentieth centuries:

- slavery should be abolished;
- the conditions for women workers should be improved; and
- in order for women to play a full social role and improve the world, they should have access to education and to political rights.

Right from the beginning, suffrage was seen as a means to achieve the above objectives. A prominent suffragette like Elisabeth Cady Stanton called for the reform of marriage and divorce laws (a demand that caused a scandal at the time). Another leader, Susan B. Anthony, called for women's control over their own wages. For both Anthony and Stanton, as for the weaver from Glasgow, the vote and women's access to education were prerequisites to other reforms.[44]

By the end of the nineteenth century, the suffrage issue had become a major rallying point. It served as a primary mobilizing factor, comparable to the abortion issue at the beginning of the present phase of the movement in the west, such as in Holland. Yet it generally continued to be perceived as a means for women to improve their condition and their societies, not as the sole and ultimate goal.

Women from various social sectors participated in the early women's movements. As we have seen, their concerns were overlapping. The idea of a split, between bourgeois women fighting for the vote and proletarian women interested not in political rights but in supporting the class struggle, was encouraged by socialist groups from the end of the nineteenth century.

In 1868, Swiss feminist Marie Goegg founded the first international women's organization, the International Association of Women. At its first congress in 1870, the participants demanded equal rights for all people from all social classes, as well as access to education, and equal pay for women for equal work. This was the first recorded demand for equal pay for women; the First International adopted this demand only in 1889. Goegg asked to appear at the First International Congress to be held in 1868, but never received a reply. Instead, the

League of Peace and Freedom (in which Bakoenin played a prominent role) did receive her. But already in 1868 Marx had decided that the League (and Goegg's Association) had no right to exist as the First International in its call for the unity of all workers should adequately safeguard peace.[45]

The relationship between Marx and the First International on the one hand and the feminist movement on the other was further impaired when the International decided in 1872 to suspend section 12. This section was established in New York in 1871. Its goals included the emancipation of workers, both male and female, by acquiring political power, and social freedom for all races and both sexes. Marx held it against section 12 that they were too concerned with the issue of 'free love' and that they thought 'the vote for women is more important than the issue of labour'.[46]

Coward points out that socialist hesitation to link with the women's movement is caused by inadequate theorizing by Marx and Engels on the family. They subsumed sexual relations under the category of 'the family', while 'the family' was in its turn subsumed under theories of class and political representation.[47] Women's struggles were thus seen as 'partial' struggles within the larger class struggle. Once the party had won, and communism was established, women's subordination would also disappear leaving the 'happy proletarian family' in place.

Although Marxist theory does recognize the historicity of the family, which explains partly the great attraction it has for feminists, for political reasons the class struggle was given priority. Thus socialists created an arbitrary division of feminist women along class lines. Only those from working-class backgrounds, or those middle-class women who devoted themselves wholeheartedly to the proletarian cause (such as Zetkin and Kollontai, but they too had their problems with their male comrades), were accepted in their ranks. The others were denounced as politically conservative bourgeois women. By implication, the demands of the women's movement for access to education and political rights were branded as reactionary demands which true socialist women should not support.

Picq asks whether it was 'political weakness or sexual bias' which led women socialists to reject the demands of legal and

political equality for women and not support bourgeois women
even when they were fighting for women workers. She concludes that socialist women 'saw the interest feminists took in
working-class women as just another indication of the
nonproletarian tendencies of the movement.' This '"theory of
bourgeois feminism" led women socialists to reject the demands
of legal and political equality for women. Instead, they spent
their energies criticizing the objectives of those they had turned
into their political adversaries.'[48]

This division, which is now almost a century old, between
bourgeois feminists who are supposedly blind to the plight of
women workers, and socialist women who dismiss feminist
demands, still plagues the women's movement. Even today
socialist women find themselves reluctant to enter a feminist
consciousness raising group, and feminist women experience
feelings of guilt for setting up a rape crisis centre instead of a
women workers' library.

The struggle for the vote became an important, though never
the only important concern in the Third World too. Reddock in
this volume provides a detailed account of Trinidadian women
fighting for suffrage. They were accused of 'changing nature
itself'. She also indicates that this political campaign was linked
to an increase in women's socio-economic opportunities.

However, women's movements in the Third World and the
west were not necessarily alike in this early phase. There were
some parallel concerns, there were also great differences between them. First, all women's organizations in the colonized
countries of the Third World were engaged in anti-colonial
struggles. The accounts of the women's movements in Indonesia, Somalia and the Sudan all demonstrate the involvement of
these movements in nationalist causes.

The colonial experience and the racialization and sexuali-
zation of the colonized peoples had far-reaching, contradictory
and complex implications for women. Indigenous forms of
women's subordination intersected with the new colonial ideology which further entrenched women in a domesticated, sexually subservient position. The emphasis on motherhood and
domesticity of women in the Victorian, European societies was
carried by the colonial powers into their overseas dominions.

Third World peoples were seen as childlike, emotional,

unreasonable and instinctive—in general, closer to nature. This perception appeared to justify white male superiority. Their arrogance was bolstered by the repeated depiction of Asian and African societies as backward, stagnant, chaotic and primitive.[49] The 'mission' of white men thus was to bring 'culture' where nature reigned and especially to improve women's degraded status. In a perfidious mixture of appeals to a 'natural' Victorian morality and a desire for 'social reforms', measures were propagated which in some instances may have benefitted women, but in other cases eroded their political, economic and sexual rights.

Thus the discourse of social reform, which grew out of and in opposition to the colonial situation, provided space to fight for women's education and against some defined 'ills' as child marriage and widow immolation. At the same time, an image of western bourgeois womanhood was being constructed. The last chapter of this volume deals with some of these violent and contradictory processes in the Minangkabau region of Indonesia, leading to the erosion of old matrilinear customs. The collection of essays on Indian colonial history edited by Sangari and Vaid[50] provide a critical and insightful analysis of these experiences and their implications for the women's movement in India.

But, and here we are concerned with the third myth indicated above, early non-western women's movements were not solely engaged in ousting colonial oppressors, however overriding this concern might have been at the peak of the anti-colonial struggle. Some examples to the contrary from the present collection: early Peruvian feminists attacked prevailing sexual relations, and anarchist women fought to incorporate women's demands in the unions In Trinidad women fought for education, political rights, better divorce laws and improved working conditions. Women were at the forefront of labour disturbances in Jamaica. Somali women protested against polygamy and their own heavy workloads.

Thus, issues related to body politics, working conditions, education and political rights, class and gender were seen as legitimate concerns in most early women's movements around the world. In addition, women in colonial settings fought for national liberation. As the cases of Somalia and Indonesia show,

nationalist male leaders of the young independent states tried
to curb women's activities after independence. That women
were 'betrayed' once a national revolution succeeded has been
demonstrated again and again.[51] The denial of the history of
women's struggles against their gender subordination in Third
World contexts only adds to this 'betrayal'. Women attempted
not only to subvert the colonial powers, they also attacked the
power of men over them.

Which is what present-day feminists in the South are engaged in doing even today. The myth that women in the South
are primarily interested in issues of food and labour while
women in the North are engaged in body politics and discourse
analyses simply does not stand up to closer scrutiny. Again,
this does not mean that there is no difference between the two
kinds of movements. What I am stressing here is that both in
the South and the North, within their specific socio-economic
and political contexts, feminists have similar concerns. It is more
fruitful to look for points of commonality than of fissure.

Granted this is not an easy process. Women's conferences
are still being held in the North where issues of race and imperialism hardly feature or are only brought up by women of
colour. And there are Southern feminists who even today dismiss theoretical debates centred around cultural analysis as ir-
relevant. But I also see increasing respect and mutual understanding. White western women are beginning to realize that
racism is not just an issue of 'helping' women of disadvantaged
colours, but something they themselves are affected by. Meanwhile, women in Peru and India, for instance, realize that racism is not only an issue of imperialism, but rooted in their own
societies, an issue women everywhere have to confront.

The strength of Third World feminism lies in its insistence
on the materiality of power relations, not only in cultural practices, but in all aspects of daily life. When women from the South
engage in theoretical debates, as several case studies in this
volume prove, they are haunted by the economic deprivation
of their sisters. This exacerbates the power of their analyses.

I have been convinced of the great potential for international
solidarity among women. Our research project went through
many difficult stages, but the process also led to a strong sense
of solidarity. It deepened our understanding, respect, insight

and analytical capabilities. What appears most urgent now is the creation of multicultural alliances among women on the basis of respect for each other's identities, struggles and analytical positions.

NOTES

1. Joan Kelly, *Women, History and Theory, the Essays of Joan Kelly*. Chicago & London: University of Chicago Press, 1984.
2. Gerda Lerner, *The Creation of Patriarchy*. New York & Oxford: Oxford University Press, 1986.
3. Virginia Vargas, 'The Feminist Movement in Peru: Inventory and Perspectives,' in: Saskia Wieringa (ed.), *Women's Struggles and Strategies*. Aldershot: Gower, 1988.
4. Kumari Jayawardena, *Feminism and Nationalism in the Third World in the 19th and Early 20th Centuries*. The Hague: ISS, 1982. p. 13.
5. Teresa de Lauretis (ed.), *Feminist Studies Critical Studies*. Bloomington: Indiana University Press, 1986. Also see Teresa de Lauretis, *Technologies of Gender, Essays on Theory, Film and Fiction*. London: Macmillan, 1987.
6. Donna J. Haraway, *Simians, Cyborgs and Women, the Reinvention of Nature*. London: Free Association Books, 1991.
7. Linda J. Nicholson, *Feminisn/Postmodernism*. New York: Routledge, 1990.
8. T. Minh-ha Trinh, *Woman, Native, Other, Writing Postcoloniality and Feminism*. Bloomington and Indianapolis: Indiana University Press, 1989.
9. Teresa de Lauretis, *Feminist Studies Critical Studies*. op. cit. pp. 10, 11.
10. Rosi Braidotti, Eva Charkiewicz, Sabine Häusler and Saskia Wieringa, *Negotiating Change: women, ecology and sustainable development*. London: Zed Books,1993.
11. Joan Wallach Scott, *Gender and the Politics of History*. New York: Columbia University Press, 1988.
12. Rosi Braidotti, *Patterns of Dissonance, a study of women in contemporary philosophy*. Cambridge: Polity Press, 1991.
13. Donna J. Haraway, op. cit.
14. Julia Kristeva, 'Woman Can Never Be Defined,' in: Elaine Marks, and Isabelle de Courtivron (eds.), *New French Feminism, an anthology*. Brighton: Harvester, 1981.

15. Mary Daly, *Pure Lust, Elemental Feminist Philosophy*. London: The Women's Press, 1984.
16. Adrienne Rich, *Of Woman Born, Motherhood as Experience and Institution*. New York: Norton, 1976.
17. Luce Irigaray, *Ce sexe qui n'en est pas un*. Paris: Minuit, 1977.
18. Donna J. Haraway, op. cit.
19. Linda Alcoff, 'Cultural Feminism Versus Poststructuralism: the identity crisis in feminist theory,' in: *Signs; Journal of Women in Culture and Society*, vol. 13, no. 3, 1988.
20. Jane Flax, 'Postmodernism and Gender Relations in Feminist Theory,' in: Linda J. Nicholson, op. cit.
21. Teresa de Lauretis, *Feminist Studies Critical Studies*, op. cit.
22. Alberto Melucci, *Nomads of the Present, Social Movements and Individual Needs in Contemporary Society*. Philadelphia: Temple University Press, 1989.
23. Verta Taylor and Leila J. Rupp, 'Researching the Women's Movement,' in: Mary Margaret Fonow and Judith A. Cook, *Beyond Methodology, Feminist Scholarship as Lived Research*. Bloomington: Indiana University Press, 1991. p. 123.
24. Elisabeth Croll, *Feminism and Socialism in China*. London: Routledge & Kegan Paul, 1978. p. 44.
25. Marjorie Topley, quoted in Janice Raymond, *A Passion for Friends, Toward a Philosophy of Female Affection*. London: The Women's Press, 1986. p. 140.
26. Janet Saltzman Chafetz and Anthony Gary Dworkin, *Female Revolt, women's movements in world and historical perspective*. Totowa: Rowman & Allanheld, 1986. p. 137.
27. Marjorie Topley, 'Marriage Resistance in Rural Kwangtung,' in: Margery Wolf and Roxane Witke (eds.), *Women in Chinese Society*. Stanford: Stanford University Press, 1975. pp. 86–8.
28. Emily Honig, 'Burning Incense, Pledging Sisterhood: communities of women workers in the Shanghai cotton mills, 1919–1949,' in: *Signs: Journal of Women in Culture and Society*, vol. 10, no. 4, 1985.
29. See Topley in *A Passion for Friends*, op. cit. and Saskia Wieringa, *Uw toegenegen Dora D.* Amsterdam: Furie, 1987.
30. Hester Eisenstein, *Contemporary Feminist Thought*. London & Sydney: Unwin, 1984.
31. Iris M. Young, 'Humanism, Gynocentrism and Feminist Politics,' in: *Women's Studies International Quarterly 8*, 1985. p. 174.
32. Nancy Fraser, 'The Uses and Abuses of French Discourse Theories for Feminist Politics,' in: *Theory, Culture & Society*, vol. 9, 1992.
33. Alison Jaggar, *Feminist Politics and Human Nature*. Totowa:

Rowman & Allenheld, 1983.

34. Chandra Talpade Mohanty, 'Introduction: Cartographies of Struggle, Third World Women and the Politics of Feminism,' in: Chandra Talpade Mohanty, Ann Russo and Lourdes Torres (eds.), *Third World Women and the Politics of Feminism*. Bloomington and Indianapolis: Indiana University Press, 1991. p.11.

35. Cheryl Johnson-Odim , 'Common Themes, Different Contexts, Third World Women and Feminism,' in: Chandra Talpade Mohanty, Ann Russo and Lourdes Torres (eds.), op. cit. p. 315.

36. Ann Oakley, *Subject Women*. Oxford: Robertson, 1981.

37. See also Olive Banks, *Faces of Feminism*. Oxford: Robertson, 1981.

38. Françoise Picq, '"Bourgeois Feminism" in France: a theory developed by socialist women before World War I,' in: Judith Friedlander, *et al* (eds.), *Women in Culture and Politics, a Century of Change*. Bloomington: Indiana University Press, 1986.

39. Ann Oakley, op. cit.

40. Barbara Sinclair Deckard, *The Women's Movement, Political, Socioeconomic and Psychological Issues*. New York: Harper & Row, 1979. Also, Olive Banks, op. cit.

41. Flora Tristan, *Unión Obrera*. Barcelona: Fontanara, 1977.

42. Ann Oakley, op. cit. p. 2.

43. Ann Oakley, op. cit. p. 9.

44. Miriam Schneir, ed., *Feminism: The Essential Historical Writings*. New York: Vintage Books, 1972. The collection contains important texts of early American feminism, including the famous speech by Susan B. Anthony: 'Woman Wants Bread, Not the Ballot!'

45. Bob Reinalda and Natascha Verhaaren, *Vrouwenbeweging en Internationale Organisaties 1868–1986, een vergeten Hoofdstuk uit de geschiedenis van de internationale Betrekkingen*, Nijmegen: Ariadne, 1989. p. 24.

46. Ibid. p. 27.

47. Rosalind Coward, *Patriarchal Precedents, Sexuality and Social Relations*. London: Routledge & Kegan Paul, 1983.

48. Françoise Picq, op. cit. p. 341.

49. Joanne de Groot, 'Conceptions and Misconceptions: the historical and cultural context of discussion on women and development,' in: Haleh Afshar (ed.), *Women Development & Survival in the Third World*. London and New York: Longman, 1991.

50. Kumkum Sangari and Sudesh Vaid (eds.), *Recasting Women, Essays in Colonial History*. New Delhi: Kali for Women, 1989.

51. See also Kumari Jayawardena, op. cit.

2
Methods and Power: Epistemological and Methodological Aspects of a Feminist Research Project

Saskia Wieringa

To my knowledge our project was unique. Not only was it multidisciplinary—researchers came from the social sciences, political sciences, history and the arts—it was also carried out on a global scale. The most salient characteristic, however, was that our political commitment as feminists informed the epistemology from which we started and the methodology we applied to our research. It will be, therefore, interesting to engage in what Kelly calls a process of 'critical self-reflexion'.[1] For although a wealth of studies is being produced which spell out the progress made by various feminist scholars in their respective disciplines, there have been comparatively few attempts to analyse the processes by which these scholars have attempted to reach their goals. And whereas the established social sciences have been severely attacked from many sides on precisely their methodology, and several propositions have been advanced as to what a feminist methodology might look like, there have been very few in-depth assessments of feminist research projects.

To understand the process of our research, the project has to be contextualized. Therefore, I will indicate the epistemological pre-history on which we built when we were designing the proposal. While we were carrying out our research, however, feminist scholars provided new epistemological insights, only some of which we could incorporated in our work. This is because there were, at times, contradictions between the nature of our project—empirical, historical research informed by a wish to use its results to empower women—and the philosophical enterprise of constructing epistemologies. I will focus on some of these contradictions as they surfaced within the project.

I would like to point out that the present analysis is based entirely on my own assessment of the research process. I was both general coordinator of the project as the Institute of Social Studies (ISS) country-coordinator of Peru, Indonesia and later of the Caribbean, and one of the researchers. As such, I was too close to some of the dilemmas and conflicts outlined below. Not surprisingly, the view I will provide is one 'from the centre', and necessarily partial.

In my defence I can say, one of the most refreshing outcomes of debates on epistemology of at least the last 20 years is that science is a social construct and 'objective science', in the sense of a science untouched by history and the social context, is a *contradictio in terminis*. What I present here is my evaluation of a research process which shaped to a large part the work and lives of the many women who were involved in it, in the hope that others will take this process of reflection further.

The project: its conception, birth and growth

The project, 'Women's Movements and Organizations in Historical Perspective', was conceived during the First Conference of the Women's Decade in Mexico, in 1975. The conference initiated the Women and Development programme of the ISS in The Hague, in which programme the research project was embedded. Women from all parts of the world met at the conference and were so excited about sharing their experiences of work and struggle, that it was suggested an opportunity should be created for women to systematically pursue such an activity, preferably combined with research on associated topics.

After more meetings and workshops had repeatedly stressed the importance of research into and analysis of the experiences of women in productive and reproductive labour, in 1979 Maria Mies was appointed at the ISS to give the first courses of what has now become a full-fledged Masters programme in Women and Development. Together with Mies, Mia Berden, Rhoda Reddock and myself took the first concrete steps in the direction of the research project in 1982.

All of us had ties with women's organizations in various

countries: Maria Mies in India, Rhoda Reddock in Trinidad/ Tobago and I in Indonesia. Our experiences became the basis for the first country projects. Almost all other countries which were included in the project had participating researchers who had had prior contact with the Women and Development programme at ISS. The Peruvian researchers were linked to the women's centre of Flora Tristan, which had been set up following a workshop coordinated by ISS staff. The initiator of the Somalia project was an ex-participant of the Women and Development course.

Sudan was the only exception. So far we had not had any direct contact with any Sudanese feminist researchers. Sudan was included at the request of the Dutch Directorate General for Development Cooperation, the financing agency of the project. The Directorate operates many development projects in Sudan in which it would like to involve scholars trained in women and development issues.

Our reason at ISS for working closely with women and institutions involved with our teaching programme was that we hoped in this way the cohesion of the research project, especially in its theoretical and methodological aspects, would be strengthened.

After intensive consultations with the country coordinators of the various subprojects, a research proposal was presented to and accepted by the Dutch Directorate General for Development Cooperation of the Ministry of Foreign Affairs.

A project structure was devised in which each country team had its own country coordinator at ISS. I, as general coordinator, was responsible for liaison between the Ministry and ISS, and between ISS and the various country projects. The country teams were set up with considerable autonomy and laid down their own research priorities. Their coordinators were responsible for recruiting team members, financial affairs, regular reporting and actual fieldwork and analysis.

A broad array of topics was included. This ranged from the analysis of a single-issue campaign (the Anti Price Rise Movement in Bombay), to an account of a women's trade union (likewise in India) or a women's theatre collective (SISTREN, Jamaica), to the documentation of the first phases of a national women's movement (Peru, Somalia, Trinidad), to the history of besieged women's organizations (Sudan, Indonesia). The overriding consideration behind each proposal was in what way research in each country could contribute to strengthening the contemporary phase of women's movements in that country.

The first general project meeting was held at ISS in 1983. Research proposals of the various country teams were refined and operationalized. Attention was paid to the strengthening of the general theoretical and methodological background of the entire research staff. There were some meetings on research techniques which were thought to be extremely useful for the project, such as oral history and group interviews.

At that meeting several differences surfaced between team members. Not only did groups of researchers hold different theoretical views, the differences also got an epistemological character where they touched on issues like the validity of certain forms of knowing. Maria Mies and some researchers mainly from the Caribbean and India, insisted that capitalism and colonialism were the major determinants of women's position and that consequently we should focus our research on those processes. Others, including me and some researchers mainly from Peru and Sudan, pointed out that precapitalist relations were also major determinants of women's subordination, and that we should analyse the social construction of womanhood in a more comprehensive way. We wanted to start our research from the divergent, sometimes contradictory experiences of women's lives and struggles.

These differences were not discussed openly at that time and certainly not as an epistemological dilemma. Mies and those who agreed with her insisted that they held the 'correct' views, and our group was pushed into a defensive position, struggling for what we saw as a central element within feminism: the pluralism of feminism. We were of the opinion that this insistence on the 'correctness' of a certain feminist position was a residue of Marxist-Leninist theorizing. There were some painful confrontations but the issue was not dealt with in a conclusive way. Fortunately, our combined political will to devise a project which would help fight women's oppression proved stronger than our epistemological divergence.

Over the next two years the researchers were 'in the field'. During this period they were supported as much as possible by ISS staff. ISS-based country coordinators made several trips to the teams to help them with their problems, and to give news about the work being done by other teams. Back at ISS they tried to collect background material that might be of use to the researchers, and kept up a regular and in many cases intensive personal correspondence with them. As general coordinator, I was supported by two members who helped edit the quarterly Circular Letter which carried news about the various research teams, and discussed theoretical and methodological issues.

In 1985, at the second general meeting, most researchers brought the first drafts of their reports. These were discussed and a first attempt was made at analysing the enormous wealth of information. Almost all of them had taken photographs with the intention of creating audio-visual shows for women who would not have access to the reports. In an extra week of audio-visual training the tape-slide series were finalized.

During this workshop the tensions between the various theoretical 'streams' came to a head. There appeared to be four divergent positions within the project team: the feminist Marxist, the feminist post-modernist, the feminist activist and the feminist empiricist. Unfortunately, these differences were not viewed as a theoretical or an epistemological issue. Rather, they were transformed into an almost personal power struggle between Maria Mies and me on the one hand, and between researchers from the South and from the North on the other. Some researchers tried to stay out of these debates, because they resented the imposition upon them of what they saw as essentially a First World debate.

When Maria Mies left the workshop and the project overnight, our political commitment to our cause kept us together.

The reports were finalized after the workshop. All country teams made serious efforts to disseminate the research findings among women in their own regions. In some cases dissemination had already started during the research process, in others it was started after the 1985 workshop. They ranged from scientific seminars to articles in the popular press, to radio talks, exhibitions, a play and several attempts at fiction.

In 1987 a last workshop was held in Bombay.

By now all participants were ready with a first draft of their reports which were hotly debated. The atmosphere was open and constructive and we were able to discuss some of our major areas of conflict. We had learnt to respect our differences and be enriched by divergent points of view.

The teams had collected valuable material collected. In several cases it was the first time a women's organization or movement was documented, or specific problems analysed. The range of women's protests recorded by the project teams varied from individual bursts of anger, women's poetry and drama, to action groups focusing on immediate political and gender issues. Many myths about women were contradicted in the process, and lies about women's actions deconstructed.

Epistemology, methods and politics

Historically, feminist critiques on mainstream 'bad science' have been preceded by leftist critiques on traditional positivist research methods. Certainly from the end of the 1960s, scholars had realized that the search for 'social facts' had resulted in a social science which reduced people to 'objects of research', making their lives quantifiable. It was pointed out that this kind of research was blind to various levels of oppression, such as those based on class, race and ethnic or cultural identity. Latin American 'liberation sociologists' even emphasized the importance of a social science practice which would serve the special interests of oppressed groups.

According to them, the hierarchical relation between researchers and subjects of research had to be replaced by a methodological approach which stressed the 'view from below and from within'.[2] A researchers was expected to consciously side with those she worked with, try to see reality through *their* eyes and work on issues which were directly relevant to *their* lives.

These sociologists demonstrated convincingly that sociology and anthropology were not value-free disciplines just as an impartial science in itself was an epistemological impossibility. Freire and many others proposed that it would be better to make conscious political choices on behalf of certain social groups instead of trying to cling to the illusion of 'objectivism'.[3]

Action research became the catchword of the day. However, these liberation theoreticians excluded gender from their analyses. Trained in traditional Marxist theories, they brought all the flaws of Marxism, including its androcentric biases, into their scientific practice.

The next attack on the positivist, objectivist bulwark came from the feminists. Oakley[4] is one of the first theoreticians to grasp the extent of androcentric bias in both traditional and liberation social theories. Rejecting male-biased research, she stressed the importance of feminist research. She indicated that not only the subjects of research but also their researchers themselves may and will change through the research process. She emphatically rejected the 'false claim' of the value-freedom of social research, and emphasized the necessity to break down the hierarchy between the researchers and researched.

Feminist scholars engaged in an overtaking manoeuvre. Women were recognized as people capable of knowing their own reality. Women's experiences were added to many existing theories; parts of other theories were re-written to accommodate feminist points of view. Also research methodologies came under fire: many feminist social scientists in those years tended to reject the quantitative techniques of sampling and surveying and concentrated their efforts on qualitative, 'soft' research methods.

That soft research techniques are not automatically feminist, was pointed out by Davis Caulfield[5] in her critique of one of the 'softest' of the 'soft' methodologies—anthropology's preferential method of participant observation. Her conclusion was that researchers should move from their aloof and 'objective' way of applying the method of participant observation, to engage in what she terms 'partisan participation'. Anthropologists should take sides openly and should set about observing in a manner which would be partial to the interests of the people they were working with.

Other feminist theoreticians started attacking more fundamental issues. Not only was scientific research seen to be permeated by androcentric biases, science itself was considered an androcentric institution (although one continued to use many of its results). Mitchell,[6] Dworkin,[7] Rich[8] and Daly[9] are but a few of those feminist theoreticians who, each in her own way, set themselves the task of criticizing forms of science which legitimize women's subordination.

They proceeded to summon feminist theoreticians to construct theories and methodologies which would contribute to women's liberation. Daly places this process of theoretical liberation in the symbolic realm, in the area of the giving of meaning and theory formation:[10]

> The method of liberation then, involves a castrating of languages and images that reflect and perpetuate the structures of a sexist world.... It castrates precisely in the sense of cutting away the phallocentric value-system imposed by patriarchy, in its subtle as well as in its more manifest expressions. As aliens in a man's world who are now rising up to name— that is to create—our own world, women are beginning to recognize that the value-system thrust upon us by the various cultural institutions of patriarchy has amounted to a kind of gang rape of minds as well as of bodies.

Against this background Maria Mies formulated some guidelines for feminist enquiry.[11] Her work shows the heritage of the liberation sociologists. She emphasizes that value-freedom should be replaced by 'conscious partiality', a hierarchical relation by a 'view from below'. She posits 'change of the status quo' as the central element in feminist research and consequently stresses that feminist researchers should be activists as well, engaged in concrete struggles against women's oppression and exploitation.

The natural outcome of such a research process should be that both the activist-researchers and the women who are being researched are engaged in a process of consciousness raising. A focal point of such research, Mies points out, should be the historical analysis of women's oppression and their struggles against it. For, she argues, if women are able to recuperate their own history, they will be better able to fight against present oppression.

These were the authors who had inspired us when we conceptualized our project. They had made us aware that feminist theorizing is comprehensive and situated at all levels of science: at the epistemological level of the philosophy of science, at the level of individual disciplines, as well as that of operationalizing research and devising methodologies.

However, in practice, conceptualizing an empirical research

project involved certain choices. In 1981, when we started putting down on paper our ideas about research, many of the issues that Harding summarized as the dichotomy between 'successor' and 'standpoint' feminist theories were still somewhat unclear. 'Successor' theoreticians, according to Harding, are those engaged in improving 'bad', androcentric, mainstream science. 'Standpoint' feminists, on the other hand, criticize the very roots of science and aim to create not only a better, but a new feminist science.[12]

We did not take sides in this dichotomy, our guideline was more pragmatic and eclectic: to commit ourselves to a research project relevant to women's struggles and organizations. Many of the tools we used were constructed in the traditional mainstream social science practice. The adherents of the 'successor' theories had a lot to offer us: their critique was directly applicable to our methodological problems.

The position of the 'standpoint' feminists was harder for us to integrate in our thinking. Although we felt stimulated by many of their insights, in practice they posed quite a few problems. How does one stop a 'gang rape' by 'renaming a universe', for instance? We tried to map out the contours of a feminist science. But for the moment we agreed with Spender's conclusion that everything we now know is only temporary and not adequate, that 'there are no absolutes', that 'meaning is socially constructed' and that 'human beings seem to have an enormous propensity for imposing order (and meaning) on chaos'.[13]

We realized, to confront this 'chaos' of women's realities, we must work with the most current methodological instruments, improved by the critique on 'bad science' and formulated by the 'successor' theorists. At the same time we needed to sharpen our minds by listening to what the 'standpoint' feminists had to say. This dilemma—how to change science while having to work with whatever resources we find in existing sciences—remained central to our project. In course of the work we decided both approaches could mutually reinforce each other and that we were not going to be trapped by this apparent dichotomy.

Another epistemological consideration we adhered to was the breaking of the boundaries of individual disciplines. We viewed women's realities as holistic constructions to be approached from various locations. Political and social scientists, historians and anthropologists and specialists in communication, drama and the arts could yield valuable insights; valuable not only in the specific knowledge they would each bring to the project, but also in the perspectives from which they looked at the world of women. We decided not to be restricted by the artificial boundaries put up between these disciplines and to consciously compose a multidisciplinary research team.

In this endeavour we were greatly helped by various feminist critiques.

The historian Fox-Genovese[14] taught us to be aware of the contradictions and uncertainties in which women's lives are lived, and to incorporate them in our research. We accepted her viewpoint that feminist history should not be linear, but try to take into account contradictions of class, race and ethnicity as well as differences in women's position in their lifecycle.

Likewise, Kelly[15] reminded us that women might experience a relative loss of status precisely in those periods of so-called progressive change. To many project members, who came from a background where women felt 'betrayed' when the struggle for national liberation they had participated in did not result in women's liberation, this sounded familiar.

We also tried to take into account various feminist critiques on the very categories of social analysis (for example, bringing the concept of gender into the center of the analysis), on the concepts used and on existing theories of social change. Thus multidisciplinarity and eclecticism formed the core of our theoretical approach.

Methodological principles

Once the central objective of the project had been formulated, the methodological objectives were identified as follows:

- The research design should reflect the central elements of feminist struggles, democracy and self-reliance. Thus hierarchical relations both within the research team and between researchers and the women they would work with should be minimized.

As we were afraid that working from a centrally formulated question might result in a design which would not reflect the interests of all researchers, we decided to ask the country teams to define their own research questions on the basis of the common theme outlined earlier. Intensive preparatory contacts were made with the teams to discuss their ideas and to formulate research objectives in line with the felt needs of both the researchers and the subjects of their research.

- The researchers should be activists as well. We hoped the results of this project could be fed directly into the groups or organizations in the countries of the researchers. We also felt that researchers who were involved in women's movements would be better able to discern the most pressing needs of those movements.

Consequently, the project members were engaged in both activist and academic work in their own countries. Only in one case, the part of the research in Indonesia for which I was responsible, we had to deviate from this position, as it was politically impossible for Indonesian nationals to carry out this particular bit of research.

- Communication should be shared within the project as well as within the various feminist groups and organizations involved. Internally, we tried to promote communication among project members through three workshops, and by producing the quarterly Circular Letter. Each country team had its own coordinator at ISS, with whom the members were in regular and often very personal contact. The country coordinators tried to solve many of the practical research problems, along with methodological, financial and theoretical ones. Each coordinator paid several visits to the team she was involved with, sharing information about other teams.

As most of the researchers belonged to some women's group, sharing of research experience with those institutions was guaranteed in most cases. The phase of sharing with the rest of the world started with the last workshop held in Bombay in September 1987, and with the production of this collection of articles.

- The research process was to help strengthen the various

institutions involved in the project. This was directly ensured by the data collected. But we also hoped that the research itself would be a learning process for individual researchers. To this end a training course for some of the junior researchers was implemented at ISS.

* Stress was to be put on the methodological commonality of the teams emerging from the political commitment of the researchers. The theoretical commonality was more clearly discernible in the basic question from which all researchers departed than in the design, implementation and consequent findings of each research team.

Research needs at a particular moment dictated the selection of an available research method. Often the direct involvement of women whose histories of struggle were being researched into was sought and obtained. As this was easier to accomplish through group interviews and oral history documentation, these techniques were more widely used than traditional surveys. Additionally, in many cases the research required the collection and analysis of archival and statistical material.

In the selection of methods and in the way we used them, we tried to avoid the biases of an androcentric, 'objectivist' mainstream approach. Our ambitions to go beyond this, to venture into more innovative terrain, were expressed in our research questions, and in the purpose of the project, to spread the acquired knowledge to a larger audience of women interested in empowerment and social change.

Methodology: how far did it work?

Box[16] lists five criteria for a successful multidisciplinary research: creative leadership, conceptual clarity, methodological virtuosity, cross-disciplinary communication and flexible financing and administration. I believe we mostly met these criteria. However, in our case 'creative leadership' meant a sharing of leadership, democracy within the project and autonomy of the various teams, rather than a strong central leadership. Our performance depended greatly on a flexible and non-hierarchical, as well as creative leadership.

Secondly, although in our workshops we had many discussions on our central concepts, we did not strive towards unanimous agreement on definitions and the use of the concepts. In fact, when that was attempted in the first workshop, there was strong resistance to what was felt to be 'attempts to impose specific views'. We ultimately decided that the most important thing was to understand what each of us meant by certain concepts. In the process, all of us were forced to acquire clarity on the concepts themselves. On the whole, the fact that we strove towards a multidisciplinary design was evaluated very positively by all project members.

Our methodological objective to reduce hierarchy in the research design had a positive impact. We were able to operate in a highly decentralized way which is, to my knowledge, rare in such a complex international project. Communication was not always smooth, reports did not always reach on time, but on the whole the teams functioned independently.

The political commitment of the members of the research teams was reinforced by the independence they enjoyed in devising their own research strategies and formulating their own questions. Thus the researchers did indeed investigate issues which were of immediate concern to themselves and the groups they were involved with. I believe the high quality, and the immense quantity of data collected were in part due to these factors, which also helped to negate any hierarchical North-South relationship.

Our researchers being activists as well as academics, contributed to the relevance of many of the research findings. As we had expected, they began disseminating some of the research findings from an early phase of the work. In some cases this had an added advantage: the reactions of the women with whom the research data were shared yielded valuable additions to the data already collected.

Initially our funding agency was not enthusiastic about the need for a thorough dissemination of research data and heavy cuts were made on this item of the budget in the preparatory phase of the project. As a result, many researchers tried to share their findings with a larger audience as best they could, often by contributing several hours of voluntary labour. Fortunately, at a later stage, officials of the Ministry realized the importance of dissemination, and the project received an extension for this purpose.

The internal communication within the project deserves some extra comments. Initially, most researchers did not know each other very well. They also had hardly any idea of the issues which concerned their colleagues in other countries. This lack of awareness became very clear during the first project workshop at ISS, in 1983. Everyone shared a commitment to feminism, but it soon became obvious that feminism meant different things to different researchers. The common elements shared by all of them were their commitment to their organizations and there belief in the relevance of the project to these organizations.

In course of that workshop many participants gradually realized there were more common elements in the project as a whole. For instance, all of them shared an awareness of the fact that our work was innovative and subversive. Also, as far as specific mechanisms of women's oppression were concerned, it appeared there were unexpected parallels between situations that at first sight did not appear to have much in common.

During the second workshop at ISS in 1985, the common link that the project was creating between all researchers was felt more strongly. In spite of the theoretical and epistemological diversity of the various members of the project team, the common methodological principles and the actual experience in the field forged one common research project out of all the independent subprojects. Contentwise, this link was strengthened because the researchers recognized the common elements in the great diversity of mechanisms of oppression. They also felt that identifying these common elements would help to analyse the specific national or regional circumstances with greater depth and incisiveness. In the last workshop, in Bombay in 1987, this process was further strengthened. The researchers showed a clear concern for the issues women in the other project countries were faced with, and all saw the importance of international dissemination of the findings.

Another methodological principle, the aim to strengthen the women's groups or institutions that the researchers were involved with, was generally met. In Bombay, India, a new women's research and documentation centre was set up. In

Sudan and the Caribbean the research strengthened the respective academic institutions the researchers were involved with. In Somalia a new women's academic department was set up, and in Peru the work carried out by the research team could be fed directly into the various tasks the women's center Flora Tristan was involved with. Only in Indonesia this objective could not be met directly, due to the difficult political situation of the country.

Before dealing with some major dilemmas we faced, I will mention two constraints. The first is related to communication within the project and the logistics involved. Communication between The Hague and the research teams was often difficult, a situation which was compounded by political problems, such as in Sudan and Somalia. Communication between the various teams created even more problems. Often the route via The Hague created less problems than direct contact between, say, Peru and Indonesia.

Another issue was the workload of the researchers. We had consciously opted for researchers who were also actively involved in the women's movement. However, in course of the project it became clear that the dynamics of research and especially of report writing and activism may clash. In periods of crisis the immediate demands of activism may appear so overriding that the relative quiet required for analysis and report writing may seem a luxury.

The dilemmas we faced

As indicated earlier, the researchers utilized a variety of feminist approaches. I will try to sift out some of our dilemmas.

As I have already mentioned, an approach that greatly influenced important feminist epistemological considerations is the division Harding[17] makes between 'successor' and 'standpoint' feminists. From their vantage position in society, 'successor' feminists see themselves as the seekers and finders of the final truth; but they leave untouched the traditional methods of data gathering as well as the basic premises of the disciplines in which they are engaged. Unknown to themselves, they are caught in a central paradox: their attacks on androcentric science are carried out with the tools that they set out to change in the first place.

Those who try to avoid this paradox, have a more shattering approach, for they attack the very basis of scientific rationality. And, as Harding notes, as 'neither God nor tradition is privileged with the same credibility as scientific rationality in modern cultures,'[18] their attack is directed at the roots of modern culture: it is aimed at the very basis of thinking. Or, as DuBois puts it:[19]

> I do believe that feminism empowers and requires us to think very differently about the purposes and methods of social science than we have been able to do within the confines of the hegemony of androcentric science and worldview.

The central premise of the adherents of the 'standpoint' theory then, is that women's subordinate position in itself provides the clue of a 'better science', of a more complete understanding of reality as it is grounded in women's experiences as understood from the perspectives of feminists. Thus it is grounded in an essentialist vision of gender relations. Rightly, Harding questions this feminist universality by pointing out that there is not one feminist experience, but that women's realities are mediated by factors of class, race and culture.

The problem which then arises is how many feminist standpoints do exist, and which of the many standpoints is 'true'? If there are only 'situated knowledges',[20] what kind of a meta-principle exists to distinguish between all these 'truths'? And how do we 'weigh' the various elements that make up the totality of women's subordination in differing class, race and cultural settings? Harding's recommendation is that of a post-modernist feminist position, which attempts to embrace all these various differences as the basis for cooperation and solidarity.

However useful Harding's approach might be, my own experiences with the project lead me to believe that the danger of post-modernist relativism can be overcome only by clear political commitment—by constantly making political choices; by making these choices explicit; and by continually refining the tools, concepts and ideas which underline these choices. This Harding herself also indicates, although rather hesitantly.

Secondly, the dichotomy between 'successor' and 'stand-point' feminism may not be as clear-cut as Harding maintains. To Harding, 'standpoint' values are intrinsically better than the 'old', male-dominated values. Thus, 'standpoint' feminism is also a better 'successor' science. Yet post-modernist relativism does not recognize criteria to assess the improvement inherent in 'standpoint' feminism.

Lastly, the division between 'successor' and 'standpoint' feminists creates another dichotomy—this time not between 'the One' and 'the Other', or between 'Nature' and 'Culture', which feminists like Strathern have rightly criticized,[21] but within feminism itself. Would it not be more fruitful to search for fusion, mutually reinforcing women who advocate these positions?

Thus post-modernism may lead to political impotence. But there are ways to overcome this. After all, human beings are not passive recipients of their identities. Subjectivity is created by a continuous process of interaction with the world in which people become gendered beings, belong to a specific racial or ethnic group, while that world too goes on changing. Being in a certain position does not automatically mean that one has the 'right' consciousness. Also, identities are composed of elements which may entail different, or even contradictory struggles. One has to choose which element of one's identity to give precedence to, or which political struggle to prioritize. Post-modernism may not allow for a meta-ethos to help one make these choices. Yet it is vital that these questions, which are essentially moral ones, are discussed.

In our project, researchers who felt attracted to a post-modernist approach were never able to forget that they were all waging very real and specific struggles, and were daily affected by their race/class/gender positions. The purpose of the project was to validate this struggle, by carrying out a reflective, self-analysing practice geared towards empowering women to re-interpret their values and reconstruct a world which has more to offer them.

In this attempt at a 'passionate scholarship' (a term borrowed from DuBois), which rejects the dichotomy between science and the makers of science and which puts political and ethical issues at the centre of the feminist scientific debate, I propose we bring to the foreground our feminist perspectives not only on women's subordination, but also on the goals we set for ourselves. Many scholars have argued that politics has never been far away from science, and critiques of androcentric biases have pointed out the extent to which male interests were served by the way science was being constructed. I suggest we take this argument one step further and bring our feminist subjectivity to the core of the scientific debate; not to 'subjectivize' science, but to bring up for closer scrutiny the central values upon which any scientific endeavour is based. In fact, opening up our own political commitments for scrutiny at all stages of enquiry makes for the creation of 'better' science.

Theoretical and epistemological divergence

Although all participants in the project generally agreed to the methodological principles outlined above, they arrived there via different routes. In course of the research it became increasingly clear that these routes were based on sometimes widely diverging epistemological and theoretical positions.

The first group of researchers that I would like to distinguish adhered to a feminist theory which was based on epistemological and theoretical axioms derived from historical materialist theories. In their feminist-Marxist analysis, private property and capitalism were considered to be the most important factors causing women's oppression and exploitation. Much attention was paid to reformulating Marxist concepts such as labour, production and reproduction in an attempt to enlighten the historical materialist inheritance with feminist views.

Paradoxically enough, despite their insistence on the primacy of historical and socio-economic factors, these researchers emphasized the use of essentially ahistorical categories of 'sex' and 'patriarchy', instead of 'gender' and women's oppression or subordination. Most of the women in this group had a background of deep involvement with leftist organizations, besides their feminist activism. They came closest to what Harding describes as logical successors to Marxism, with historical materialism as a major part of the methodological baggage. They did not question the basic tools of historical materialism, nor many of the basic premises of various disciplines to which these tools could be applied. Epistemologically they insisted that their line of 'knowing' was the most 'correct' one.

Another group was much more hesitant about the central position of historical materialism. To differing degrees, its members emphasized that to understand women's subordination other factors besides socio-economic ones should be taken into account, like sexuality, socialization and other political, ideological and psychological issues. They also pointed out that pre-capitalist forms of women's oppression so far have not been dealt with adequately within feminist-Marxism.

Women in this group emphasized the use of the term 'gender' in trying to understand the social construction of the relationship between women and men. Also, they questioned some premises of disciplines such as history, and epistemologically moved into a closer scrutiny of 'male' ways of thinking and the 'male' basis of science itself. They rejected the monocausal and unilinear path of history and some of them (especially the ones from Peru) stressed the importance of 'rethinking' mainstream history, including the historical materialist versions of mainstream history.

To most participants belonging to this stream, their feminist present was of more importance than their leftist past. They could in no way be seen as a monolithic group, since various approaches were suggested embracing a wide range of theoretical positions. For the sake of convenience I shall call them 'feminist post-modernists'. Sometimes their ideas were rather vague and inconsistent. Although they rejected essentialism in principle, some of them were interested in a re-evaluation of women's values. Their viewpoints were probably closer to Harding's 'standpoint' theoreticians or to Alcoff's 'cultural feminists'.22

A major problem was that questioning science in general, or the basis of history in particular, was all very well, but they were not as successful in coming up with methodological tools to support their position. As their political activism and academic background were of a similar nature as that of the researchers in the first group, they ended up moving more or less within the same methodological realm as the other researchers.

The third group I would identify as the feminist-activist one, which was not so concerned with constructing theories or issues of an epistemological nature, but concentrated on the activist sides of the research. Although members of the first two groups belonged both to the ISS-based staff and the country teams, part of the resistance of the third group towards 'too much theory' was based on the fear of being overly influenced by theoretical positions perceived as formulated in the North. But, as one of them put it later, by keeping aloof from major theoretical issues, they also lost their chance to develop their own Third World perspectives on feminist theory-building. Their theoretical position mostly consisted of elements of the 'successor' theory, while methodologically they insisted on the importance of an early dissemination of the findings and devoted a lot of energy to that effort.

I would describe the members of the last group as feminist empiricists—those of us who stayed outside the theoretical struggles of the first two groups and at the same time did not prioritize activism in the same way as the third group did. The major concern of this group was to carry out the research as well as possible. The members selectively used whatever they thought would be of interest to their own work from the discourses of the other groups. Politically, they endorsed the basic premises of our research.

The major conflict within the project related not so much to the existence of these positions, as to the fact that the first group hardly wanted to recognize the existence of the others, and especially of the second group. Trained in Marxist-Leninist principles, they were convinced they walked the 'correct' path and that there could be no other.

As Maria Mies, who had to a large extent influenced the formulation of the methodological premises of the project, was one of the major protagonists of the first group, it commanded a certain prestige. I belonged to the second group and thus came into conflict with her.

It soon became apparent that the 'correct' line was not the tenable one, just as it proved quite impossible to squeeze all the various women's groups, movements and organizations researched by the members of the project staff into one single theoretical framework.

It was unfortunate that this struggle took up so much time

and energy that might have been spent more fruitfully on creative solutions to other major issues that came up as we went along.

However, the struggle was a necessary phase we had to pass through, and after Mies left, the conflict in effect strengthened the unity of the team. As one of us put it: 'The tears and confrontations proved that the solidarity between us was real, that we did not skip lightly over our major disagreements, nor were they swept under the carpet.'

Surprisingly, in the final analysis our differences had few methodological consequences. All of us subscribed to the basic premises and shared the political commitment necessary to sustain the research activities. The divergence within the team did, however, have an influence on the internal dynamics of the project, and forced us to look far deeper into issues that we in our different ways had taken for granted.

The common ground

The methodological principles all researchers strongly supported were the need to minimize the negative effects of the project hierarchy, the view that the combination of researchers and activists would be a major impetus to the research process, and that it was vital to disseminate research results among as wide a range of women as possible. As far as fieldwork was concerned, the researchers used those techniques most appropriate to the questions they were asking, drawing from a wide range.

As I have already indicated, researchers who questioned the mainstream periodization of history, took the present periodization as their starting point when it came to data collection, as did all other researchers in their historical work. It still remains to be seen how far the differences within the team will provide the basis for an alternative analysis of the research results.

Project politics: money and hierarchy

The hierarchical relationship between ISS/Ministry on the one hand, and the researchers in the field on the other hand as the recipients of the funds from the North, caused unavoidable strains.[23] The Directorate General for Development Cooperation of the Dutch Ministry of Foreign Affairs provided the funds for the project, while the ISS project team fulfilled a mediating function between the Ministry and the researchers. While the Ministry remained virtually invisible, the researchers were constantly aware of the neo-imperialist relationship between the donors and the ISS staff, which sent out reminders if reports were late, checked out accounts and, if all obligations were fulfilled, transferred the next instalment of funds.

In addition, there were some factors which, despite our efforts to the contrary, further emphasized the inherent hierarchy. For one thing, the research was to be carried out entirely in the South. This was partly because we felt there was no dearth of feminist researchers in Europe and the USA already working on the same issues. We also wanted to avoid a possible preponderance of western concerns. Nevertheless, we should have realized that the absence of a Northern team would further strengthen the idea of Southern countries being treated as permanent objects of research.

Another factor working towards hierarchical relations was the methodological principle that only researchers actually living in the countries concerned could be involved in the research. The unintended result was that the ISS team, like a spider in its web, became the sole central administrative body and financial guardian of the project. The fact that I, the general coordinator, was one of the researchers, did not change this situation, neither did the return of Rhoda Reddock, the ISS-based coordinator for the Caribbean, to her country of origin. It simply meant that I took over as the country coordinator. It did not lead to the researchers becoming more involved in the administrative burdens of the project, and we could find no way to draw them closer to the financial centre.

The pyramidal structure was further reinforced by two more factors. In the first place some important decisions were taken at the apex of the pyramid that neither the researchers, nor the ISS-based project staff could control. For instance, initially, the Directorate General reacted very positively to the research part of the project, but showed no enthusiasm for disseminating the findings.

Secondly, ISS became the theoretical and methodological axis. Communication on issues relevant to the researchers was done via ISS. It was in The Hague that some junior researchers received extra training in research methodology. It was the ISS team that sent out methodological guidelines to researchers in the field. Although everyone had the freedom of choice, this did constitute an attempt to retain some comparability and commonality in the project.

The negative effects were aggravated by the fact that some of the epistemological differences were fought out within the ISS team, and several researchers felt they were drawn into this battle against their will.

My own position was very vulnerable. Both as general coordinator and as researcher, I was firmly opposed to those among us who felt that their position was the only 'correct' one. But when I became one of the main antagonists of this position, although I was struggling to create room for all points of view, I was seen as a person from the North engaged in a battle some researchers from the South were not even interested in. Regardless of the views I held, the mere fact that I was one of the vocal Northern theoreticians branded me as a racist in the eyes of some.

Only after a major outburst did we realize that this had happened. This realization opened the way to a discussion on the relation between theory and racism.

Most of the researchers concluded that theory in itself has no colour, although many specific theories do, and that it is vitally important that researchers from the South formulate their own theoretical positions.

In the end, we can truthfully claim we did try to do away with some of the negative side effects of the inherent hierarchical relationship between donors and recipients of funds. But while we swept out what we could see through the front door, other problems related to this issue entered through the back door and settled firmly in the midst of the research process.

Some conclusions

In attempting to gain meaningful insights into a complex and incessantly changing social reality with the help of a scientific tradition which we, rightly, have come to suspect, feminist science has set for itself a staggering task. In this context, it is more fruitful to attempt to find ways of scientific cooperation, rather than stress epistemological points of divergence, however useful it may be to analytically distinguish these differences.

Creating dichotomies is a favourite western philosophical pursuit which may sometimes take away from the more important task of building bridges between opposing points of view. Working with a clear political commitment, and recognizing the validity of various approaches seem to me to provide a methodological practice which may yield the most promising results. It is important that feminist scholars create among themselves new forms of discourse which will lead to a collective pursuit of knowledge.

Meanwhile, our research has taken a modest step towards recuperating women's history, while contributing to the building of new feminist theoretical and epistemological insights. The richness of the data may give us some insight into the relation between struggles for 'equality' and the affirmation of 'difference', a fascinating area of enquiry.

My own emphasis on a flexible, eclectic, open and dynamic feminist epistemological approach does not mean that I lean towards the post-modernist position of an extreme relativist and essentially apolitical feminism. It is not only a matter of letting a thousand flowers bloom, but of carefully trying to pick those which form the best combination.

Feminism, as a politically motivated scientific set of theories can only be nurtured by a constant process of assessing the political positions taken, and by making conscious choices about strategic issues. And for that we have to be brave enough to work without a safety net of clear rules and guidelines. If we accept that feminism is a political position, and if we agree that science is a political process, that its assumption of value-free objectivism is false and politically loaded, we will have to realize that working within a feminist scientific approach means that every step we take we are affirming some political understanding.

In this process, distinguishing between the different theoretical positions, as Harding does, may be illuminating. Yet the underlying danger, of the dichotomies thus created being sterile, can only be overcome by consciously resorting to feminist politics. The only way to proceed, then, is by constantly assessing and reassessing our decisions, and each time sharpening to a fine edge the criteria by which we assess them.

NOTES

1. Joan Kelly, *Women, History and Theory, the Essays of Joan Kelly*. Chicago and London: University of Chicago Press, 1984.
2. Gerrit Huizer and Bruce Mannheim (eds.), *The Politics of Anthropology, from Colonialism and Sexism toward a View from Below*. The Hague: Mouton, 1979.
3. Paolo Freire, *Pedagogy of the Oppressed*. New York: Herder and Herder, 1971.
4. Ann Oakley, *The Sociology of Housework*. New York: Pantheon Books, 1974.
5. Mina Davis Caulfield, 'Participant Observation or Partisan Participation?' in: Gerrit Huizer and Bruce Mannheim, op. cit.
6. Juliet Mitchell, *Woman's Estate*. Harmondsworth: Pelican, 1971.
7. Andrea Dworkin, *Woman Hating*. New York: Dutton & Co, 1974.
8. Adrienne Rich, *On Lies, Secrets and Silence, Selected Prose 1966/1978*. London: Virago, 1980.
9. Mary Daly, *Beyond God the Father: towards a philosophy of women's liberation*. Boston: Beacon Press, 1973.
10. Ibid. p. 9.
11. Maria Mies, *Towards a Methodology of Women's Studies*. The Hague: ISS, 1979.
12. Sandra Harding, *The Science Question in Feminism*. Ithaca and London: Cornell University Press, 1986, and Sandra Harding and Jean O'Barn (eds.), *Sex and Scientific Enquiry*. London and Chicago: University of Chicago Press, 1987.
13. Dale Spender in Gloria Bowles and Renate Duelli Klein (eds.), *Theories of Women's Studies*. London: Routledge and Kegan Paul, 1983. p. 28.
14. Elizabeth Fox-Genovese, 'Placing Women's History in History,' in: *New Left Review*, 133, London, 1982.
15. Joan Kelly, op. cit.
16. Louk Box, 'Multidisciplinary Research in Development, How to Get There?' in: *Imwoo Bulletin*, Jrg 7, no 9, December 1989.
17. Sandra Harding, op. cit.

18. Sandra Harding, *The Science Question in Feminism*. op. cit. p. 16.
19. Barbara DuBois, 'Passionate scholarship: notes on values, knowing and method in feminist social science,' in: Gloria Bowles and Renate Duelli Klein (eds.), op. cit. p. 109.
20. Donna J. Haraway, *Simians, Cyborgs and Women, the Reinvention of Nature*. London: Free Association Books, 1991.
21. Marilyn Strathern, 'No nature, no culture: the Hagen case,' in: Carol MacCormack and Marilyn Strathern (eds.), *Nature, Culture and Gender*. Cambridge: Cambridge University Press, 1980.
22. Linda Alcoff, 'Cultural Feminism versus Post-Structuralism: the Identity Crisis in Feminist Theory,' in: *Signs: Journal of Women in Culture and Society*, vol. 13, no. 3, 1988.
23. Honor Ford-Smith, *Ring Ding in a Tight Corner, a Case Study of Funding and Organizational Democracy in SISTREN, 1977–1988*. Toronto: ICAE, 1989. Ford-Smith attempts an interesting analysis of the structures of power and inequality operating in the SISTREN theatre collective of Jamaica.

3
Women's Movement in Peru: The Early Years

Maritza Villavicencio

A heterogeneous country characterized by sharp contrasts and great inequalities, Peru evolved independently until 1535. The ethnic and cultural variety typical of the Andean world proved no hindrance to its high level of technological advancement, or to the development of its complex economic, political and social fabric. When the Spanish conquest took place, this process of development was abruptly halted. The 'trauma' caused by the conquest gave way to the structural problems Peru continues to suffer from today: profound gender, race and class differences, and sharply varying economic, social, cultural and political conditions.

The Republic of Peru came into being in 1821, under the rule of native born Spaniards, known as *criollos*. Identifying themselves more with their Hispanic roots than with the New World, the *criollos* governed Peru by turning their backs on the people and working against the interests of a majority composed of large numbers of native Indians, mestizos and blacks. Towards the end of the last century, with the inflow of modern ideological currents and the appearance of new social pressure groups, the existing social order began to be questioned. Parallel to this movement, the first controversial women's groups emerged. This process continued and reached its highest point during the first 30 years of this century.

Since 1978, a new and significant women's movement has flourished in Peru, specifically in its capital, Lima. Along with the challenges the movement posed, many questions arose as to what its ultimate destiny would be, and how to best articulate its demands. This led to reflection.

A first result of this process was recognizing that the movement was pluralistic and diverse. It had simultaneously emerged in three distinct streams: popular-urban, feminist and political. Searching for satisfactory answers to our questions, we came face to face with history. We found clear evidence that a process similar to the one we were undergoing at present had taken place at the turn of this century. This led us to ask why had the struggle of the women who preceded us not helped our own struggle? Why had their legacy been lost? What had happened to their organizations? Why and how had the women before us been silenced and forgotten? Would we suffer the same fate? What mistakes did they commit that it was important for us to avoid, and what had they done right that we might reclaim?

This article addresses the past from the point of view of the issues we are faced with in the present.

Rebel women writers

In 1876 the first *veladas literarias* (literary evenings or soirées) were inaugurated in Lima. This cultural event was the public expression of advances achieved by a whole generation of women intellectuals. The peak moments of these *veladas* are linked to the personal and collective history of a particular group of women writers. All of them had been educated at home by private tutors, under paternal surveillance.[1] Universities in Peru were closed to women until 1908.

Under the circumstances, what these women accumulated from their learning process was necessarily of an individual and intimate nature. This condition, I believe, determined the development of independent thinking, clearly differentiated from that prevailing among the men of their generation.

Another element common to these writers was their self-esteem, mainly founded on respect for their own intellectual production, all achieved with great personal effort and despite family and social opposition.

They contested the Catholic and colonial ideology, which looks upon women's intellectual capacities as inferior. They were aware of the constraints imposed on women, and of the fact that women were educated in a frivolous and superficial manner because of the attitudes fostered within the *criollo* middle and upper classes.

By demanding that women's education be reformed, they

were the pioneers of feminist assertion in Peru. They were the first women to openly intervene in the ideological-philosophical debate about the 'nature of the weaker sex', instituted in intellectual and religious circles from the colonial period onwards. It was because of them that for the first time a crucial issue was addressed: the constraints women faced in combining their domestic roles as wives and mothers with extra-domestic, intellectual activities in the public domain.

There is abundant proof of this: Mercedes Cabello de Carbonera wrote about her colleague Manuela Villarán de Plascencia: 'Once, with that noble wit of hers, I remember she said to me: "if you could only see me writing, my friend, you would feel sorry for me: I write surrounded by four or six children—while one takes away my pen, the other takes my eraser, this one screams at me because he thinks I haven't heard what he's asking for, and in the middle of all that racket and confusion, I finish off my composition and go on with my other occupations."'[2]

To the outside world these women writers appeared unaffected by the obstacles they met, primarily to defend themselves against attacks launched by men, who saw in the emerging contradictions an opportunity to further restrain women within the strict confines of domestic work.

However, the strength of reality made itself felt, and the women have documented their experience of being impelled to abandon conventional restraints after being married or having become mothers.[3] It seems more than a coincidence that the most prolific women writers, who played a leading role in Peru's social and cultural life, were either single women or widows. In effect, they were women who recovered their personal independence when the masculine guardianship under which they were placed disappeared.[4] Carbonera and Clorinda Matto de Turner were foremost examples of this phenomenon.

Although some women poets found literary inspiration in their own faith, the fact that they wrote at all entered them into conflict with the Church. As a consequence, with a few exceptions, this generation of feminists was anti-clerical. The social critiques launched by de Turner against the clergy's power over the native Indian population—as well as the feminist interpretation of the Gospel and the promotion of lay female education proposed by de Carbonera—influenced and marked their generation. Their points of view were highly controversial for the times. Having to defend the very existence of their literary craft, they also had to assert their political and ideological positions, questioning the Catholic Church's power, and defying the country's elite ruling class.

Both women expressed and supported their ideas through literary and journalistic writing, making use of existing cultural media or even creating new ones. They inspired the launching of the first two women's magazines in Peru: *La Alborada* (The Dawn, 1874), founded by Angelita Carbonell de Herencia Zeballos, and the weekly newspaper *El Album* (The Album, 1874), founded by the Argentinean writer Juana Manuel Gorriti and her Peruvian colleague, Carolina Freire de James. The best exponents of the female pen, and the most distinguished women intellectuals from this part of Latin America, contributed to both these periodicals.

The *veladas* were promoted by Gorriti, with the unswerving support from de Carbonera, who organized and conducted them. Sessions were held at night in the homes of the founders. Women writers thus reclaimed a previous experience dating back to the times of the colonial and early Republican periods, when women had promoted *tertulias* (chats or discussions) in their own homes. The *tertulias* had brought together politicians, intellectuals and military figures who determined the country's destiny. It was a strategy by which women indirectly influenced the political life they were barred from in public.

Thus the space that patriarchy had ordained for women to actually exclude them from all others, was revived to increase women's power. In contrast to the *tertulias*, the *veladas* allowed women to be key figures for the first time. They could address themselves directly to public opinion, without go-betweens. The central topics discussed always dealt with women's issues, even if the lecturer happened to be male. The programmes held were fundamentally of a cultural nature: music or poetry recitals, a lecture offered by a special guest speaker, and then discussion by those present. Very often these cultural events lasted through the night.[5] Although political and government matters were not discussed—at least not officially—philosophical and ideological subjects of a topical, political nature were dealt with.

Besides, as the *veladas* grew in importance, it became notewor-
thy in itself who was invited or not, who attended the sessions
or had stopped going to them. The *veladas* in Lima were interrupted during the war with Chile, but they later resumed and
reproduced in other cities such as Cuzco and Arequipa.
Throughout the history of our republic, Peruvian women have
never had the same political and ideological weight they earned
for themselves during this period.

It is important to stress that after the war against Chile (1879),
these women promoted the creation of private schools for female pupils, thus broadening and modernizing the limited Peruvian educational system.

This group of women writers made theoretical contributions
to the history of ideas in Peru, and influenced later generations
of rebel women. They introduced a specifically feminine perspective into the debate on women's status, not only redefin
ing the way issues already under discussion were dealt with,
but making possible new paths of exploration leading to other
focuses of interest. In this sense, what was particularly refreshing was the reflection springing from their own experiences as
women, that is, the pooling of cultural insights they had internalized in their gender relations, from the private sphere of their
domestic lives. Thus although there were differences among
them, they eventually acquired a common understanding, at
variance with the male point of view, and ultimately, in total
disagreement with men.

It is evident from their writing that, when approaching any
social dilemma, these women were concerned with modifying
the quality of human heterosexual relations, more than with
actually providing or regulating norms within the prevailing
perspectives of the State. The latter issue was more crucial to
the interests of liberal politicians. One of the themes showing
this difference in attitude is the issue of matrimony. Male liberals had become staunch defenders of civil marriage versus the
prevailing Catholic one. These men battled fiercely with the
Catholic Church to undermine its power over the State, and
attempted to build new civil spaces within Peruvian society.
Their proposal to introduce civil marriage in Peru, though indirectly dealing with women's freedom and women's rights,
was in truth only one more weapon in the anti-clerical struggle.

Advocating of civil marriage for these men did not mean they were actually taking women's opinions into consideration. This becomes clearer if we consider the subtle or direct demands women were voicing at the time in their own publications.

As far as marriage was concerned, most women writers did not much question the institution as such, nor did it matter excessively to them if the marriage was civil or religious in nature. Instead, many of their reflections centered upon the importance of love in marriage, and their severe condemnation of arranged marriages. These 'romantic or idealistic notions', as so many authors have called them, were for their time genuine social critiques of marriage, in defiance of patriarchal authority. This is most likely why men did not bother to listen to them.

Women of the elite classes married, or rather were married to, suitors selected by their fathers. The selection criteria did not take into account the feelings or opinions of marriageable daughters. Selection hinged on the economic and political convenience of the match, among other things, and was undertaken by an oligarchic and pseudo-aristocratic class interested only in continuing to reproduce itself. In this sense, daughters were a negotiable asset for men to remain inscribed within the social sphere of power.

Contradictions in terms of discourse between women and men were blatant. Male politicians participating in the debate completely ignored this aspect of the issue, focusing solely on the formal aspect of marriage and its public and institutional relations, while feminist discourse appealed to a sense of the moral and humanitarian, in order to modify internal relations, but without linking this to political and civic instances of formal power.

However, although women's digressions on daily life were not associated with formal politics, they did relate to politics in terms of an imaginary social paradigm in which women would have a full role, and that could not occur without women being involved in it. De Carbonera was the most lucid exponent of this Utopia. In dealing with topics like marriage and other issues, political discourse became disjointed from feminist discourse, because the profound logic of the latter was essentially of an ethical nature, while Peruvian politics left much to be desired in this respect. Women, already marginalized, chose to evade this field because they disapproved of it unanimously, and instead addressed themselves to a regime of ethical human relations.[6]

1900–1930: Three mainstreams of the urban women's movement

The trail opened by the women writers of the 1870s was followed by new generations of women, who continued to generate discourse on women's issues in a more complex fashion, incorporating new female practices resulting from the modernization of Peru's society, and creating new channels to broaden and improve their position in the public sphere.

New spaces for feminist practice and reflection are associated, from the end of the last century to the 1930s, with formal education, industrial training, social welfare, health, labour, union activity and direct political commitment. Three mainstreams of the women's movement branched out during this period, two of them directly connected to women writers: the feminists and the politically involved. A third, an urban-popular movement of women who belonged to the working class, emerged alongside Peru's industrialization and urbanization processes, at the turn of the century.

The political mainstream

In dealing with the political stream I am referring strictly to leftist movements that have existed since the beginning of this century. These were of a reformist or revolutionary nature, anti-oligarchic, anti-imperialist and anti-capitalist, mobilizing women for political change. It is necessary to clarify this, since right-wing politics has never produced an organic movement of any permanence which was interested in mobilizing women.

Anarcho-syndicalism reached its peak between 1911 and 1924, a period which coincided with the publication of its main organ, *La Protesta*.

This trend displaced the mutualism which had until then been prevalent among workers, incorporating certain aspects of working class culture. The mutualists had focused on both production and reproduction. They did not see workers only as individual labourers, nor were their demands aimed exclusively at wage improvement. Instead, the entire working family was considered the social subject of their actions. Thus mutualism strove to satisfy the needs of all its members: children, youth, women, the aged, etc. It addressed several issues, such as education, health and the 'social evils' threatening the family. Women's role was confined to providing assistance in events like illness and death.

The conflicts identified by mutualism had also been taken up in a collective fashion, as 'class' conflicts. So, for example, both mutualism and anarchism promoted women's organizations, or women's sections within the structure of workers' committees. Women belonging to these groups were encouraged to develop educational activities geared towards working class youth. The first technical schools for women in Peru were actually created under workers' initiative.

With the advent of anarchism, workers' activities took on another dimension. Hierarchies were redesigned under the logic of new doctrinal elements: the inevitability of class contradictions between proletarians and capitalists, focusing on the relationship of economic exploitation. This relationship acquired the character of struggle and confrontation: workers had to reshape their existing organizations with this purpose in mind. Syndicates and strikes came into being.

The creation of union structures served to exclude women from the workers' movement. First, because most workers were male.[7] Second, because as the unions emerged, they were bogged down by discriminatory ideological elements already in existence: women could not participate in a struggle that would inevitably involve violence, because violence was alien to their nature. Third, the movement developed as a channel for public political action, which automatically accepted society's unchallenged sexual division, restricting public activities, especially those of a political nature, to men. Women workers, therefore, were prohibited from joining the unions, even if they worked in a factory where men had formed one; they were also considered a threat to labour stability.[8]

However, both the women workers and women from working class families challenged this discrimination, utilizing the experience they had gained while participating in the former mutualist associations. When the unions called for a strike, networks established by women made it possible for the strike to continue, not only through the collection of funds, but also through other actions in support of the striking workers. Women's committees appealed to the solidarity of different social sectors, as well as to bourgeois political leaders, for intervention on behalf of the workers. They helped to popularize the workers' sruggle, and were directly involved in the conflict, organizing the *olla comun* (collective pot), and undertaking defensive actions in response to police repression.

The nature of women's participation under these crucial and dramatic circumstances caused a certain change of attitude in the male workers. Some unions started accepting women in their general assemblies, and several women were even elected to leadership positions. Even so, the participation of women remained an exception rather than the rule. Female segregation from the internal dynamics of syndicates had no correlation with the other working class and union activities, because parallel to all events, women kept up their mutual assistance strategies, and participated in recreational union activities.

Direct involvement of working class and intellectual women in ongoing debates, in propaganda, teaching and other activist practices, allowed them to create their own spaces within the general dynamics of the workers' movement. It made it possible to create and sustain a relationship based simultaneously on solidarity and confrontation with their fellow workers.

Women founded cultural centres and workers' libraries throughout Lima and the provinces, and managed to keep them functioning. Through these structures they established an organic network among the different nucleuses of workers. In the same way they entered the domain of the workers' press. They brought to both these activities their reflections on women's issues, fighting through them for the mobilization of all women.

This was possible because, on an ideological plane at least, anarcho-syndicalism held that women workers were submitted to the double burden of economic exploitation as workers and sexual exploitation as women. Thus, prostitution, abortion, child illegitimacy, etc. were depicted as calamities to which working class women in the capital were particularly vulnerable. The anarcho-syndicalist project was supposed to ensure a two-fold liberation of women workers.

This discourse, however, exempted male anarchists from feeling guilty about the sexual harassment of women in their own class. Furthermore, this approach turned women workers into one more object of controversy and rivalry between workers and employees. Just as women were labelled 'unstable elements' within the framework of male labour stability, they were also considered unstable in terms of anarchism's global project, as they were mostly illiterate. Women were thus considered particularly susceptible to conservative ideas, above all to the ideas transmitted by the Catholic Church. The heirs of liberal thinking fought for lay women's education as a factor of progress. They were under the impression that by modifying the ideological content of women's roles as mothers and educators (while not questioning the functions attributed exclusively to them), women would be better suited to the type of social change anarcho-syndicalism promoted.

The difference in the analysis of gender issues of anarcho-syndicalist women in contrast to their fellow male workers, resided in the fact that they always defended women's interests. Their discourse alluded permanently to the Utopia of 'liberty and equality between the sexes' offered by the anarchist project. The group of anarcho-syndicalist women always formulated its analysis and reflection on women's situation from this perspective. Therefore, besides decrying how capitalism made women into objects with the Catholic Church's complicity, these women also confronted the male workers, bringing into limelight the fact that violence against women was widespread in the working class. This helped demystify the idealized image anarchists had contrived regarding common-law unions, which was very popular then among workers in Lima at the time.

Different articles published by anarchist women on themes like morality, sexuality, freedom and equality of rights and duties for both men and women, subtly highlighted women's essence as human beings, while male writers still tended to portray them as mothers, wives or daughters of the workers. This differentiation on an ideological plane was best expressed by the independent press. *La Crítica* was a newspaper edited by Dora Mayer and Miguelina Acosta Cárdenas. Although

Mayer did not militate in the anarchist rank and file, her original ideas and actions linked her closely to female anarchists, especially to Cárdenas, a reputed anarchist leader.

The 'Apristas'

The Alianza Popular Revolucionaria Americana (APRA), or the Popular American Revolutionary Alliance, was founded as a continental political block. It became a political party in Peru in 1928, under its founder and historical leader, Víctor Raúl Haya de la Torre. Up to this time the intellectual generation nurtured by the 1919 University Reform had remained unified. The Aprista Party created a gap in this unity. When José Carlos Mariátegui founded the Socialist party also in 1928, the division became clear-cut. The controversy between the two parties was bitter and frontal.

For feminist intellectuals and activists the consequences of this division were even more drastic. In the first place, because the sectarian political option divided them into opposing segments, especially when the Socialist Party became the Communist Party in 1930. In the second place, the intellectual pioneers of feminist political theory opted for independence and even distanced themselves from the parties, when they realized that the newly-formed structures created no space to include their platforms. Ultimately this is what caused the silencing of feminist demands among the new militants.

This marginalization was directly experienced by the poet Magda Portal. She was a founding member of APRA, on its first Executive Board, who was put in charge of organizing its women's section with Carmen Rosa Rivadeneira.

To understand APRA's position regarding women at this stage, we must distinguish between what it preached and what it practised. Only thus can we explain how the platforms dealing with women's issues, which were approved in its First National Congress in 1931, were later retracted in favour of other political manoeuvres and party interests.

When the Congress was held, APRA advocated equal political rights for men and women, female suffrage from age 18 on, and women's right to hold public office, among other things.[9] Later on, APRA's proposal for universal female suffrage was substituted for the notion of qualified voting. Women were considered essentially housewives and barred from voting; they were said to be very conservative, and it was thought therefore they would cast their vote for the reactionary party. Even members of the Women's Section of APRA justified this shift in position. This is what constituted the break between the Aprista women and feminists.

Political and historical conditions favoured APRA's second leap backwards. Soon after Sánchez Cerro became president (1931), he launched an intense persecution of Apristas. Massacres, tortures, imprisonment, deportations, became daily occurrences. Under these repressive conditions, Aprista women formed support committees for detainees and their families, gave aid to the sick and wounded, and began international campaigns of protest. When in 1933 APRA became legal once more, the *protective* role women had played had become entrenched in such a way at the heart of the party, that it became a central element reinforcing its patriarchal profile.

The party was conceived as 'one great family', its leader as the father, the militant as offspring; women were supposed to be the mothers, and their main function was to watch over the integrity of 'their' large numbers of Aprista children. 'Motherhood' was supposed to become a supreme value for Aprista women, to the extreme that this trait was to constitute the axis of their political and personal identity.10

Women were only to define themselves in relation to others: there was no recognition of their militant capacity, and they were seen only as wives, mothers, sisters and daughters of Aprista males. All other aspects dealing with women were totally subordinated. The ensuing periods, when the party had to go underground, justified for its members the postponement of anything that did not involve the direct defence of the party's structure.

Internal conflicts reappeared once the party was no longer forced to remain underground. Its leaders continued to insist on the role of 'Aprista mothers' for all female members, trying to place them at the service of Aprista propaganda and indoctrination. They justified relegating women to perform the party's invisible tasks, at the cost of reducing their rights as citizens and as party militants. Magda Portal spoke out against these contradictions.[11] This led to her rupture with the party, which launched a campaign to discredit and intimidate her.

Socialists and Communists

The women who helped found the Socialist Party, later to become the Communist Party, were artists and intellectuals, since 1926 clustered around the publication *Amauta*, a monthly review of literary doctrine, art and controversies, that lasted until 1930.

The group's ideological scope was evidenced among other things in the encouragement it gave women to display their literary skills and express feminist, political or simply modern ideas about women. The foremost points of view expressed in the publication centred on the impact of capitalism on women's lives, and issues such as their entry into productive or 'outside-the-home' work, effects on maternity and child raising, and gender relations within the public activities women were entering: the labour market, politics, sports, etc.

The space generated by the *Amauta* nucleus remained open even after the Socialist Party was founded, but closed completely once this party became the Communist Party. Once it joined the Third International, it bound itself to the official standpoint, and became doctrinarian.

'Class', was seen as the axis of political analysis and practice, and women's problems came to be understood under this category. Women were seen exclusively as workers. Communists believed women's entry into the labour force would have disastrous consequences for the institution of the family, but thought women should organize themselves in the fight against capitalism, at least as proletarians.

Thus experiences derived from the private sphere were completely excluded from analysis, and even women's roles as mothers and educators were denied importance. The category of 'women' as such disappeared, and women only prevailed as workers. The feminist movement, which focused on gender demands and favoured female suffrage, was branded 'bourgeois', and as such, disqualified.

Even under these trying circumstances, the journalist Angela Ramos and the poet Adela Montesino from Arequipa have to be remembered because they remained true to their feminist ideals.

The feminist mainstream

There were two important stages of development of the feminist movement during this period, structured alongside the introduction of women into education, professional occupations, and other segments of the labour market, and through a multiplicity of interventions by women in the artistic, cultural, social and political fields.

On 28 October 1911, María Jesús Alvarado delivered a lecture entitled 'Feminism',[12] which was the first modern, political expression of the feminist movement in Peru. The character of her proposal was fundamentally political. This linked Alvarado to the liberal project on women's social emancipation at the end of the last century, and to suffrage movements in Europe and the United States. Alvarado took the thinking of her predecessors, and of the mutualist and anarchist mainstreams of thought one important step forward.

According to Alvarado, women's so-called inferiority was due to historical causes that required changes in conditions external to nature. She saw the need to provide women with paid work to achieve economic independence, and the requirement for a different education that raised women's awareness. She believed with these changes, women were bound to become active protagonists of national progress. All this meant that women must first enjoy the political and civil rights granted to men alone. Therefore one of Alvarado's central demands was women's suffrage, and right to hold public office.

Alvarado saw the State as the ordainer of social relations, and thus also as the agent of discrimination against women. She therefore appealed to the State and to institutionalized power. The assertive nature of her proposal led her to consider the need for concerted action among women themselves to achieve these demands. This is how the idea of forming a group was born, and how the first feminist association in Peru, Evolución Femenina (Feminine Evolution) emerged in 1914. The group undertook activities such as the creation of the Labour and Moral School-Workshop, and a campaign to seek women's holding of public posts within the cadre of Public Welfare Societies. These efforts synthesize the feminist-political character of Evolución Femenina.

Evolución Femenina

The new economic and social order, brought by the early industrialization process, caused the proletarization of large masses of the population, in particular of migrant Indians, blacks, and some foreigners like the Chinese. Slums sprang up in some urban areas, and shortages of public services, epidemics, prostitution, delinquency, and other new social phenomena appeared. Women were particularly affected by the new modalities of domestic service and by prostitution.

The affluent, aristocratic part of Lima reacted with shock to these phenomena, especially since it felt their effects: venereal disease reached epidemic proportions, and the upper classes became concerned with and discussed the problem in a sexist, racist and classist manner. For them it was merely a question of hygiene, of washing and cleaning the Indians, blacks and Chinese, so that white *criollo* members of the aristocracy did not get infected.

From its feminist position, Evolución Femenina adopted a diametrically opposed attitude. It saw the causes of prostitution in the socio-economic conditions faced by poor young women. With little formal education and no prospects of work, they fell a prey to prostitution because they needed to survive. To this was added the excessive power men held over women, and the impact it had on women (the fate of abandoned single mothers was often referred to).

Evolución offered as an alternative that women be trained for work, so that they could have the opportunity to earn an income without going against their human dignity. They proposed opening a school for this purpose, specifically geared towards 'fallen' women. Led by Alvarado, Evolución looked for and gathered support from certain political sectors, especially liberals, who at the time were relatively powerful. It also appealed to such information media as *El Comercio*, intellectual and political anarchists, and finally to so-called 'ladies of high society'.

Launching the school was a process of constructing social and political alliances, in the course of which the initial project had to be modified. It was initially conceived as a school for prostitutes who were still active. But in an effort to keep unity among those who were willing to support the effort, it had to address the issue of the prevention of prostitution first, eventually concerning itself mainly with very young women with little or no incomes.

In keeping with the principles of Evolución, women's entry into the public sphere was given priority. This was expressed in different ways, such as the demand for their right to suffrage, the reform of the Civil Code of 1853 and several other campaigns. A campaign to obtain the participation of women in the Sociedades de Beneficencia Pública (Public Welfare Societies) was a first step in the campaign to win the right to public posts.

The decision to choose this space as the first one to be fought for was not taken at random, but was rather a tactical measure, taking into account Peru's political and cultural context. It was easily accepted that this was 'an aspiration nobody could contest because these functions were not in conflict with female aptitudes and circumstances'.[13]

Many women in Peru from the upper and middle classes, intellectuals and fledgeling professionals, already belonged to modest charitable associations geared towards women. They, however, never entered the decision-making spheres of such institutions. Only men held the executive posts, because such public pisitions offered prestige and real power.

Once the social space to be fought for was selected, Evolución began waging a political campaign, which had a lot in common with the previous one on behalf of the School-Workshop, only it was wider in scope. The demand for women's involvement at the highest executive levels of the Public Welfare Society was presented as a legislative project before the National Congress. It thus raised a highly publicized debate.

A system of alliances extended to the members of Parliament. Two liberal representatives placed the project before the Small Chamber. Before and during the debate in the Chamber of Representatives, Evolución Femenina developed a broad campaign through the media, to sensitize the public. At its peak, this campaign caused strong confrontations with conservative sectors in and outside the Parliament.

The Legislative Project was approved in the Chamber of Representatives on 31 August 1915. This is considered the first feminist victory in our history.[14]

Introducing feminist ideology and praxis was no easy task in conservative Lima. However, the specific circumstances under which the movement thrived were favoured by the political and cultural climate of the time. Unfortunately, the situation backslided when this newly-emerging feminism reached its second stage of development in the mid-1920s.

Feminismo Peruano

Feminismo Peruano (Peruvian Feminism), another Peruvian feminist organization, was the second feminist endeavour in this century. It was created in 1924 by Zoila Aurora Cáceres at a time when every democratic channel was rapidly closing in the country. All opposition to the regime of President Augusto B. Leguía was being met with repression, especially opposition originating from or identifying with popular demands. One of these repressive measures—the imprisonment and later deportation of María Alvarado—was a rude blow to the feminist movement, and Feminismo Peruano ended up being a solitary voice in a hostile environment.

Adversity also came from the democratic sphere. The consensus needed for dealing specifically with women's issues, had begun to disappear due to growing political hegemony. Around 1930, when Cáceres returned to Peru and attempted to re-activate Feminismo Peruano under its original premises, the polarization of forces—between the oligarchy of landowners and the workers and syndicates—was identified with opposing political parties. The confrontation moved momentarily to the arena of the Constituent Assembly in 1932. One of the themes debated there was women's suffrage.

Cáceres, who since 1924 had campaigned in favour of women's suffrage through newspaper articles and lectures, concentrated her efforts now on winning the favour of the various political parties. But these parties, absorbed in waging a relentless war against one another, failed to understand

Cáceres's independent posture, and harshly criticized her for not adhering to a particular party option.

In truth, for feminists of anarchist and socialist roots to which Cáceres herself belonged, the situation was very complicated. On the one hand, the Unión Revolucionaria (Revolutionary Alliance) led by Sánchez Cerro, a right-wing party of anti-APRA and anti-Communist tendencies, was in favour of women's suffrage. During its short period in government it had legislated some of the measures feminists demanded, such as defending the rights of illegitimate children, reforms which had won Cerro the sympathy of women from the poorer sections of society. The Communists, on the other hand, completely ignored these demands, while the Apristas, who had acknowledged them at the time of their first Congress, later disowned them due to political manipulation.

Thus although the feminist struggle for suffrage had identified itself with popular union activism, an identification fostered by Cáceres and other feminists for more than two decades, a new dilemma now emerged because of the extreme polarization of political forces.

The controversial image of Cáceres that lingers, is due precisely to the fact that she did not accept the separation of both struggles; because under those conditions, separating them meant sacrificing one on behalf of the other. Cáceres insisted on keeping her political independence at all costs. Finally women were granted suffrage, but only in municipal elections.

Feminismo Peruano's other major action front was the creation of a women's union. Cáceres, encouraging workers to organize themselves in syndicates and calling for a general strike as she had done since 1916, kept alive her strong ties with the Comité Pro Abaratamiento de Subsistencias (Committee for Lowering Prices of Staple Products, 1919). This set Cáceres radically apart from Evolución Femenina. Although the latter expressed solidarity with the struggles of the Committee, particularly protesting reprisals taken against those leading the struggle, it did not participate directly in their activities.

In 1930, Cáceres, on behalf of her organization, supported the founding of the First Union of Sewing Mistresses of the State, involving herself in its internal conflicts, when adherents of the APRA party strove to impose themselves on its Board of Directors. In 1931 she also assisted the telephone workers of the Peruvian Telephone Company in drawing up a petition, and backed their ensuing strike. Cáceres's participation in the union movements meant another confrontation with left-wing parties, because she did not permit them to impose party interests while disregarding the interests of the women workers.

With the closing of democratic spaces, feminists became less outspoken, withdrawing into small circles which continued to advocate civil and political rights for women, but had little or no resonance on the political scene.

The urban-popular mainstream

The creation and development of the urban-popular mainstream was linked directly to the transformation of the economic order, principally due to industrial growth, which diversified the female labour sector. Changes in the material conditions of a large part of the urban population stimulated the introduction of women into the labour market, as well as the expansion of certain income-generating activities. If we take into account the fact that poor women have always worked, as part of native Indian servitude, black slavery, or as domestic workers, the events in the first three decades of the twentieth century led to some fundamental changes that carried within them the seeds of a major transformation in the social and political status quo.

One of these changes was the appearance of female labourers. The social and ideological repercussions of this new phenomenon were not so much because it was a novelty for women to be directly involved in production, but more due to the fact that they now worked long eight- to twelve-hour shifts in factories, and could spend very little time at home. On the other hand, although women's wages were lower than those of men, the fact that women were earning an income at all was indisputable.

From a conservative outlook, the very presence of women in the labour force questioned and undermined patriarchal hierarchy.[15] To this was added the fact that women in their new status as factory workers would experience first-hand the organization process of the worker-syndicate movement.

Although women workers might objectively have been considered progressive, what in practice occurred was that the real protagonists of the feminist movement in Peru were the wives, daughters and other female relatives of the workers. In fact, during the period of gestation of the workers' movement, this popular women's movement composed of relatives of male workers was closely connected with the early union struggles and even depended on the workers' movement in this first phase. The participation of women in syndicate organized strikes focused on providing the infrastructure needed to keep the strike going. However, the prolonged character of the strikes and the radicalization of the forces used to repress it, created an unexpected reaction of solidarity.

From being passive and staying subordinate to the union leadership, women progressively carved out a role for themselves in the development of strategies. For example, the female relatives of striking workers from the region of Huacho also stopped work. Since a majority of them sold food in the city, their strike cut short the city's food supply. Huacho women also took part in physical clashes, with tragic results for themselves.[16] The women of Vitarte struggled in a similar fashion.

The multiplying effect of women's mobilization took both politicians and union workers by surprise. But the popular feminist movement evolved to acquire a profile of its own, and became an organization seeking to promote women's interests, specifically during the second stage of the movement (1918–19), which was marked by the beginning of the struggle for an eight-hour working day. This period ended in a general strike protesting the high cost of living.

The general strike of January 1919 was the product of concerted efforts of different labour sectors, in Lima and its surroundings. Its central demand was the eight-hour shift, which had been legislated a few months earlier in 1918 for women and children. Union leaders suspended the strike once this goal was reached, leaving unsettled other platforms and petitions, like an increase in wages.

Not every one was satisfied with the strike being called off, in particular a large section of the popular movement that had joined the struggle in solidarity, but did not benefit directly from a shorter working day. This group was being seriously affected by the high cost of staple products, which had caused the standard of living to decline considerably. The feminist contingent was located within this part of the movement. In contrast to previous mobilizations, its composition had diversified. It no longer included only relatives of the workers, but reached out to all women united by their common interests as housewives.

When the Comité Pro Abaratamiento de las Subsistencias was founded in April 1919, its women's committee came into being almost immediately. Its starting point was the first Assembly of Women in the social history of Peru, which in its turn organized the First Women's March on May 25 of the same year. A few days later a general strike demanding that prices of staple products be lowered took place. The high level of women's militancy attracted the attention of the national media. After several days the strike faltered without the Committee having obtained any of its demands. From this moment on, the union movement under anarchist leadership retreated from the struggle, practically abandoning the Committee. In contrast, the women remained active and added new demands to the struggle, like the demand for lower house rents.

The third stage of the popular union movement was characterized by its retreat after the 1919 defeat, and by the intellectual middle-class stratum entering the political scene. This was fundamentally an ideological moment led by the student movement, which also received popular support.

In contrast this period marked the peak of convergence of the three mainstreams of the women's movement. When the decade of the 1920s drew to a close, poor urban women had managed to articulate their interests and establish their unity. Shortly afterwards, their leadership became divided into two factions belonging to two political parties: the Revolutionary Union and the APRA. This subordination to political interests meant a strategic defeat for the women's movement.

Convergence of the three mainstreams

Between 1910 and 1930, the three mainstreams, which also characterize the contemporary women's movement in Peru, gathered strength for the first time, acquiring content and form. No matter how the history of each stream was shaped, what was their ultimate destiny and the challenges each faced during this time, the history of the women's movement would remain incomplete if we were not also to reconstruct the links that existed among them—their junctures and their differences. It was precisely that day-to-day convergence, sometimes slow and silent, at others dynamic, ebullient and radical, which determined the weight of women's historic presence. It was also their failure to communicate which determined their disappearance.

During the initial period of growth of anarcho-syndicalism in the workers' movement, women intellectuals established links with women workers. But these contacts were always mediated by men, first because male leaders played a key role in the political struggle, and second because the very same activities carried out by the women were geared towards mixed groups.

In other words, although women-only spaces formally existed—for example, women's clubs were organically composed exclusively of women, and newspapers like *La Critica* were addressed solely to women—the rallying points for action were heterosexual. Political spaces were conceived as heterosexual.

Feminists were invited to the meeting point between women politicians and women workers, the other two streams of which the movement was composed. These feminists maintained stronger ties with the more anonymous sections of poor urban women than with women politicians. Thus in the unions, female anarchist intellectuals linked up with female workers, basically in their capacity as political activists. In the sphere of formal politics, especially in 1914 and 1915, the feminist movement was the cohesive force. The most notable characteristic of this period was the parallel action of both blocks, each using a different leverage point to open social and political spaces of and for women, the one through strikes and the other through organized campaigns.

As time passed, the union movement gathered momentum and crowded out all other ideological, political and social streams. Women from the urban-popular mainstream became the focus of the feminist movement, exerting a centripetal attraction on the other two currents. The peak of the alliance was reached in 1919, during the struggle for lower prices.

The character of the women's movement was exclusively

female, cutting across all classes and multi-ideological, and it was under the hegemony of interests held by women of the popular mainstream. Nevertheless the control which this mainstream exercised did not last, having grown out of the heat generated by the syndicalist movement. When the momentum of the syndicalist movement declined, the popular women's movement lost its perspective, as did the other mainstreams that had converged on this unique historical occasion.

The following phase was one of disintegration, and with it, the first great feminist cycle in the republican history of our country came to an end.

NOTES

1. Jorge Basadre, *History of the Republic of Peru, 1822–1933*, vol XV and XVI. Notes for an Educational and Cultural History, seventh edition, Lima: Ed. Universitarias, 1983.
2. *El Peru Ilustrado*, No. 77, 1888. p. 459. Data obtained with the generous help of Gaby Kuppers.
3. Elvira García and García, *Peruvian Woman Throughout the Centuries*, 1924.
4. Maritza Villavicencio, 'The Roots of the Women's Movement in Peru,' working paper, Women's History sub-series. The Hague: ISS, 1987.
5. Juana Manuela Gorriti, *Literary Soirées in Lima 1876–1877*. Buenos Aires: Imp. Europea, 1892.
6. Maritza Villavicencio, op. cit.
7. Marfil Francke, 'Women's Work in Lima 1876–1920,' working document of the 'Roots of the Women's Movement in Peru Project'. Lima: Peruvian Women Center Flora Tristan, 1985.
8. Frida Both, 'Women and the Workers Movement in Lima 1900–1930,' unpublished MA thesis, University of Amsterdam.
9. Magda Portal, 'Aprismo and Women,' Appendix 2: Papers presented by the Feminist Section of PAP Lima, to the Departmental Congress and to the First National Aprist Congress, and approved unanimously. Lima: Edit. Cooperativa Aprista Atahualpa, 1946.
10. Ibid. p. 52.
11. Magda Portal, 'Women in the People's Party.' First National Convention of Aprista Women, meeting from 14 to 24 November 1946 (Annotations for a history of the people's party). Lima:

Imp. El Condor, May , 1948.

12. Maria Jesus Alvarado, 'Feminism,' conference paper read on October 28, 1911 in the Geographical Society of Lima, 1911.

13. Maria Sara L. de Castorino, and Dora Cordova, *Feminist Evolution, An Extraordinary Woman: Maria J. Alvarado Rivera, Synthesis of the Crusade for the Recognition of the Rights of Women, Children and All the Oppressed*. Lima: 1962.

14. Jorge Basadre, op. cit.

15. Alejandro Deustua, 'The Fatal Transformation of the Family', *The National Culture*, Chapter.XII. Lima , 1937.

16. Carolina Carlessi, *Women in the Origins of the Syndical Movement. Chronicle of a Struggle, Huacho 1916–1917*. Lima: Lilith and Tarea Editions, 1984.

4
Women's Movement in Peru: Rebellion into Action

Virginia Vargas

In the past decades, women in Latin America have spoken out in different ways, with different voices, in shouts and whispers, in what already amounts to a historically significant rebellion. Having been confined for too long to private, invisible spaces, women throughout the continent are now invading the streets, town squares and other public terrain, demanding to be heard.

This experience has not only contributed to changing women's daily lives, their values and ideas about social and personal relations, it has also implicitly or explicitly served to confront societies' established structures, and is contributing a new vision of social conflicts and social transformations.

The present-day women's movement in Peru bears special significance in the Latin American context. The characteristics of the movement and the circumstances under which it continues its struggles, makes the Peruvian experience the basis for analysing the potentials and constraints of women's social movements throughout Latin America.

The women's movement in Peru is one of the largest in the continent, with probably the most diversified forms of expression and organization. This is regardless of the fact that Peru remains one of the most traditional and patriarchal societies. The influence of the Catholic Church and historically deep-rooted male authoritarianism have greatly affected women's status in the country.

Peruvian reality is exceedingly complex, and the variety of ways through which women choose to cope with their lot reflect this complexity. The country is a microcosm of Latin America's multiracial and pluricultural reality, presenting, as Calderon[1] points out, not only cultural and ethnic differences, but also a simultaneous mix of stages of historical development:

combining the pre-modern and modern with the post-modern.

This makes for a complicated process of transformation. The juxtaposition of different societies and historical stages results in a more intricate accumulation of unresolved tasks than in most other countries. The fragmentation of its social fabric, and the deep polarization evident in its society, make it difficult to think of Peru as one nation.[2] Diversity and inequality are therefore the country's main characteristics.

On a broader scope, and exerting great pressure on all of Latin America's social movements but particularly on the women's movement, is the economic crisis. The effects of the crisis on Peru's economy are among the most profound on the continent. This, coupled with an extremely heterogeneous reality, has made Peru's sharp social, ethnic and gender-based contradictions impossible to resolve throughout its history. Perhaps for these very reasons, the effects of terrorist violence on different sections of society are so marked. Meanwhile, the State has proved ineffective in providing even a partial solution to either the economic crisis or the escalating violence.

Regardless of these factors, the last two decades the ordinary people of Peru have gained in strength. Civil society was strengthened through the coming to power of reformist populist governments, in particular Velazco Alvarado's military government, which for the first time successfully pierced Peru's long-lasting oligarchic hegemony. At the same time, diverse social sectors, traditionally excluded from the social and political scene, began creating political spaces for themselves, demanding the right to participate in the process of nation building. This is the soil that nurtured Peru's new social movements during the last decade.

Basic assumptions

Along with other analysts, I too believe that the new social movements, and in particular the women's movement, by the very fact of their existence, have come to question radically the way societies are structured. In so doing, they have made evident the complexity of social dynamics, highlighting the existence of many more areas of conflict than the ones related to class alone.

The new social movements stress the links between daily life and power relations, within which it is possible to bring about social transformation. These activated spaces, seen from a fresh perspective, permit new collective actions, and allow for the presence of multiple social subjects that have come to contribute strategies for attaining political change, change which until now had been untested.[3]

For Peru and Latin America as a whole, the complex social and political processes these new movements initiate may very possibly prove to be the primary base for constructing more democratic societies. Their novelty does not lie only in the agents they draw attention to, but also in raising (and attempting to deal with) new issues, giving fresh interpretations to old problems and advancing new social practices.

The Peruvian women's movement presents a plurality of processes showing the diversity of women's realities throughout the country. In this respect perhaps we should refer to several women's movements. But I prefer, for the sake of analysis and to better explore interrelations, to speak of a *single* women's movement, of which heterogeneity is an outstanding feature. Variations give to it a richness and a clearer sense of reality, reflecting the complexity and variety of female existence.

The women's movement in Peru has developed different dynamics and goals according to the specific every-day contexts in which women live. Within this pluralistic movement we can distinguish three distinct streams: the feminist stream, the popular women's stream, and the stream emerging from traditional public spaces.

These mainstreams touch and intersect with each other continuously. Women from political parties and slum areas may equally think of themselves as feminists; women from the feminist stream may identify with and accept the political views of certain parties, and so on. But the streams also develop their own actions in different spaces and combine different goals. They can even appear to clash or be at odds with each other. In other words, each stream continues to develop its own mechanisms of interrelation and solidarity.

Here I would like to refer to two important approaches in relation to the study of social movements, that have been presented by Alberto Melucci[4] and Chantal Mouffe.[5] Melucci warns against the risks involved in considering social actors as a given or static reality. On the contrary, he points out:6

> Collective actors are themselves...the outcome of complex processes which favor or impede the formation and maintenance of solidarity, shared cultural and organizational ties, which render common actions possible.... Collective actors are social products, as a set of social relationships and not as a primary datum or a given metaphysical entity.

Mouffe develops another important approach when she affirms the existence in each individual of different subject positions, corresponding to diverse social settings. Each position is built around a specific discourse and cannot be considered the ultimate or fundamental interest *a priori*.

There is no single way to express gender subordination. The existence of the three streams demonstrates that the movements contain a plurality of levels and social practices, which can have different meanings and forms of action.7 They can also have the potential, through social practices originally centred perhaps on a single issue, to reconcile different tasks and goals simultaneously. For example, some social practices point to new values and the possibility of constructing new identities, in which women's roles are no longer rigidly considered 'natural' and therefore unchanging.

Mouffe states, individuals can be democratic in some positions while maintaining non-democratic approaches in others. At the same time, introduction of equality within one subject position can be extended or generalized to positively affect other subject positions, thereby democratizing the rest. This process does not occur once and for all. 'Subjectivity,' for Mouffe, 'is always precarious and provisionally fixed.'8

The ability to construct more truly democratic subject positions cannot be easily delinked from gender, because this is a crucial point in dealing with why women have not obtained rights at the same level as men. Possibly this is due to the fact that all women's subject positions are built upon the basis of women's subordination.

If, for example, a democratic modification of the position of women as workers was to begin, all kinds of factors associated with gender would necessarily have to be considered: the fact that enterprises are legally permitted in the first place to pay women less than they do men for equal types of work; the sexual hierarchy of the labour market; the constraints double standards place on more active female participation in trade unions, etc.

This is not to imply that the only way of developing this process is through overt feminist stands, or by placing gender issues *a priori* as of the 'first and foremost interest'. On the contrary, we must realize that everything relating to women's interests or roles within the family and society includes gender subordination, and if the issue of gender is raised explicitly it can enlighten the complexity of interrelations touching upon women's subordination.

I treat the sex-gender system[9] as that which explains, among different cultures and societies, or even within the same culture and society, the specific way in which men and women relate and how, throughout the world in almost all cultures and societies, the subordination of women has been part of each historical context.

A multidimensionality of situations of power, subordination and exploitation constitute the female identity. To connect specific experiences, realities and differences of Peruvian women by focusing on gender does not mean there is a common or static consciousness inherent to all of them. On the contrary, each stream has developed its own elements to reach specific ways of understanding and modifying their circumstances.

Focusing on gender has a great potential value, but the process is not a simple or automatic one. We have clear examples of how women can link up the struggle, for example, for subsistence, with a new concept of democracy and citizenship in which awareness of gender subordination is always present. In many other cases, visualization of the conflicts surrounding gender simply does not take place, because of the different influences that women's practices receive by way of discourses that point to pre-established patterns of behaviour and eclipse the real significance of gender awareness.

On the other hand, there can also be a kind of restricted gender subordination awareness, permitting the creation of democratic links with other subordinated subject positions at personal and collective levels, while at the same time maintaining a narrow, hierarchical view of others. Some women can be quite clear about their rights in relation to their work or their bodies, but may hardly be aware, for instance, that racism pervades their relationship with women who perform paid domestic work in their homes. Another expression of the difficulty of integrating existing dualities is the shortcomings various streams of the urban women's movement have encountered trying to develop a non-racist approach in their relations with rural or black women.

The last few decades

The women's movement of the last few decades differs in various respects from that at the beginning of the century, but there are also important similarities: the struggle undertaken by women at the turn of the century, their demands for better education, jobs, suffrage, and the right to have their own organizations and magazines, also had deep political meaning and strongly questioned society's structures in much the same way as the present movement has.

Today, clearly the partial defeat of the oligarchic domain, the modernization of Peru's economy, the growth of urban areas and social services, have all contributed to women's having greater access to schools, universities and the labour market, specially in the cities. A very important fact resulting from the increase in opportunities is that women now have more access to information about controlling reproductive functions. While shifts in education, labour opportunities and ideology have not done away with sexual discrimination altogether, women's horizons have definitely widened.

Here it is important to recognize the process of political antagonism described by Laclau and Mouffe.[10] This antagonism emerges, they say, when a collective subject constructed in a specific way, to a certain existing discourse, finds its subjectivity negated by other discourses or practices. But it can also emerge when subjects, constructed on the basis of subordination by a set of discourses, are at the same time convoked as equals by other discourses, producing in such a fashion a contradiction that opens the possibility to desconstruct the previous subordinated construction.

The basis for the emergence of political antagonism was given to women when new ideas and discourses about their roles and their destiny began to appear in society, not only due to the existence of feminist ideas, although these made a great contribution to this process, but also because of society's and the economy's requirements to have women incorporated into the labour market. At this point contradictory discourses began to appear. The majority still addressed women calling upon their traditional roles, but others began referring to equality and democracy, denying their 'subjectivity of subordination'.

These facts do not ascertain how political antagonism is formed, but rather provide its background. Along the same lines, for example, Lourdes Arispe[11] speaks out about the importance of knowledge about and access to contraceptive methods for women, whether they decided to use them or not. The mere fact that women could use surer methods of contraception opened up new possibilities, dramatically changing their vision of their destinies. If a woman's destiny was no longer only motherhood, we had to question ourselves and search for alternatives.

If we accept Heller's[12] assumption that social movements originate from unsatisfied needs—which may well explain the emergence of political antagonism—two kinds of needs surface in the case of Peruvian women. Changes in social structures opened up new spaces and brought new expectations, but did not provide access to better jobs, truly egalitarian educational opportunities, etc. At the same time, changes within family structures resulted in an increasing number of women-headed households.

The recent period of intense social developmen for a time also generated a convergence with the new demands that women were making. New social practices and discourses demanded more mass participation, questioning authoritarian ways of doing politics hitherto imposed by traditional organizations. Although women began to be protagonists in this process, they did not benefit directly from the resulting changes. Discourses reinforcing their traditional role still pervaded most political institutions and the whole of civilian society.

During the early 1970s, many women from different social sectors, but especially from the middle class, felt that the only possibility of rebelling against and rejecting their traditional roles was through political parties, particularly leftist ones. They soon found out that the left was just as uninterested in raising women's issues as the right.

Two other recent circumstances have deeply affected the course of Peruvian women's lives: the severe economic problems and the deepening political crisis. The economic problems have caused a great increase in many women's daily work load, pushing them outside their homes on a massive scale in quest of any kind of work, or forcing them to seek alternative ways of cutting down on their household expenditure. Most of the time they have developed collective strategies. Although the economic crisis first affected women in the slum areas, it has also been felt by women workers and middle-class women. At the same time, the nonexistence of a strong welfare State has also forced women to seek communal solutions to minimal health, water and sanitation, and child-care needs.

The deepening political crisis and increasing violence also affected women's lives by further restricting their channels of expression. Women from all classes began to seriously question prevailing social structures and reject the traditional notions of female destiny, voicing their objections even while they were active members of left-wing parties. In the eyes of countless Peruvian women, many institutions and political parties lost credibility and legitimacy during the 1970s and 1980s.

These structural changes and the existence of conflicting discourses regarding women's roles were the basic elements contributing to the emergence of the different streams of the women's movement in Peru. There is a growing trend today towards viewing the economic crisis as the main factor leading to the rise of women's organizations in Peru. The economic crisis of the last decade did give a significant push to women's organizations, but it did not cause the movement to materialize. The crisis has merely accelerated processes that were already developing throughout the country. We will attempt to see later how, instead of fostering the women's movement, the crisis is actually limiting its development.

It is important to remember that unlike in other Latin American countries (such as Chile, Brazil, Argentina), the recent women's movement in Peru grew in strength, plurality and diversity not during a period of dictatorship, but within the process of democratization of Peruvian society, following nearly twelve years of military rule. It was during the military regime itself that women began to confront different discourses about their roles, and develop new forms of participation.

This resulted in a somewhat contradictory process because, as Maruja Barrig[13] points out, it was the military government which fostered untried ways of representation and important organizational channels. For the first time in Peru's history, the State developed fresh policies in relation to women, addressing women's dignity and equality. Despite government control, people could exercise new forms of participation; new notions of citizen's rights thrived. It was also an important period of development for new left-wing political parties.

These factors lend credence to Bourricaud's[14] contention that the period was one of 'soft' dictatorship (*dictablanda*) rather than 'hard' (*dictadura*), a Spanish pun on words I can only approximate. While it is true that during the military government's last days in office important mobilizations took place at local, regional and national levels, these had more to do with economic demands than with a genuine desire for a more democratic regime. Women joined these struggles primarily to port the men, although they did assume active roles during street barricades staged in slum areas.

What I wish to emphasize here is that despite the broad deployment of the women's movement during the present democracy, the democratic spirit has never been too strong in Peru, a factor that is bound to influence all movements for change. It also helps explain why civil society continues to regard new expressions of social conflict with suspicion.

Discovering alternatives to construct their own organizations and exert influence as citizens has effectively influenced women's lives. But the country's authoritarian legacy perpetuates the difficulties women continue to have in believing they can create more democratic relations among themselves.

Building the streams

There is a clear continuity between the early streams of the women's movement which appeared at the turn of the century and the movement that has flourished in the last few decades. My personal feeling is that after 40 years of hidden efforts under the most adverse circumstances, the recently emerging streams also reflect the hopes that the first generation of these women could not achieve.

The first feminist group, Alliance of Peruvian Women (ALIMUPER) appeared in Peru during the early 1970s, fighting in public for the first time against the image of women as sexual objects, against the all-popular beauty pageants, etc. Struggling on alone for close to five years, the actions they engaged in lacked acceptance from society or even from other women. In 1975, under the momentum of the International Women's Year promoted by the United Nations, the reformist military government formally established the first State effort to 'revalue' women's status.

This opened an important channel to discuss and produce some insights concerning women's marginalization in society. All such initiatives remained isolated, but they gave important impetus to the women's groups and organizations that appeared towards the end of the decade. From below, women's pressure was represented by ALIMUPER, and from above, at the State level, by the National Commission of Women.

Some women's organizations sprang up in slum areas, most of them with a very patronizing approach, through Mothers' Clubs and other traditional organizations closely linked to the large conservative wing of the Catholic Church. In any case, these women's groups revealed the existence of women's potential to become organized in those communities, and to establish informal networks of solidarity to help each other in their daily problems and with their family obligations.

Towards the end of the 1970s, women's critical voice faded away in the left political parties, mainly because, aware of their subordination, these vocal women eventually left and formed separate groups, which became the real feminist stream.

By 1979, the complex process of development of all three mainstreams had become more visible and forceful. They started with parallel development, and at first there were no significant links among them. Even within each stream, women in different geographical or interest areas hardly knew one another. However, in the last few years the situation has changed greatly and true bonds of support and solidarity have formed both within and between the streams.

How gender complicated our lives

In 1979 a number of middle-class women, at first with no links among them, began to organize ourselves. These groups (Manuela Ramos, Flora Tristan, Socialist Front of Women, Autonomous Women, and ALIMUPER) evolved into a feminist stream. We questioned the conditions we faced as women, our conflicts within the family, female participation or lack of involvement in Peruvian political spaces, and so on.

This stream was composed mostly of women who had first been strongly militant in left-wing political parties. This background gave important political dimension and scope to the emerging feminist movement, but also represented, as it still does at times, one of the most significant limitations of the movement. The leftist origin also explains why one of the main problems we had to confront was believing the issues we were raising had legitimacy in themselves, for us and for society. Our initial struggles as feminists were not against our oppression as women, but against the exploitation of workers. We went out and supported miners', workers' and teachers' strikes We formed part of the left spectrum, almost without differentiation as women. Our central objective remained the fate of the ordinary woman, perhaps in the beginning more out of leftist ideological influence than from a conscious political feminist approach.

We learned in a very brutal way that party politics was not our space; that if we did not raise our own issues, nobody would do it for us. The first demonstration we organized demanding women's right to decide on their own reproduction, and opening the controversy on abortion, got a tremendously hostile reaction from men, and also from many women inside and outside the political parties. From being perceived as competent, intelligent women who had been supporting the general struggle, we were now seen as hysterical middle-class women, trying to divide the people's unity under the influence of western feminism.

It was through reflection and self-critique that we began to criticize traditional political action, acquired an intuitive knowledge about the complex web of realities, and became aware of the right each particular subject must wield to organize and express his or her own demands to society.

In recent years, feminists have developed a relatively strong presence in Peru. There are several independent feminist groups in different cities, linked through local, regional and national networks around specific issues such as reproductive rights, violence, human rights and communications; age or sexual preference (like the lesbian feminist collective); religious options (like the Christian feminist collective), etc. There are feminist magazines and periodicals; there are thriving groups of poets, journalists, film makers and experimental theatre groups. A large documentation centre has been established, which supplies legal and medical services and so on.

The feminist stream has a visible presence in several endeavours, such as actions around human rights and world peace, and takes the lead in national and international commemorations such as March 8, July 22 (the Day of Domestic Labour in Peru) and November 25 (the Day Protesting Violence against Women, also in Peru). These celebrations help to spread the notion of gender perspective throughout the country: for the past five years mass demonstrations have been held in slums, factories, town halls and political party headquarters.

The movement has also initiated feminist institutions such as non-governmental women's centres. These have contributed to strengthening the movement itself, particularly because they reinforce interaction between the feminist branch of the movement and the other two mainstreams.

Rebelling mothers

Women from the slum areas too have begun organizing themselves anew, sometimes by giving fresh content to the traditionally male-oriented organizations they were already part of. At first this process was related to existing local organizations, in which women had so far been assigned responsibilities within structures considered less important, such as health and social affairs, but kept away from any decision making.

The initial thrust of the popular women's movement was

determined by their basic needs. They struggled within their homes, just to gain the right to become involved in these activities. Later, they began to speak about domestic violence within their new organizations, and discovered that it was not just their individual ill fortune, but a social malaise. Outside their homes, they strove to form their own groups, socializing their poverty and sharing it with other women. They also had to confront their original local organizations, which sought to benefit from and manipulate these newly-emerging groups.

The popular stream is the largest in Peru. It includes many different types of organizations, with specific goals and dynamics depending on the kind of outside agencies and institutions they interact with. There are several operative organizations centred around specific tasks, such as the community dining rooms, or some municipal programmes, such as the 'glass-of-milk' programme. Some of their leaders are deeply committed to women's issues, and consider autonomy of their organizations a principal feature to be maintained.

Changing traditional spaces

The third women's stream evolved in a slower fashion, because the traditional spaces from which it emerged are usually the most resistant to change. In trying to distance themselves from the traditional political arenas in order to heighten their own perspective, some women, mostly from left-wing political parties, began to set up women's commissions or sub-groups within their own political organizations.

At first their attempts to organize were more in terms of seeking and offering an alternative discourse as a counter-proposal to feminism, than a heartfelt desire on their part to examine women's status outside their political organizations, or even within the context of their own party's policies and programmes. But these initial efforts brought these women together allowing them to modify their views. They thus began the intense and fruitful process of looking at themselves as women and not only as political militants.

Women from political parties and trade unions too started to realize how their own circumstances were tied to their being women. Making this process even more heterogeneous and complex, peasant women began to organize within the scope of traditional peasant associations in significant numbers.

These peasant women, particularly from provinces with a history of organizational efforts like Puno and Cuzco, have demanded land and credits, the right to found and lead their own organizations, to produce their own radio programmes, etc. In some cases, they managed to become actively involved in heavily male dominated organizations, such as the *rondas campesinas* (farmers' patrol groups) in Cajamarca. *Rondas* are committees created by rural communities to defend their lands against terrorist attacks. Today some women form part of its leadership. They are also extending the *rondas'* actions to oppose domestic violence against women. When such a case comes up, women discuss it openly at the general assembly of the women's committee. Most of the time they draft and carry out their own sanctions, but in some instances they do appeal to male leaders and ask for mixed public sanctions.

Women from trade unions also make up a special group within this stream. Although the industrial labour force is not very large in Peru, it has its own distinct conditions and important levels of organization. Women have faced strong opposition in this sector, because Peru's trade unions combine a highly traditional classist orientation with an absolute lack of interest in women's demands. In spite of these circumstances, women in the industrial sector have established feminine commissions in the Central Union of Peruvian Workers (CGTP), and have undertaken within their own unions the struggle for what they feel are their most pressing demands.

The dynamics of the movement

The preceding look at the different streams allows us to examine more closely the dynamics of the women's movement today. Its complexity makes it hard to understand the sense and direction of many actions, or their not yet so visible effect on women and society as a whole. Most of the time this is true for all social movements, because of the lack of new methodological approaches and the resistance met in discarding old ideas about social conflicts. The difficulties tend to increase when analysing the women's movement because there are still too many preconceptions about women's roles. I will approach its dynamics by looking at some of the specific tensions the women's movement has encountered in its daily development.

The ambiguity of subordination and rebellion

We have seen how women have different subject positions as a product of different structural conditions. This fact explains why women's practices are heterogeneous and do not necessarily point in the same direction. Instead, they are marked by a continuous, opposing process of submission and rebellion: on the one hand is the need to find alternative ways of dealing with the world, hinged on more democratic and egalitarian values, on a more autonomous conception of life itself, etc. On the other hand lies the marked influence of traditional ideas and practices considered the only valid ones not just by society but too often by women themselves.

Women seek external legitimacy, while at the same time confronting and rejecting external influences. Women also learn to recognize the presence of discrimination but at the same time find security in it. As Pires de Rio Caldeira[15] suggests, this ambiguity between the new and the traditional is one of the characteristics of women's social practices. It is not good or bad in itself; it is simply part of the very difficult process of growing as persons and as a collective.

Women have the potential to give other meanings to their traditional roles in the public sphere. They can insert themselves in public life not along masculine lines but by holding on to their values and keeping the dimensions of their specific roles and personal experiences in the private sphere. In practice this signifies they question the separation between the public and the private. Women also acquire a kind of intuitive political calculation. They cannot fight all the battles at once. They negotiate, use traditional forms of arguing to preserve the most highly-valued goals, for example relegating for the time being the need for substantial changes in the sexual division of labour within the home, because they know it is one of the most difficult changes in societies like ours. Women in the slum areas opt for getting up very early and completing household chores before leaving for their organizations, but at the same time they are quite capable of fighting fiercely to defend their right to be out of the house until very late if need be. Though still submissive by upbringing and in role expectations, they are organizing against male violence.

These social practices may also contain traps that really hinder the advancement of social causes. The problem is, these traps are backed and legitimized by almost all prevailing discourses pertaining to women and their roles. Often the process of transformation, though furthering the hope of new social identities, is also prone to ambiguity and falls a prey to it. The process of growing as individuals and growing as a social movement at the same time implies many heart-rending moments women which can withstand only by drawing upon their personal and collective strength.

The ghost of old paradigms

The women's movement has a visible presence now in Peruvian society, and must be taken into account. However, most political discourses speak of and address the different mainstreams as groups battling and counteracting the effects of the crisis, rallied in defence of their families.

These discourses vary according to whether they come from the right- or the left-wing parties: the first places more emphasis on women's roles as mothers and as natural guardians of the family, and the second stresses their roles as mothers, opposing the government or institutions to preserve family subsistence. But both the right and the left do not break with the traditional vision of women's roles, and concentrate most of their attention on the popular stream of the movement. The problem is, only one aspect of the ambiguity or duality women are faced with is thus emphasized.

It is true, for example, that many women are mothers, and no matter what their social circumstances, the majority feel a strong commitment to seeking the security of their families. But women are also in the most marginalized sectors the poorest of the poor. 'Feminization of poverty' is an indisputable phenomenon of the last two decades or more, and conditions faced by women in the slum areas or mines are far worse than those of other women. Given that all these elements are part of reality, we cannot lose ourselves in them. Examples abound of how better material conditions do not necessarily change women's subordination. Reductionism denies what women are realizing and seeking: to be heard as persons, to have their own voice as women.

A basic guideline that can capture the true sense of women's actions or lack of actions, includes examining the obstacles, problems and options women face within the context of their spaces to articulate their different subject positions from a more democratic gender position.

In this respect I want to point out the risks much of the research done on women's movements in Peru is prone to: the risk of hiding the specificity of women's struggles among all other subject positions and contradictions women confront, and that of subsuming all other contradictions to gender. The first risk comes from holding traditional patriarchal views about social conflicts; the second is incurred when adopting a narrow, sectarian form of feminist understanding.

The traditional view tends to analyse the dynamics of the women's movement according to pre-determined notions of what actions and awareness should consist of. For example, while recognizing the pluralistic reality of the women's movement, proponents of this approach still seek homogeneity, and tend to apply, in a mechanical way, categories related primarily to an economic class approach. Most frequently this perspective validates work and activities carried out by what is categorized as the popular stream. All merit is attached to this all-purpose, seemingly magical word: popular. Following the same line of reasoning, the feminist stream of the women's movement is labelled *petit bourgeois*. In this disparaging term is supposed to reside its limitations.

This traditional approach views the effects of women's demonstrations and other actions in quantitative rather than qualitative terms. Women's protagonism is viewed not as the complex, frustrating but enriching process of seeking a new identity, but rather as women's capacity to rally against the State, to support the 'general' struggles and respond to family needs.

This quantitative view also ignores the potential for change within the women's movement, or even within other movements, such as that of gays and lesbians. In Latin America's conservative environment, gays and lesbians have confronted immense obstacles when trying to organize. They have been exposed to violent condemnation, physical aggression and rejection by almost the entire society.

This explains in part why the homosexual movement in Peru does not have too many people organically linked to its organizations. The movement's value is not quantitative, of course, nor is its central merit the fact that it is struggling for a specific minority, although that is important. Its major significance lies in the fact that it is fighting for sexual freedom. Much more than fighting for a specific right, it has opened an until now unexplored space to question one of the most fundamental aspects in the lives of individuals: sexuality. Because sexuality is the object of authoritarian repression, opening the door to confront sexuality and question compulsory heterosexuality in our society permits the flourishing of more democratic relations, respect for diversity and the option to be different.

A vision stressing solely gender also has its own risks: gender may become a reductionist concept, in the sense that it will not reveal the different subject positions of women. This approach does not take into account that gender only gives women a theoretical unity, since a multiplicity of living conditions exists among them. It transforms women into an abstraction, forgetting the complex individual differences inherent in people, due to circumstances, environment, beliefs and practice. Gender may easily become an empty concept, not accounting for the specific articulation it evokes on other subject positions of the women's movement.

Both these approaches tend to take some elements of the movement's reality and attempt to pass them off as the whole. Striving for a more flexible approach, it is important to realize that all streams of the women's movement experience conflicts, have contradictory practices and bear a multiplicity of meanings. We are after all referring to collectives made up of people with their own life histories and limitations, who have suffered to varying degrees from social exclusion and domination. Many times they show solidarity, but not always. Many times they have knowledge, but they also make mistakes. They have many unfulfilled needs, both material and emotional. As individuals they are also in permanent interaction with a world radiating enormous hostility—a world that develops macroplans for them, speaks in their name, but ultimately and almost always decides without them.

Crisis and violence

Violence and political and economic crisis have greatly intensified during the past year. We mentioned how the crisis first appeared as a circumstantial factor that gave important momentum and visibility to the process of raising awareness and organizing as women. Peruvian women have displayed enormous creativity in resorting to new collective strategies for subsistence. These processes have generated and sustained powerful links of solidarity.

But by now the crisis and increasing violence have created immense obstacles not only to the further development of the women's movement, but also to sustaining what it has achieved so far. The question at present seems to be whether the accelerating crisis in the country has not already become a structural component of the women's social movement, hugely influencing its options for development. Violence has escalated to such proportions and its impact is so widespread, that it is difficult to consider it any longer as a transitory phenomenon. The most irrational expression of this violence is the terrorist group Sendero Luminoso (Shining Path).

The impact of the crisis can be felt at all instances of daily life. Women's daily routine, especially for those living under the worst material conditions, has lost its relatively fixed space where internal and external certainties were built. This has critical consequences. On the one hand, women are losing hold of previous historically-rooted ideas about their roles and personal and social values: the opening of new contexts of reference is changing their symbolic horizon. On the other hand, deep personal and social changes are making women feel a great sense of insecurity towards the present and the future. The crisis has accelerated a process that should have had more time to evolve. Its effects can be felt not only in daily life but also in its influence on the movement's dynamics.

The weight of the economic crisis makes networking and solidarity among women more fragile. It diminishes the time available for them to organize themselves and attend meetings or implement strategies. It also facilitates outside manipulation, and reinforces the passive and receptive aspects of some women's organizations.

Violence is not only placing the incipient democracy at risk, but is also creating a sense of vulnerability that is powerfully affecting women's lives. The women's movement has recently expressed its commitment to the defence of human rights and peace, aware that these are the only options left in order to attain a more stable ground for any further development. If the economic crisis and political unrest continue at the same pace, current efforts to stop violence may change to a despairing sympathy for reprisal actions. Violence may then be seen as the only way to oppose violence.

An example of how the economic and political crisis affects the dynamics of the movement occurred in Lima in November 1988, allowing the most primitive human feelings to surface. A rumour spread throughout the city about the *sacaojos*, men purported to take out children's eyes in order to sell them. In a few days the whole city was in turmoil. No matter what their social class, culture, education, women of each neighbourhood assigned to these mythical beings the characteristics that most expressed their own hidden fears. For poor women in the slum areas, the *sacaojos* was a white, blond man, who owned a big car; for middle-class women, he was a dirty, haggard-looking black or Indian.

Throughout Lima, women reacted in similar ways. Women from the middle-class and the slum areas alike, did not send their children to school. Many women opted for staying at home with them. Most women from slum areas who belonged to any organization, including the leaders, did not attend meetings or demonstrations for almost a week, or curtailed their participation and took their children along for the short periods of attendance. None had in fact seen the *sacaojos*, but one and all, not excluding myself, believed they were lurking around, waiting for our children to wander off alone on the streets.

I highlight this experience because it was a case of mass hysteria that particularly affected women and summarized many symbolic fears. To take out children's eyes has great symbolic meaning: in a country like Peru, in spite of all the efforts and richness of its social movements, there is an underlying, deep and unconfessed feeling among adults that our children have no future, or at least a very bleak one. In this vision, there is also the fear that nobody can really do anything to change the panorama of desolation in the long-term, and this may approximate being blinded.

It also shows that there are many fears and guilt feelings among women concerning our families and the pressures contemporary living conditions have on our time and affections. Even when we feel we are doing our best for our children, and even if awareness of our own rights as humans has increased, there are mixed feelings in relation to our practices as mothers, mothers who leave the home much more, by choice or by necessity, than our mothers and grandmothers ever did, and must leave children alone or in someone else's care.

How to change the world without losing ourselves

There is a fundamental tension common to all social movements: the need to preserve their own autonomous space, and the need to achieve specific goals without compromise, or the necessity acquire visible power over other members of society.

Elements that make this tension more complex are the particular 'time' and 'rhythm' of the dynamics of social movements. Social movements are cyclic in two senses, because they respond to changing circumstances and because they tend to have their own life cycles.[16] In this sense, collective actors do not develop in a linear process, going from a state of unconsciousness to a high level of awareness through ordered stages.

Melucci refers to latency and visibility as two interrelated poles of collective action. Although visibility is measurable through public demonstrations and actions, a social movement's existence would not be possible if an underlying, invisible knot of social relations were not also a fundamental part of it. These hidden networks become visible whenever collective actors confront public spaces.

Latency is the other and possibly the most important dimension of all social movements. It allows its actors to appropriate their own lives and pre-figure what could be new social relations. Such a process makes us think that, even if the explicit objectives of the Peruvian women's movement are never achieved, nothing will ever be the same for women who dared to break their silence, and step out of their predestined space.[17]

Tension continues to be a part of social movements. It has been dealt with by many authors. Evers[18] refers to the two choices invariably confronting social movements: conquering power spheres within dominant structures at the risk of remaining in permanently subordinate positions; or retaining identities without negotiating, at the risk of remaining weak, isolated, and full of contradictions. Possibly, as the same author points out, the best alternative resides in the precarious balance of both choices, and both expressions are part of its dynamics.

An important concept in any discussion about the women's movement is the concept of autonomy. But this is only part of the problem: the practice of autonomy is a complex one, and there is a tendency to think of it as a term with one unique meaning, for good or for bad, without considering that within movements there are no fixed and homogeneous practices with regard to autonomy.

Only when a woman acquires personal autonomy, although neither in practice nor in theory can any individual totally achieve it, can she be said to have taken the first step towards developing a collective understanding of autonomy. This will then be expressed in the willingness and capacity to defend women's common interests, in accepting that women's demands can no longer be postponed and are of high priority, and in refusing subordination. This political will is developed in relation to other groups, movements and institutions. The concept of autonomy is therefore a relative one, and does not refer only to individual or isolated practices.

Seeking and finding autonomy is not an automatic process. The ways people struggle for and demand autonomy do not necessarily include a vision of plural democracy. This also means defending their own rights may lead many to deny other specificities and demands; this is exemplified in the case of workers struggling to end long-lasting oppression, while systematically ignoring women workers' plights.

We can distinguish separate levels of autonomy in the streams of the women's movement, corresponding to different ways of acting out the process of autonomy. Most of the time women's demands for equality have been denied or considered at best struggles of a secondary nature. This is also linked to the absence of women at significantly decisive levels from public institutions, where mostly men continue to be in charge of policy-making. At the same time, the women's movement has created new and different spaces for female participation, where women are more at ease, discovering self-confidence, self-esteem, and feeling more among peers. These feelings may cause defensive reactions in women regarding the whole public sphere, and reticence to create or accept the opportunity to exchange experiences with others. Here autonomy becomes a defence mechanism that can lead to undue isolation, and even ghettoization of the movement.

Women may also feel greatly committed to specific demands and have a sense of autonomy without becoming isolated, but at the same time fail to realize there are other aspects of female subordination the movement must address. Such is the case of racial issues. Lelia Gonzales, a black Latin American feminist, argues that the women's movement in Latin America is a kind of neutral movement in terms of colour and race, and this means in practice to be racist by omission.[19]

There might also be autonomy at an organic level, but this does not necessarily mean that the overpowering and long-lasting codes about how women are supposed to act have been done away with. As an example, take the case of some women's groups that have their own space and mandate, while continuing to be subordinated ideologically to the discourse and influence of diverse political parties or Church institutions. In contrast, women can also have organic links with parties or Church associations while retaining a clear autonomous vision and practices in relation to women's issues and the movement.

These are only some of the complexities associated with autonomy in the women's movement. What is indisputable in all this is that ambivalence in relation to autonomy does exist within the movement and is expressed through women's social practices.

Paradoxically, although the movement is probably the most dynamic of Peru's current social movements, there is no real correspondence of women's achievements at the spheres of decision making within local structures or sources of local power.[20] Women have forced society to listen to them, but are still not taken into account.

In the case of political parties, there is another paradox: although there was great opposition from the parties to a separate women's movement, a number of its leaders, especially those belonging to the popular stream, are still militants, mostly in left-wing parties. This does not necessarily mean they are always comfortable within those structures. They have encountered strong attempts at manipulation to which most often they have reacted by trying to preserve the unity and autonomy of their women's organizations.

Within the feminist stream, unresolved tensions have provoked some of the most audacious responses. The most important one was its participation in the electoral campaign of 1985. Two of us ran as feminist candidates: for a Deputation in Lima, and the Senate at the national level. We were inscribed within the lists of the United Leftist Front as 'independents' (not the party's officially designated candidates).

Because both of us were visible leaders of the feminist autonomous stream, there was a strong identification between the feminist movement and the leftist political parties by public opinion. The experience of joining the electoral campaign was important to us and to the whole movement. The point I want to raise is that we took the decision to run as candidates at a time when we were running the greatest risk of becoming isolated.[21]

The move allowed us to open new spaces and consolidate our capacity to create pressure and dialogue, but we could not hope to change the rules of the game, and the leftist front did not change substantially its approach to women's issues either. We lost the elections, but participating in the electoral process made us decide there were also other important ways to gain public visibility for the movement itself, utilizing elements that are not commonly used in social movements. We changed our internal structure, electing our own leaders to make sure there was always an organic channel through which to articulate our points of view and demands to society.

The feminist stream was not alone in making incursions into the electoral process. Some of the most prominent leaders of the popular stream offered themselves as candidates during the

November 1989 elections. Some of them ran for posts of more limited scope, but others, with the support of the strongest organizations, ran for and were elected to important posts. Such is the case of Maria Elena Moyano, president of the Federation of Popular Women of Villa El Salvador (FEPOMUVES), who was elected to the position of Lieutenant Mayor of Villa El Salvador, the largest shanty town in Lima. [22]

Are these attempts to gain political power really valid or necessary? Are we perhaps putting more emphasis on the visible aspects of the movement and not on its rich and strong internal processes? I feel at this point in Peruvian history this is a difficult but crucial battle. Regardless of the risks involved, we must realize social movements are not only recruiting agents, but should keep being dynamic subjects with the capacity to formulate their demands again and again as society changes or stagnates.

We know incursions at the formal level of politics do not guarantee necessarily that women's rights will suddenly acquire priority on a predominantly man-made agenda. But that is not the only thing we are seeking. For women to put forth their demands at the level of formal politics does not exhaust other options, or diminish the long-term goals and vision of the women's movement. We have also acquired enough confidence, through experience, to know that when the State recognizes even one claim women are making, it has a tremendous effect: the women's movement acquires a political dimension, which yields gains that belong to the whole of society.

Take the example of the long struggle of women from different streams for political action concerning violence against women. One demand—only one of many—was the establishment of a police branch for women's claims, to be run by women police officers. Some of us were then participating in a Council for the Defence of Women's Rights just created by the government. The Council took up this struggle and the first Women's Precinct was created in 1988.

Incredibly, the first day it opened its doors to the public, there were almost 2,000 complaints filed by women, beaten by their husbands, raped, etc. The feminist stream with its limited legal aid and other support services would not have had the capacity to deal with such numbers even in three months. Now we are struggling to have Women's Precincts in every district, and pressuring for better legal and psychological assistance.

Myths that come between political ideals and social practice

Finally, there is another tension within the movement: the distance between what we think or feel we are and the reality in which we live—the old dilemma between theory and practice. I mentioned earlier how ambivalence already exists in women's practices, referring more to the popular stream. Now I will demonstrate how it operates inside the feminist stream, because I feel it reveals what is happening across the movement.

Tension is expressed in not having a realistic perception of what we are and what we want as a movement. Our Utopia, sometimes more charged with defence mechanisms than with creativity, is taken all too often as a norm. But, Utopias should rather be seen as a horizontal referential,[23] a way of imagining the impossible in order to determine what is possible, not as a goal in itself. Yet we try to place our social practices in it without stopping to analyse which elements of these practices are deforming or enlightening our way. Thus we are prone to replace analysis or deny the contradictions by constructing myths about our existence as a movement.

Some of the participants of the Fourth Latin American and Caribbean Feminist Encounter, which took place in Mexico in 1987, got together to talk about these myths. We highlighted a few of the most prevalent myths that erode our long-range political vision: that feminists do not want power; that they engage in politics in a different way from others; that all women are equal; that we have a natural unity because of being women; that feminism is the politics of women by women; that any group is the whole movement; that women's spaces are in themselves a guarantee of a positive process; that because a woman feels it, anything is valid; that the personal is automatically political; that consensus is democracy.

In reality, none of these affirmations are true. We have innate contradictions, adopt traditional behaviour patterns when engaging in politics, and not all women are equal, even though every time this is verbalized it provokes authoritarian responses that heatedly deny our differences. Unity among women is not

given, but rather is something we must build, supported by
our differences. Feminism is not, nor do we want it to be, a
political approach only for women. One of my highest aspirations as a feminist is that the fight for women's rights be taken
up by the entire society. Women's subjectivity can also become
an arbitrary imposition when considered only in its individual
dimensions. The personal has the potential to be transformed
into the political when both awareness and will are combined.
Consensus can be a very authoritarian practice because it can
conceal differences. These are the kinds of statements that make
up part of the irrational elements all movements have.[24] Only
by recognizing them can we begin to change them and give
space to more creative social practices.

Raising contradictions openly is part of the healthy practice
we want to develop, not by denying conflicts and differences,
but by trying to establish a new system of ethics, new 'rules of
the game' that let us find more humane practices for ourselves
and society. I have offered you a personal reading about the
contributions, traps and knots of our movement. Regardless of
its doubts, ambivalence and bewilderment, we are sure it will
keep moving forward.

NOTES

1. Fernando Calderon, 'America Latina, identidad y tiempos
    mixtos (o como tratar de pensar la modernidad sin dejar de ser
    indios),' in: *Revista David y Goliat*, No. 52. Buenos Aires:
    CLACSO, 1987.
2. Sinesio Lopez, 'Sociedad y estado en el Peru actual. Un intento
    de interpretacion.' Lima: mimeo, 1989.
3. Vargas, Virginia, 1986, 'El aporte de la rebeldia de las mujeres,'
    in: *Revista Paraguaya de Sociologia*, Paraguay, Reprinted in V.
    Vargas, *El aporte de la rebeldia de las mujeres*. Lima: Ed. Flora
    Tristan, 1989.
4. Alberto Melucci, 'Social Movements and the Democratization of
    Everyday Life,' in: John Keane (ed.), *Civil Society and the State*.
    London: Verso, 1988. Also see Alberto Melucci, *Nomads of the
    Present*. London: Ed. Radios, 1989.
5. Chantal Mouffe, 'Towards a new concept of democracy,' in: C.
    Nelson and L. Grosberg (eds.), *Marxism and the Interpretation of*

Culture. Urbana: University of Illinois Press, 1988.

6. Alberto Melucci, 'Social Movements...' op. cit. p. 247.

7. Alberto Melucci, *Nomads of the Present*. op. cit.

8. Chantal Mouffe, op. cit. p. 90.

9. Gayle Rubin, 'El trafico de mujeres. Notas sobre la economia politica del sexo,' in: *Nueva Antropologia*, vol. VII, no. 30, Mexico, 1986.

10. Ernesto Laclau and Chantal Mouffe, *Hegemony and Socialist Strategy: Towards a Radical Democratic Politics*. London: Verso, 1985.

11. Lourdes Arispe, 'Democracia para un pequeno planeta bio-generico', Prologue in E. Jellin (ed.), *Participation, ciudadania e identidad*. Geneva: UNRISD, 1987.

12. Agnes Heller, *Anatomia de la Izquierda Occidental*. Spain: Ed. Peninsula, 1985.

13. Maruja Barrig, 'Democracia emergente y movimiento de mujeres,' in: *Movimientos sociales y democracia: la fundacion de un nuevo orden*. Lima: Desco, 1986.

14. Francois Bourricaud, *La oligarquia en Peru*. Lima: IEP, 1969.

15. Teresa Pires de Rio Caldeira, 'Mujeres, cotidianeidad y politica,' in: *Participation,...* op. cit.

16. Gunder Frank and Martha Fuentes, 'Ten theses on social movements,' in: *World Development*, Feb., 1989.

17. Jose Nun, *La rebelion del coro*. Buenos Aires: Ed. Nueva Vision, 1989.

18. Tilman Evers, 'Identidad: el lado oculto de los movimientos sociales,' reproduced in: *Materiales para el debate contemporaneo*. Buenos Aires, n.d., 1985.

19. Lelia Gonzales, 'Women Organizing for Change: Confronting the Crisis in Latin America,' in: *Isis International*, in coordination with Development Alternatives with Women for a New Era (Dawn), Book Series 1988/2.

20. Cecilia Blondet, *Las organizaciones femeninas en época de crisis*. Lima: IEP, 1989.

21. Vargas, Virginia, '1986, Vota por ti mujer,' in: *Isis Internacional*, Edicion de las Mujeres, 1986. Reprinted in *El aporte...* op. cit.

22. In February 1991, Moyano was brutally murdered by members of Sendero Luminoso, the terrorist organization which has gained in strength in recent years, holding most of the country hostage with its acts of senseless violence.

23. Norbert Lechner, *Los patios interiores de la democracia*. Santiago: Ed. FLACSO, 1989.

24. Claus Offe, *Partidos politicos y nuevos movimientos sociales*. Spain: Ed. Sistema, 1989. Also see Agnes Heller, op. cit.

5

The Early Women's Movement in Trinidad and Tobago, 1900–1937

Rhoda Reddock

Trinidad and Tobago is a small, two-island State situated at the southernmost end of the Caribbean archipelago just six miles north-east of Venezuela. It was captured by the British in 1897, ending over 300 years of Spanish colonial rule and just under 100 years of French settlement.

By the beginning of the twentieth century, its population comprised a majority of Africans—ex-slaves and descendants of enslaved Africans—indentured and ex-indentured labourers from India, small numbers of Chinese and Madeirans who had also been imported originally as indentured labourers, and Europeans who were predominantly plantation owners, merchants and colonial officials.

As a Crown Colony, Trinidad and Tobago was a late addition to the British colonial possessions in the Caribbean (or West Indies as it was more popularly referred to). The old representative system of government which had provided some degree of national sovereignty to the local plantocracy, was never instituted in Trinidad, whereas Tobago had lost its elected legislature in 1874, even prior to union with Trinidad in 1889. Up until the mid-1920s, therefore, the country was governed directly from Britain through a nominated legislature and expatriate colonial officials.

Historically, in Trinidad and Tobago and indeed for most of the Commonwealth Caribbean, women's organizations prior to the 1970s were supposed to have been concerned primarily with social welfare. This was true only to a certain extent, as shall be shown in this paper.

Material available on the early women's movement points to a majority participation of middle-class, educated and cultured women. These women were increasingly excluded from wage-work and through their participation in women's organizations sought to improve the lot of their sex and race. As with similar movements in the rest of the world, their demands reflected the influence of liberal ideas. They wanted education for girls, citizenship and other political rights. But they were also strongly influenced by nationalist sentiments of the time, and central to their struggle was their confrontation with the growing prevalence of European sexual division of labour as part of the modern western family.

The early women's organizations took a variety of forms. This chapter examines the experiences of the organizations of middle-class women who combined women's rights activism with social welfare during the first part of the twentieth century, prior to World War II. Feminist women could also be found within nationalist and labour organizations of the time, a topic we shall not discuss here.

The Women's Self-Help movement

One of the earliest examples of women organizing in their own interests in the English-speaking Caribbean was the Women's Self-Help movement. In Trinidad and Tobago, this took the form of the Trinidad Home Industries and Women's Self-Help Association. Initially founded in 1901, it drew its inspiration from the Lady Musgrave Self-Help Society formed in Jamaica in 1865.

According to its founders it aimed 'to provide a means through which all gentlewomen in reduced circumstances should be assisted to add to their incomes.'[1]

Although traditionally perceived as a charity, this organization provided income-earning possibilities for women. It encouraged and facilitated economic activities centred around the 'womanly skills' which all women were supposed to have learnt in their homes and which benefitted their class and status in society. These societies are testimony to the fact that even in the elite classes of the white and 'highly coloured', women could not afford to depend totally on their male breadwinners.

Their activities included work such as embroidery, lace making, plain needlework—sewing, mending and darning for private individuals, hotels, clubs and the constabulary—and 'housekeeping' or the making of preserves, jellies and cakes for local use, export and catering. They also operated a tea room, serving light refreshments primarily for 'ladies while shopping', which sold incidentals like flowers, stamps, postcards and photographs.[2] In addition, classes in 'womanly skills' were organized for the 'better class of young women'. These included cooking classes and needlework demonstrations. In 1911 a small lending library was opened.

To some extent this organization challenged the prevailing view of women's inherent 'selflessness'. Its members defended their right to earn an income rather than work only for charity. In May 1931, a profit of $15,000, its first for three years, was paid out to the members. The organization was active until 1938.

Audrey Jeffers and the Coterie of Social Workers

By the 1920s, black and coloured women began organizing themselves. The most important women's organization of this period was the Coterie of Social Workers. Founded in 1921 in Port of Spain, the capital of Trinidad and Tobago, by 1935, it had branches in San Fernando and Tobago. It comprised mainly women of middle-class black and coloured communities, who by the mid-1930s were being increasingly excluded from careers in the civil and teaching services. The Coterie helped relieve some of the frustrations of inactivity faced by these well-educated women, since even their housework was taken care of by domestic servants. It also served as an avenue to improve the status of black and coloured women.

For example, its founder, Audrey Layne Jeffers, was herself from the small black property-owning class. Her family home was in St Clair, the most prestigious upper-class district in the country and she also owned property herself. Jeffers received primary and secondary education at Tranquility Girls Practising School, including the 'higher Class for girls', then completed a diploma in Social Science at Alexander College, North Finchley, in London.[3]

Prior to 1921, social work was the prestigious preserve of white and coloured ladies of the upper classes. By organizing around social work, Coterie members sought to bring some of this prestige to their race and sex. In 1928 the St Mary's Home for blind girls and women was founded; in 1927, Mother's Day was introduced and in 1935 came the Maud Reeves Hostel for

Working Girls and the Anstey House for 'respectable', that is middle-class young ladies was opened.

Despite strong British and US influence on the Coterie, there was little emphasis on the family as a unit or on women as wives. Rather their work met the needs of working women, mothers and children. This can be explained by the fact that Jeffers herself never married, although other members did.

While studying in Britain, Jeffers had been one of the founders of the Union of Students of African Descent, later the League of Coloured Peoples. She served among the West African troops during World War I and, supported by the West Indian Committee, started a West African Soldiers' Fund and cigarette fund.[4] After the war she became a member of the Society of Peoples of African Origin, led by fellow Trinidadian F.E.M. Hercules, which campaigned in London during the post-war period of 1918–1919.

This combination of nationalist and women's rights activities characterized many of the early women's organizations in colonial countries. This supports the assertion of Kumari Jayawardena[5] that the fight for women's emancipation in colonial countries during the late nineteenth and early twentieth centuries was necessarily bound up with the fight for national liberation and other democratic struggles of the period.

Jeffers's concern for the changing condition of black middle-class women in Trinidad and Tobago was also shared by Captain A.A. Cipriani of the Fabian-oriented Trinidad Workingmen's Association (TWA), resulting in close collaboration between them on many occasions.

Beatrice Greig and the women's struggle

Next to Audrey Jeffers, Beatrice Greig was the most important women's rights activist of this time. Although more radical and socialist-oriented, she accepted the Victorian housewife ideal and notions of 'uplifted womanhood', even when in fact she challenged many of these notions by her own actions on behalf of working women.

Daughter of Scottish-Canadian missionaries, she was born in Newfoundland in 1869, but had lived in Trinidad with her parents from the age of 16. She spent some time in India where

she was strongly influenced by the Indian nationalist movement and the Theosophist movement. While there, she be-
friended Catherine Mayo, author of the controversial book
Mother India, which dealt with the subjugation of women in
India. Around 1891, she returned to Trinidad where she married a planter, William Greig of Couva. Eventually widowed,
she spent the rest of her life in Trinidad participating in an as-
tounding range of social and political activities.

Greig worked actively with the Teachers' Union (TTTU) and
the TWA (later Trinidad Labour Party). As part of her work
with the Teachers' Union, she sought to break down the barriers against the full participation of women.[6] Earlier, she had
formed the Trinidad Union of Girls' Clubs, with a membership
of working girls in 24 centres throughout the country.

As a writer, her letters to the editors of the various newspa-
pers joined those of other feminists and activists on issues rel-
evant to women and workers. In 1931, for example, she joined
Audrey Jeffers and R.M. Scott in letters supporting the new
Divorce Bill. In this they acted counter to their traditional ally,
TWA leader Cipriani who, as a Catholic, supported the Roman
Catholic lobby.

In a letter to the *Labour Leader* on this subject, Greig raised
the issue of civil marriages and questioned religious jurisdiction over civil unions. She further argued:[7]

> The assumption that divorce laws would have a disastrous
> effect on marriage assumes that people live together only
> because of compulsions. It is an admission of the failure of
> marriage as a social institution. Those who so argue are more
> cynical than the partisans of divorce, who because of their
> faith in the stability of human beings, do not fear such disas-
> trous consequences.

An important focus in the work of Beatrice Greig was the
'Upliftment of Indian Womanhood'. Her experiences in India
had made her a lifelong supporter of its life and people. In the
absence of visible activists on behalf of Indian women in
Trinidad and Tobago, Greig herself assumed this task.

In the late 1920s, as a contributor to the *East Indian Weekly*,
she consistently raised issues related to Indian women. It was

on her suggestion that during his visit to Trinidad in 1929, Pundit Mehta Jaimini gave a public lecture on 'The Ideals of Indian Womanhood'. In September the same year, she was officially made associate editor of *The Beacon*, a literary journal, and in addition to the 'India Section', contributed a regular column, 'The Library', which presented life histories of remarkable women.

In October 1936 Greig joined Jeffers as the first female candidates to municipal office in the country. She presented herself as an independent candidate for the northern ward. As we shall see later, this was not to be.

The struggle for seats for women on the City Council

On the 8 September 1924, in the climate of legislative reform, a delegation of women was received by the Governor to discuss the issue of votes for women.[8] But it was not until 1927 and at the municipal level, that the issue of the participation of women in politics and public life really came out in the open.

In August that year, TWA President and Deputy Mayor Cipriani moved a motion to amend the Port of Spain Corporation Ordinance and make women eligible for seats on the Council. In support of his motion, Cipriani stated that this had already been done in other parts of the British Empire and that since the war, women were now to be found in banks, commercial houses and business firms doing jobs and holding positions which men had done before the war. The motion was referred to a committee for one month during which time a major public debate ensued.

One of the first responses was from the *Trinidad Guardian*. On 28 August, in an editorial entitled 'Women in Council', it pointed out that so far women had given 'no public demonstration of their views' and worse still, when the case was being put forward in the Council, none 'of the leading feminists of Trinidad (if there were any)' had been 'present to encourage and applaud their champion.' From this it concluded that the political consciousness of women had not yet 'reached the articulate state'.[9]

This was only the beginning of a struggle which would take many years to resolve. The resulting debate was extremely interesting, giving many insights into contemporary thinking on 'the woman question'. The *Labour Leader* pointed out that women had made no public demonstration because they knew it must come sooner or later, and they were correct, because Cipriani had put forward the motion without being canvassed or approached.[10]

On 15 September, the St Andrews Literary and Debating Club held a mini Legislature on the motion—be it resolved that women are made eligible to seats at the legislature. The motion in favour argued that entrance should be based on merit, educational and property qualifications; restriction was seen as selfish and four eminent women in England were mentioned.

Against the motion, it was argued that women's place was in the home. 'If she wanted to make and administer laws, the home was adequate avenue for her.' It was stated further, 'God never intended women to take a leading part, Jesus Christ did not have one woman disciple.' The conclusion was that Trinidad could not be compared to England as women there had centuries of evolution of nationhood before them. The motion won 10 to seven, with one abstention, but this was not the case in the real Council.[11]

As would be expected, the right-wing press led the criticism against the motion. Articles and extracts were reprinted from British newspapers, as well as quotations from Lady Clara Bevan, English author of *The Secrets of Getting a Husband*. This book was reprinted in Port of Spain, indicating its apparent popularity during that time.[12]

In another article in the *The Port of Spain Gazette*, entitled 'Time and The Woman', 'A.C.' recalled a discussion with a friend on the issue of women in the Council in which the friend queried, 'Do you like to see a woman screaming to crowds from a platform or at street corners? I loathe it, in her own proper sphere...' was the reply. The rest of the article sharply criticized the feminist movement in the following words:

That's the basic error of the so-called *feminist* movement which is really a *masculinist* movement. The perversity of this philosophy is the false assumption that men and women are the same kind of being; and that women have been kept down by men and have lapsed into an inferior position. Hence it urges women to force themselves on to the same level as men learning to do all the things men do and behaving as men behave but this is trying to change nature itself.

It went on to accuse 'modern civilization' of destroying the basic and essential unit of Christian civilization—family life.[13]

Bearing in mind the antagonistic climate which had been built up against the motion, it should not be surprising that the report the committee presented to the City Council on 29 September 1927, recommended that the ordinance *not* be amended. In the ensuing debate, the position taken by the supposedly progressive City Councillors of the day is quite revealing. Tito Achong, for example, supported the recommendation, stating that in this city, women were not educationally qualified enough to deal with the issues of taxation, sanitation and engineering with which the Council dealt from time to time. In addition, he continued, they were not on the same plane psychologically, 'At a certain state of a woman's life she was not even fit to give evidence before a Court of Law.'[14]

Alfred Richards, founding member of the TWA, suggested that first men of intelligence and experience be allowed to come to the Council before bringing in women of high social rank from the areas of St Clair and Stanmore Avenue, which was what the motion was asking.

Two other Councillors, Monteil and Potter, noted that the women had not asked for it, concluding they preferred to leave such responsibilities to the men and were content to advise their husbands, brothers, etc.

The arguments against the recommendations far surpassed those for it in literary eloquence. Councillor J.M. Thorne stated that it was men's pride and conceit which made them want to keep politics their special preserve. Councillor Archibald criticized *The Port of Spain Gazette* for suggesting that women qualified for the Council only because they had put their husbands' property in their names. He accused the Council of being like the Mad Hatter in the tea party in *Alice in Wonderland* who shouted 'no, no', to which Alice replied 'There is plenty of room' and seated herself in a large armchair at the head of the table.

Councillor Pollard in his maiden speech criticized Potter and Monteil for suggesting that women should 'exercise influence from their drawing rooms'. He suggested that the ladies should not be saddled with the responsibility for having inspired the views hitherto voiced in the Council.

In his reply, Cipriani asked the Council whether they wanted the women to return to the days of suffragette demonstrations and clashes with the police to impress the men of 1927 that they wanted to claim their rights and privileges, and referred to the campaign of the Independent Labour Party (founding member of the British Labour Party) to recruit the women forces of the Empire. In closing, he asked the Mayor not to use his casting vote and the Council to let the people decide whether women were ripe for the position or not.

At the end, the committee's recommendations not to make women eligible were accepted and carried by the Mayor Gaston-Johnson K.C.'s casting vote.[15]

Throughout the campaign only one woman was mentioned in the press as having publicly supported the motion; this was Beatrice Greig. She asserted that women were ready to serve because among other things they paid taxes and voted. *The Port of Spain Gazette*, however, refused to accept her arguments as being representative of the women of the city.[16]

Even after the vote, the *Gazette* continued its campaign, but campaigning by the other side was also taking place. On 13 March 1928, Beatrice Greig gave an address at the Richmond Street Library and Debating Association on 'The Position of Women in Public Life'. It was chaired by Cipriani.[17] During 1928, articles were carried in the *Labour Leader* on women in politics in other countries.

On 22 April 1929, Cipriani again put forward the motion to the City Council. The Mayor (the same Gaston-Johnson K.C.) told Cipriani that since the last meeting he (Cipriani) had not held any meeting on this subject to get a mandate from the city's women and only seven women were in the audience that day. This was taken to represent an absence of popular demand. In the vote which followed, five voted against, six in favour and it was again rejected by the Mayor's casting vote.[18]

In supporting the last motion, the *Labour Leader* was joined by *The East Indian Weekly*, edited by C.B. Mathura, a friend and colleague of Cipriani, and to which Beatrice Greig was a regular contributor. In an editorial, it condemned the decision and stressed the importance and increasing participation of women in business and politics, expressing surprise at the sexual inferiority complex that was evident in some of the Councillors.[19]

The campaign continued in the *Labour Leader* with articles on British women politicians; including pen-portraits of women in the British House of Commons, such as Margaret Bonfield and Susan Laurence, the latter the newly elected Chairman of the Labour Party.[20]

They also drew attention to the fact that in Jamaica it had recently been moved that women be eligible for seats on all Boards and the Legislative Council, while in Trinidad Miss Masson had been appointed to the Board of Education.[21]

On 29 May 1930, the motion 'that in the opinion of the Council persons of the female sex shall be qualified to be elected and to be Aldermen and Councillors of the City of Port of Spain and also to be elected Mayors of the City,' was put forward by Councillor E.W. Bowen. It was seconded by Councillor Thorne. By this time Cipriani was Mayor of Port of Spain. It was passed by nine votes to eight with Cipriani giving the casting vote. Over 50 women attended the session.[22]

However, the motion did not become law until 1935. In November 1934 it was laid before the Legislative Council and accepted. On 3 January 1935, the Port of Spain Corporation accepted the amendment to Section 11 of the Principal Ordinance. When the draft was being considered, Alderman Rigsby once more recorded his dissent but by then it was too late.[23]

On 4 September 1936, a similar position was moved in the San Fernando Borough Council. It was moved by Councillor Victor Ramsarran and carried by a majority of eight to two. It made all qualified burgesses 21 years and over (30 had been originally proposed) eligible to sit on the Council. One year later, on 22 October 1937, a bill to this effect by Acting Attorney-General E.J. Davies was introduced into the Legislative Council and passed.

Not until 1936 and 1937 therefore did the enfranchised women of Port of Spain and San Fernando become eligible for municipal office. Yet this again was relevant only to a very small minority of women.

By 1937, very few women or even men were eligible to vote and to sit in the Borough and City Councils. Fewer still were eligible to vote for the Legislative Council and women were not eligible for political office.

First conference of women social workers

Collaboration within the region has characterized the Caribbean women's movement from its inception. Not surprisingly, therefore, in 1936 Jeffers and the Coterie hosted the little remembered 'Conference of British West Indies and British Guiana Women Social Workers' in Port of Spain. The examination of newspaper coverage of the conference suggests that it was an extremely important, large-scale and far-reaching event. Held between 30 April and 10 May, at the Princes Building, Port of Spain, it marked the 15th anniversary of the Coterie.

In her opening address, Audrey Jeffers called for a regional federation of women social workers to form closer intercolonial bonds in matters of educational, political and social interest and for the loosening of insular ties.

The conference created quite a stir since, for the greater part of its duration, men were not allowed to speak. On 5 May however, the 'speaking ban' was lifted. Jeffers announced that men might say a few words provided they asked no questions.

On the same day Beatrice Greig made one of the most significant presentations of the conference: 'The New Age and Women's Place in it'. She noted that in primitive societies the magnitude and power of women's mind had been recognized and that this had reached its height during the Roman civilization when she claimed women had attained a position of almost complete independence and equality with men.

Human development since then, however, had been based on unrestricted individualism described by Darwin as 'the survival of the fittest'. This had resulted in the accumulation of wealth on the one hand and of comparative poverty on the other. This was true not only of industrial England, but was also evident in the filth, squalor and overcrowding of the slums of Port of Spain.

She went on to argue that the violent dislike and distrust that Schopenhauer and his followers showed of women's minds was evidence of women's power; and it was now becoming clear that only the influence of woman's mind which put the good of humanity above self—could ensure the future of the human race. In her own words:[24]

> What is to be the science of power in the New Age? The science of the emotion of the ideal in the social integration. What is the calling for which woman has been trained through long years of subordination and suppression. It is the knowledge which she instinctively holds, if often unconsciously the ideal of other regarding rather than self-regarding and that the race is better than the individual.

In her presentation on the following day Mrs George Masson noted that up to the present the women of Trinidad and Tobago had not shown themselves to be politically-minded, but this was not surprising, as up till then they had no political background. She called on the women to lay the foundation for future generations of women. In concrete terms, she called for the inclusion of women on the Housing Commission as 'No one was more directly interested in the home than the housewife'; for the voting age of women to be lowered from 30 years to 21 as for men; and for women to be eligible for seats on the Legislative Council as they were now eligible for seats on the City Council.[25]

Gertie Wood of the then British Guiana, in her speech 'Political Aspirations and Achievements of Women in British Guiana', reflected clearly the contradictions in the consciousness of these women at this period. She pointed out that a great army of women were engaged in domestic service, and 'bear the brunt of their sex' silently, without ever realizing it. In this way these 'women workers' put in 'far more consistent self-sacrificing service' than did men. She added that for so long women had been taught to bow and smile to men, accept what they condescended to give and not to ask for anything more; that now in this 'New Era' when things were changed, women were still too timid and shy to do otherwise. But, even in the hearts of shy women there was an aspiration for something more.

Like the speech by Greig, this was one of the more radical speeches of the conference, which reflected the very definite feminist consciousness of some of the speakers.

She concluded however, in that conciliatory manner which is not so uncommon even today:[26]

> I am an advocate of 'Women's Rights' but not an extremist and have no patience with extremists for I know and believe that there is much that men alone can do so we still have need of them.
>
> But we aspire to a fair and square deal to be meted out to women workers....

The highlight of the conference was perhaps the address given by Audrey Jeffers on 8 May entitled 'The Urgent Needs of Women in Trinidad'. She began by stating:

> The needs of our women—to my mind have been seriously neglected in the past. The men made it a transient concern, and the women in high places—socially and intellectually, took a rather lukewarm interest in their own sex. Hence it is that Trinidad's women have had the poorest chances of nearly all the East Indies of a sound education, unless there was opportunity to travel abroad.

She went on to identify three types of women in Trinidad. The first type was totally dominated by her husband, who prevented her from taking an interest in anything outside the home except for religious duties. She never even read the newspapers and was at the beck and call of her husband and children. The second type chose to stay at home and delighted in the gossip brought into her home from outside. The third type she found the most irritating of all: she assumed a culture she knew nothing about; carried a superiority complex about everything; was critical of all she saw; discouraged others from doing anything worthwhile; herself doing nothing, she was 'a respectable nuisance in the community, but unfortunately the most prevalent type.'

As far as possibilities for women's employment were concerned, Jeffers found this very limited. The greatest sufferer was the 'middle-class educated negress' whose father had been a faithful civil servant or professional man, but who was now virtually excluded from the Civil Service. To support her point, she noted that in her private census there were three 'negresses' in the government service, six to eight on the whole of Frederick Street, none in the groceries and only two in the leading business firms. For the majority therefore the only alternatives were teaching or nursing. Those who worked in the small stores, did so from 7 a.m. to 8 or 9 p.m. and earned only $1.50 per week.[27]

On a social level, she noted that immorality and prostitution were on the increase in Port of Spain and that social workers were finding it difficult to cope. In addition fathers, including professional men, were not supporting their illegitimate children financially, although they were legally required to pay the minimal amount of half a crown per week.[28] To solve these problems, Jeffers suggested the following. First, that no later than September of the following year, a scholarship for girls be introduced, for this she herself intended to raise funds; second, that a high school for girls, along the lines of the government Queen's Royal College, be established; and third, that a Women's Police Force be set up especially to scour certain commercial houses 'on the job of clearing, cleaning and rounding up and saving innocent girls from becoming victims of this form of livelihood.'[29]

In conclusion, she called upon women to:

...come together and join hands and encourage our women to lead healthy lives—to learn that laziness is a crime—not to scorn any work, but to know that it is better to lift their characters by doing honest work than otherwise.[30]

At the close of the conference, the resolution to form a West Indian and British Guiana Women Workers' Association was accepted. Other resolutions called for the greater participation of women not only in welfare activities, but also on official committees and boards and in municipal and legislative councils. Jeffers's statement on women's education was welcomed and the new association agreed to induce girls to spend more years in school. It was also agreed that the next conference would be held in British Guiana.

Commenting on the conference, a *Sunday Guardian* editorial entitled 'Awakening Women' noted that it was doing a great service by making the public aware that women in the colonies have other ambitions besides those of darning socks and cooking. But it hoped that the Conference would go further and stir in the women themselves the desire to take a more active part in political and social work. It stated·31

> It is not for instance the fault of the public—certainly not that of the male members of the public—that no women have yet come forward as candidates for seats on the city council. These positions were opened to them about 2 years ago. Nor can any reluctance on the part of the government be claimed as a reason why the sex had not yet found a place in the Legislative Council, for the Red House made it quite clear since 1930 that it was perfectly willing to admit women if they wanted to come in.... We are not aware that any request has come from women either before or since....

In other words, although recognizing the problem, the blame was laid fairly and squarely at the feet of the women: another instance where women's lack of action is given as the reason for the continuation of discriminating legislation.

Even so, the conference apparently had quite an effect on the public. Inspector-General of the Constabulary, Col. A.S. Mavrogordato, expressed his doubts about the introduction of women police in Trinidad. He noted however, that women police could be very useful in dealing with social services, the children's court and the reformation of girls who had gone astray. At the same time, he did not feel Trinidad had the kind of women who could make such a force a success.

Ironically, parallel to the conference, the new Education Code, retroactive to 1 January 1935 was being implemented, striking a final blow against the employment of married women teachers. Except for brief and general mention, this issue was not discussed during the conference.

The City Council election of 1936

As if to follow up the resolve of the regional conference, in September 1936, Jeffers and Greig announced their candidature for the elections to the Port of Spain Council. Jeffers was proposed for the western ward (Woodbrook and surrounding areas) while

Greig was proposed for the northern ward. Although entering as independents, both women were supported by the Trinidad Labour Party (TLP), in particular Cipriani, who had success-fully piloted the motion which made this possible. In present-ing these candidates to the public, Cipriani said to the *Trinidad Guardian*:[32]

> Both of these ladies are specialists of the Colony's social work and, with the support of the Labour Party at their backs, they should find no difficulty in ousting any nomination from the opposite sex.... We hope it will not be long before similar qualification will be open to them on the Legislative Council....

The *Trinidad Guardian*, in an editorial, 'Challenge by Women', welcomed the news, seeing it as a stimulus to the women's movement in the West Indies. It concluded by advising their male opponents that in the event the women won, the men could feel that they had lost gloriously to 'foemen—albeit from the weaker sex—entirely worth their steel'.[33]

This campaign was not going to be an easy task and from the start questions were raised about Labour Party support for non-members, particularly in the northern ward, where a TLP Councillor had been originally considered. But the 'battle be-tween the feminists and anti-feminists' in this ward, predicted by Spectator of the *Guardian*, did not take place as, due to an oversight, Greig was forced to withdraw from the fray.

On 16 October, Audrey Jeffers was nominated candidate of the western ward against Councillor A.P.T. Ambard, editor of *The Port of Spain Gazette*, and Felix Griffith, auctioneer and com-mission agent. Objections to her candidature were concretized in a protest lodged against her nomination by one Patrick Jones. He argued on the grounds that she did not fulfill the property qualifications. This was only part of the general antagonism which had emerged in some circles to Jeffers's nomination. Her main rival, Ambard, used the pages of his *Gazette* to wage a campaign against her. He also took the unusual step of being nominated in four wards—the western, southern, south-east-ern and the north-eastern.

Jeffers defended her candidature in a special interview in

the *Sunday Guardian*. She noted that no other topic was being more discussed at that time than the upcoming election and 'the advent of a woman to the Polls'. This fact, she added, had moved some to mirth and others to wrath. This wrath she suggested was because she, 'a mere woman', had dared to contest a seat on the City Council and especially from the western ward. She pointed out that the person accusing her of dishonesty in accepting Labour Party support had done the same himself in previous elections. If she was successful however, she would not repeat his ingratitude.

Throughout this statement (and indeed her campaign) the fact that she was a woman was central. She reminded readers that there were 500 women burgesses in the ward and asked 'Why should a woman not represent them?'[34]

The election turned out to be a source of great excitement. Meanwhile, in the *Sunday Guardian* in a letter to the editor, Greig thanked all those who had supported her in her attempt to contest a seat on the City Council. She expressed regret for the unforeseen circumstances which had caused her nomination to be withdrawn, and for the disappointment which it had caused to many. She concluded however that she was not downhearted, but still lived to fight another day.[35]

In justifying Labour Party support for Jeffers's campaign, Cipriani argued that workers stood to gain from her 'socialistic tendencies and public service' and explained that though supported by the TLP in the past, Ambard had acted against the interests of the working class after being elected. In the prevailing atmosphere of anti-Fascism and popular feeling against the 1935 Italian invasion of Ethiopia, he denounced Ambard as a Fascist. Ambard, he argued, had declared himself on the side of the Spanish rebels who were on the same side as the representatives of Italy and Germany, hence he supported the Fascist cause. Cipriani concluded to a cheering audience, 'Those who vote for Italy vote for Ambard. Those who are voting Ethiopia are voting Miss Jeffers.'[36]

Understandably, women of the Coterie saw this as part of their struggle. In her manifesto, Jeffers argued that a woman in the Council was what was needed, pointing out that what she had done for the people and children of Port of Spain, men in the Council had tried and failed.[37]

On 3 November 1936, women rallied to the polls, that is, those few who were eligible to vote. In the previous election, few women had been seen at the polling station. Jeffers beat her two opponents. She received 369 votes against Ambard's 299 and Griffith's 98. The poll was said to have been the largest since 1917. In the words of the *Guardian* editorial of 5 November, 'Hail the Woman', 'the issue was a clear one—whether a woman was or was not to secure a place in the City Council.' It concluded soberly:[38]

> The Woman's Movement has scored a notable victory. Those who supported the entry of Miss Jeffers into the City Council will thereby have their confidence increased and their willingness to work strengthened.... To continue 'stern and unbending' towards the Woman's Question in Trinidad after Tuesday's spectacular triumph would be futile and we submit, foolish.

Like a number of other organizations in 1938, the Coterie submitted a memorandum to the West India Royal Commission (WIRC). This Commission of Enquiry had been sent out by the British Colonial Office to investigate the social, political and economic factors which had led to widespread riots and disturbances in the region between 1934 and 1938.

The memorandum called for the establishment of a women's college with qualified teachers, where girls could be adequately prepared to compete for the Island Scholarship; an independent scholarship for girls who wanted to pursue a vocation; the institution of a school of Home Economics for adult women who had had no previous opportunity to acquire this 'valuable education' during their school years; a vocational school for girls; separate (and simpler) school exhibition examinations for girls; provision of clothing by the government to needy children; an end to the practice of transferring young female assistant teachers to schools distant from their homes; control over the proliferation of cinemas and the content of shows; and the nomination of an equal number of women and men on the Board of Censors.

A second section dealt with the issue of women's employment, calling for examinations or the establishment of a Board (as for male teachers) to prevent colour discrimination in the appointment of female teachers; improved wages and conditions for store clerks and shop assistants; improvement in the status of nurses; and protection of the independent trades of women, such as dressmaking and laundering. The problem of young unmarried mothers, aged 11 to 15 was discussed, calling for an institution for homeless girls and for women police to operate as rescue workers. In addition, the memorandum called for the Bastardy Ordinance (requiring fathers to support their illegitimate offspring) to be rigidly enforced and for nursery schools to be established.

On the general position of women, it demanded the removal of the prohibition on women in the Legislative Council; the appointment of women jurors in cases where women were on trial; and the appointment of women to all Boards in connection with housing and welfare of women and children.

In conclusion

Evidently, in the early part of the twentieth century, women in Trinidad and Tobago already recognized the need for increased rights and socio-economic opportunities. As in most colonized countries of the time, the women's movement was placed within a broad nationalist framework using social work as the main mechanism. While the black and coloured middle-class women sought to improve their status vis-à-vis white women and men, they never questioned their own position in relation to women of the working class.

Despite its contradictions, the gains of this early movement, and the tradition of regional collaboration it established, provided a basis for future periods of women's activism in Trinidad and Tobago.

NOTES

1. Trinidad Information Bureau, *Trinidad: The Riviera of the Caribbean*, Port of Spain, 1919. pp. 35–36.
2. J. Aldric Perez, *A Review of the Trinidad Home Industries Association (1901–1920)*. Port of Spain, 1920.

3. Olga Comma-Maynard, *The Brierend Pattern: The Story of Audrey Jeffers O.B.E. and the Coterie of Social Workers*. Port of Spain, 1971.
4. Ibid. p. 2.
5. Kumari Jayawardena, *Feminism and Nationalism in the Third World*. London: Zed Books; New Delhi: Kali for Women, 1986.
6. *Trinidad Guardian*, 8 October 1933, p. 1.
7. *Labour Leader*, 5 December 1931, p. 9.
8. *Mirror Almanack*, 1925.
9. *Trinidad Guardian*, 26 August 1927, p. 6 and 28 August 1927, p. 10.
10. *Labour Leader*, 3 September 1927, p. 8.
11. *The Port of Spain Gazette*, 21 September 1927, p. 9.
12. Ibid. 25 September 1927, p. 1.
13. Ibid. 27 September 1927, p. 4.
14. *Trinidad Guardian*, 30 September 1927, p. 9.
15. *The Port of Spain Gazette*, 30 September 1927, p. 12.
16. Ibid. 16 September 1927.
17. *Mirror Almanack*, 1929.
18. *Trinidad Guardian*, 23 April 1929; *Labour Leader*, 27 April, 1929.
19. *The East India Weekly*, 4 May 1929, p. 6.
20. *Labour Leader*, 10 and 12 August 1929.
21. Ibid. 24 May 1930, p. 8.
22. Ibid. 31 May 1930, p. 6.
23. *The People*, 5 January 1935, p. 11.
24. *Trinidad Guardian*, 7 May 1936, p. 11.
25. Ibid. 9 May 1936, p. 12.
26. Ibid. 8 May 1936, p. 8.
27. Ibid. 20 May 1936, p. 7.
28. *The People*, 23 May 1936, p. 6.
29. Ibid. p. 12; *Trinidad Guardian*, 10 May 1936, p.1.
30. Ibid.
31. *Sunday Guardian*, 10 May 1936, p. 4.
32. *Trinidad Guardian*, 1 October 1936, p.1.
33. Ibid. 3 October 1936, p. 6.
34. Ibid. 18 October 1936, p. 3.
35. *Sunday Guardian*, 25 October 1936, p. 4.
36. *Trinidad Guardian*, 30 October 1936, p. 3.
37. Olga Comma-Maynard, op. cit. pp. 90–91.
38. *Trinidad Guardian*, 5 November 1936, p. 6.

6

Women and Colonial Policy in Jamaica after the 1938 Uprising

Joan French

Labour disturbances in British West Indies in the 1930s are generally regarded as marking a turning-point in the relationship between the British Imperial Government and the West Indian colonies. In Jamaica, the uprising of 1938 shook the foundations of the colonial State, and forced a number of important reforms.

Most of these reforms, implemented in the 10 or so years following the uprising, were based on the recommendations of the West India Royal Commission of 1939. Chaired by Lord Moyne, it became popularly known as the Moyne Commission.

The Commission was appointed in August 1938 as a direct result of the uprising in Jamaica, the largest in the chain of labour disturbances in the West Indian colonies of the period. Its terms of reference as spelt out in the Report of the West India Royal Commission were: 'To investigate social and economic conditions in Barbados, British Guiana, British Honduras, Jamaica, the Leeward Islands, Trinidad and Tobago and the Windward Islands.'

The purpose of the Commission's report and recommendations was to provide a guide to British colonial policy as it related to remedial action after 1938. The main concern was the prevention of further disturbances and the maintenance of British control in the colonies.

The full text of the Moyne Commission report was not published until 1945, for fear that the conditions exposed might lead to further rebellion. However, a statement of the recommendations was published in 1940, for the specific purpose of providing a guide to those responsible for the administration and implementation of colonial policy in the West Indies.

The Commission's investigation was perhaps the most extensive and participatory in the history of British West Indian colonial relations. The Commission heard formal evidence in 26 centres from 370 witnesses or groups of witnesses, and received and considered 789 memoranda of evidence in its visits throughout British West Indies.

The seriousness with which the Commission's investigation was regarded is clear from the numbers, status and range of organizational affiliations of those giving evidence, and from the high level of public interest. In Barbados, for example, large crowds gathered in Queens Park to listen to the proceedings relayed by loudspeaker. In every territory the Commission was the big event of the day. Both those who gave evidence and those who had been in active rebellion saw the Commission as the channel through which reforms might be achieved.

The reforms implemented as a result of the recommendations did contribute in a general way to improvements in the condition of women, but were limited in relation to women as a specific group. The limitations arose partly from the manoeuvres of the rich and powerful to protect their interests in the face of a popular onslaught on their positions of power, partly from that of men to protect their interests in relation to women, and partly from the approaches taken by women themselves in their struggle for improved conditions.

While a considerable amount of literature has emerged on these reforms where they relate to political organization, the union movement, regional integration, education, etc., little has been written about them in relation to the status and situation of women. Similarly, recommendations on education, public health, trade unions, agriculture, etc. have been studied as part of courses in our schools and university for years, but no studies have been carried out on how the recommendations affected women. This is perhaps not surprising. While the other topics are explicitly dealt with in specific sections of the report, ideas on the role of women, though central, or perhaps because they are central, are spread throughout the various sections.

It is the intention of this chapter to demonstrate:

• that specific policies towards women were contained in the report;

• that the content of the Colonial Development and Welfare Act of 1940 and the programmes of the Development and Welfare Office, Jamaica Welfare and Jamaica Federation

of Women (JFW) were in line with these policies;
- that the policies impacted on both middle-class and working-class women, although differently, but in ways that significantly affected the manner of their integration into the workforce;
- that these policies greatly helped promote ideas about the roles and obligations of women and men which are linked to the concept of the male breadwinner and dependent housewife—ideas which largely define the parameters of discussions on male-female relations in Jamaican society to the present day.

Gender relations and the economy prior to 1938

Historically, the economy of Jamaica since colonization by the British had mainly centred on large sugar estates based on slave labour. During the latter years of slavery, both female and male slaves were given access to land to grow their own food, primarily to relieve the estate owners of what had become an increasingly burdensome and expensive task.

Women got equal access, because under the common oppression and exploitation of the system every slave was a slave regardless of sex, and women and men were 'equal under the whip'.[1] The ownership of their bodies and labour, and the power of the slavemasters to dispose of them and their children at will, gave rise to this equity in relation to land. This was despite occupational inequalities on the estates, where women dominated field work and men the skilled occupations. The slavemaster's ultimate power and control undermined the male slave's assertion of power over 'his' woman, which may have had a negative effect on him, but proved positive for her.

Land was the main means of production and the primary source of economic advancement, which both male and female slaves were able to use to their advantage. They worked harder on their own plots than on the *backra* (white) master's estate, eating what they needed and selling the surplus. With the money earned, they were able to develop a level of economic independence, even to the point of buying their freedom when this was allowed.

It was women who controlled the marketing of the produce.

In addition to returns from their own plots, they got a nominal share of the profits from the produce they sold for their partners, and sometimes for their masters. Their strong position in relation to land was also evident in the fact that it was as common for men to have a variety of women as a form of economic security, as it was for women to have men. As Edward Long states: 'One of them perhaps has six or more *husbands* or *wives* in several different places: by this means they find support when their own lands fail them.'[2]

In the transition from slavery to emancipation however, women lost more than men. One of the reasons was that the European monogamous marriage was promoted among the slaves from the final decades of slavery, as a way of encouraging population growth to replenish the labour force in the wake of the abolition of the slave trade in 1807. Even where slaves resisted the legal form of marriage, the ideology of the male breadwinner and property-owner and the dependent, non-earning housewife spread among the ex-slaves.

With the lion's share of responsibility for children, the sick and the aged, it was harder for women to take the plunge to move away from the estates. It was also more difficult to confront *backra massa* (the white master) over unjust treatment if they stayed, since he could throw them and their dependents out of the estates at will. And when they did move away, it was harder for them to establish an independent land base.

The European family norm was not quite the same as that which the slaves had known in West Africa, where families were predominantly polygamous, with a man taking a number of wives. Women's value, apart from sexual services, lay in the labour they provided in the fields and at home and in their capacity to produce children, especially male children. Male children brought wealth and labourers into the family through marriage. Female children depleted family resources since the marriage required the payment of a dowry to the husband. Sons stayed home, daughters moved away to become the servants of other families.

What the European and African family systems had in common was the element of male dominance and the subjection of women to male will.

However, West African culture supported women's access

to land. Many of the West African societies from which the slaves came, notably the Ashanti, allowed family lands and goods to be passed from one generation to another through the female members who had the main responsibility for growing and preparing the family's food.[3]

Equitable access to land in the new conditions allowed the development of new relations between the sexes. Slave women could assert their independence and autonomy in relation to their men, which contrasted with both the domestic oppression of the women of the slave-owning classes and the subjection of women under West African polygamy. Slave women did not want either. In a famous, 'Conversation on Marriage' involving the slaves Quashie and Quasheba, Quasheba states that she has no desire to marry as the missionaries advocated. This, she says, would give Quashie the right to demand domestic services, lord it over her, and deprive her of the right to reject him with ease if she can no longer put up with his bad habits.[4]

These new relations were threatened by the British system of matrimonial and property laws into which the ex-slaves became increasingly, though never predominantly, integrated. According to British law, a married woman could not own property. If she had property before marriage, it passed on to the husband, to be used and dispensed with as he saw fit.

Resistance to these and other injustices inherent in this model of male-female relations, was evident in the low rate of marriages despite the best efforts of the missionaries and some planters. African customary law is undoubtedly responsible for the strong tradition of family land, which developed in Caribbean societies and became a refuge for many women whose land rights were assaulted by British culture. Reading between the lines of Edith Clarke's *My Mother Who Fathered Me*, one gets a clear sense of the ongoing conflicts generated by the contest between the African and British systems, even in relation to family land.[5]

However, it was British ideology which thrived, and in the post-emancipation period there was a gradual weakening of control of women over their own land. The ideology informed State policy and became institutionalized in a variety of ways which induced some level of conformity. For example, married slaves were given preference in estate housing in the late slave period. When land settlement schemes began to be established under governor John Peter Grant in the 1860s, the concept of the 'farm family' with a male head was used as the basis for allocating land. But while this imposed system became characteristic of all land settlement schemes right into the twentieth century, it did not go uncontested. The authorities were forced by circumstances to give land to female heads of households, although within the 'farm family' the wife had no land rights.

While women constituted two-thirds of the field labour force on the estates throughout slavery, in the transition to wage labour women's position in the agricultural labour force changed. Men came to constitute the 'real' labour force, with stable jobs and more regular employment on the estates. Women were used as 'supplementary' labour as it became more widely accepted that a woman's place was in the home.

For the missionaries, this was seen as a way of removing women from the brutality and hardships of field labour, and as a transition to a finer style of living. For the ex-slaves the arguments were seductive, given their past experience. In practical terms, however, it meant that women were increasingly deprived of direct control of the main material base—land—and placed in a subordinate position to men in their earnings. Dependence on a man became a necessity for more and more women.

During the post-emancipation period and up to the end of the nineteenth century, while the number of women working in agriculture increased, the form of their insertion underwent changes. Unlike the features we will observe for the twentieth century, their involvement in domestic work declined.

Main sectors of female labour: 1844–1891

	1844	1871	1881	1891
Agricultural	132,192	143,698	208,587	271,296
Domestic	20,571	16,453	15,048	26,686

Source: Census of Jamaica 1871, 1881 and 1891 and *Free Jamaica 1839–1865: An Economic History*, Douglas Hall, Caribbean University Press, 1969. p. 266.

At the same time, the category of 'indefinite and non-productive' labour doubled between 1844 and 1871, from 143,779 to 289,784, declining again to 265,970 as the increased birth-rate after emancipation levelled off. This expansion was also partly due, however, to more women working for their own families rather than as domestics in other people's homes.

In the years of the First World War (1914–1918) sugar prices rose to 10 times their pre-war level, and the sugar industry was vibrant. The 1880s had also seen the start of a huge expansion in banana production on the initiative of the US. This banana boom continued into the 1920s.

The construction of the Panama Canal and migration to the sugar and banana plantations of Central America and the US at the end of the nineteenth century operated as a safety valve, providing income-earning opportunities for thousands of Jamaican males. From 1880 to 1920, an estimated 146,000 persons, almost exclusively male, migrated from a population that ranged between 580,000 and 858,000.[6] By 1934 a total of 275,624 men had migrated.

By the 1930s, however, the Jamaican economy was experiencing inescapable problems. The 'world economy' was undergoing the Great Depression which came to a head in 1929. In addition, banana production in Jamaica was affected by leaf spot disease which by 1931 had already taken 24,000 acres out of production in the parishes of St Mary and Portland.[7] Between 1927 and 1937 there was also a slump in sugar prices, which almost halved the price per ton by 1937.[8] To compound matters, migration as an outlet began to decline around 1914, and was closed off as an option by the mid-1930s.

Women now found themselves working more and more, not as directly paid casual workers, but, along with their children, as 'family labour', and supplementary to men. Many who were not blood relations of the men, were sub-contracted by them to assist in fieldwork. This relegation of women to a second- or third-level workforce was a response to the pressures on the colonial State brought about by the return of thousands of male migrants from the Central American republics. The primary right to wages was increasingly reserved for males.

As early as 1935, the report of an unemployment commission estimated the 'genuinely unemployed' as men only. In the

Orde-Browne report of 1938 (on which the Moyne Commission later relied heavily) rates for work on relief schemes were recommended based on the minimum needs of a single man without dependents. Women were not considered. By 1937, female employment was seen by ordinary working men as a threat to male employment, and men were accepting the idea that women had less right to wages. The justification was obviously linked to women's role as housewives. 'No man wants to employ us when he can employ a woman.'9

The returning male migrants refused to work for the pittance or in the limited capacities being offered locally. They had, moreover, been exposed to labour organization and unionization in the course of their work abroad, and spoke against the prevailing conditions in such a way as to contribute significantly to the radicalization of the island's politics.

By 1938, local conditions were sub-human: wages were low, especially for women, health services and housing were poor, and the majority were unable to afford many basic necessities at current prices. Riddled by disease and plagued by exhaustion, thousands (including women) roamed from estate to estate in search of seasonal work.

At the same time increasing educational opportunities and the benefits of migration had further developed a black and coloured middle class influenced by the ideas of the time: the black self-reliance and pride of Marcus Garvey, the socialist ideas of the Russian Revolution, the growth of the international workers' movement and the growing self-assertion of the colonies worldwide.

All these factors combined to produce the explosion that was the uprising of 1938. There can be no dispute that the uprising resulted in broad and beneficial changes. The wages of labourers and workers were upgraded, unions were formed and recognized, the black and coloured middle class made advances in the civil service and in the professions, and the males became leaders of the political parties which were formed. Adult suffrage and limited self-government were achieved in 1944, leading to full self-government in 1957 and eventually to independence and the end of colonial status for the island in 1962.

For women, special provisions for advancement were contained in the Sex Disqualification (Removal) Act of 1944. As workers their wages were upgraded, and they gained improved rights to unionization. More opportunities were provided for their progress in the professions. Black women were accepted in the civil service other than as clerks and typists. Their access to education was expanded and they gained the right of election or nomination to the Legislative Council, boards and local authorities. They became the backbone of the political parties.

Despite all this, women did not emerge from the period with equal decision-making power or equal access to material resources. The balance of their relationship with men in the society changed in favour of men. That change was a result of the particular concept of womanhood contained in the recommendations of the Commission and all other instruments of colonial policy of the time.

As already noted, the full report of the Commission was not made public until 1945, although its recommendations were published in 1940. In June 1945 a 'Statement of Actions Taken on the Recommendations' appeared. It is these documents which provide the source material for our examination of the policy towards women as defined by the Moyne Commission and implemented by the British State. To use the recommendations of 1940 alone would deprive us of the opportunity to examine the reasoning and approaches behind them. References to the action on the recommendations allow us to assess progress in the implementation of policy up to 1945.

The Moyne Commission and women

In Jamaica, women giving evidence before the Commission included Amy Bailey of the Women's Liberal Club, an early black Jamaican feminist and outstanding fighter for the economic and political rights of women; May Farquharson, daughter of a white planter and initiator of the early birth control movement in Jamaica; Una Marson, black Jamaican feminist, author and radio broadcaster who eventually settled in Britain and promoted Caribbean and Jamaican interests as an announcer at the British Broadcasting Corporation; Edith Clarke of Jamaica Welfare Limited and later author of the famous study of the Jamaican family, *My Mother Who Fathered Me*; and Edith Dalton-James, educator, who appeared before the Commission as one of the representatives of the Jamaica Union of Teachers.

According to Howard Johnson, the evidence indicates that the colonial office made a conscious effort to include women on the Commission.[10] This 'conscious effort' resulted in the appointment of two women to the Commission of 10: Dr Mary Blacklock and Dame Rachel Crowdy. Dr Blacklock was an expert in tropical medicine who had served as a medical officer in Sierra Leone and as Professor of Pathology at Lady Hardinge College in Delhi, India. Dame Crowdy was a distinguished social worker with international experience. Though a member of the Commission, Dame Crowdy also gave evidence before it in support of proposals for reform and for the advancement of women.

Much of the content of the Commission's report in relation to women is based on the input of these and other women who testified before the Commission. In examining its report and recommendations, we are therefore also examining to a large extent the ideas of the women's movement as it manifested itself in Jamaica at the time, and insofar as the views of women were heard in the halls of power.

The report and recommendations do contain a central focus on women apparent from the three things the Commission saw as basic to a solution of social problems in Jamaica after 1938. They were, the status accorded to women; the. lack of family life; and the absence of a well-defined programme of social welfare.

The main pillars of the proposed policy were:
- promotion of the ideology of the male breadwinner and dependent housewife, and, as a means to this end, the promotion of 'stable monogamy', preferably through marriage;
- promotion of the ideal of voluntary social work as the most laudable and prestigious occupation for middle-class women;
- increased opportunities for women in the professions;
- increased participation of women in the civil service and government, and access to higher posts;
- use of the same procedures (nominal equality) in selecting male and female candidates for appointment in the civil service.

The bias towards the concerns and interests of middle-class women is obvious. The needs of 'women of the labouring classes' were to be addressed only tangentially through social work and the promotion of 'proper families'.

There are no recommendations for equal pay in respect of female workers, though one of the findings of the Commission was that West Indian women were paid miserably low wages as compared to men, and this was impractical in a situation where many women were heads of households.[11]

This clearly conflicted with the other ideas which dominated in the report: ideas related to the promotion of the European monogamous family. Elsewhere it was argued that if women were poor and families destitute, it was because women did not have families with a man at the centre. The report states that where there was no 'father'

the whole (financial) responsibility falls on the mother.... In such circumstances cases of extreme poverty are inevitable, for the standard of living must be lower than it would be in a family group where, even if both parents were not employed, more money would be available, since the wages of men are normally higher than those given to women.[12]

The solution to female poverty then, was not to pay women proper wages for the work they did, but to deprive them of what little wages they had by establishing families in which men were seen as the providers, and therefore as having the primary right to a wage.

It was lack of this 'proper' family which was blamed for all suffering—for poverty, for infant mortality, for venereal disease, and for 'the lot of their unfortunate children'.[13] This was also the reason given by women of the middle classes for overpopulation. In reality, the rate of infant mortality differed little whether the parents were married or unmarried, and the birth rate among married couples was actually higher than that among single or common-law mothers.[14]

As a corollary to the establishment of the male-headed household, the Commission proposed a campaign against, 'the social, moral and economic evils of promiscuity'. 'Promiscuity' was defined as all those forms of relations between the sexes

which were non-marital or non-monogamous. Multiple con-
secutive unions, the most common among the masses, were thus
condemned. Faithful concubinage was tolerated because its
presumably monogamous and 'stable' nature resembled marriage in all but its legal form. The children of those unions were,
however, like the children of 'promiscuous' unions, condemned
for their 'illegitimacy'.

That there was some struggle around the imposition of the
monogamous nuclear model at the time of the Commission is
evident from the following comment in the report:[15]

> Some witnesses averred that the West Indian prefers cohabi-
> tation without marriage, but no convincing evidence on this
> point was put before us. Other witnesses alleged that the
> failure of West Indians to marry is a legacy from a time when
> the institution of wedlock was discouraged among the slaves.

It was never in fact possible to get practical acceptance of
the model in its pure legal form. Marriage remained a minority
activity: common-law unions and female-headed households
remained the order of the day.

The report goes on to give a glimpse of the racism inherent
in the Commission's inability to be convinced of the West Indian preference for cohabitation without marriage. It alleges
that, being primitive, West Indians were incapable of consciously deciding for themselves what they wanted.[16]

The findings of the Commission included the need for the
establishment of hostels in town for domestic workers and shop
assistants. This was the single material provision in favour of
working-class women, but in practice it was never established
out of public funds. In fact, when the 'Statement of Action Taken
on the Recommendations' was published, it noted that despite
war expenditure, much had been done to implement the recommendations in relation to the setting up of social welfare
bodies and programmes. By contrast we are later told that 'ow-
ing to war expenditure no action has been taken on the recommendation that more hostels should be provided for women
workers.'[17] The same excuse is given for failure to address the
problem of nutrition.

Other 'actions taken' on behalf of working-class women were

limited to the provision of a completely revised curriculum for primary schools, to include instruction in hygiene and domestic science for girls. (Boys were to be given manual and agricultural training). Whatever other little help was extended to women of the labouring population, was given through the voluntary labour of middle-class women, as in the case of the two central kitchens and 70 school canteens established by 1945. Some clothing donated by the US was altered by girls in schools under the supervision of female teachers and given to needy children. These, then, were the only practical measures taken for the benefit of the poor, which were made explicit in the Statement of Actions. The play centres recommended for schools did not become a reality, perhaps because of controversy over paying the girls a small fee.

For middle-class women, on the other hand, 'equal' secondary education and 'equal terms' in the island scholarships were 'generally already true or receiving consideration'.[18] The Sex Disqualification (Removal) Law of 1944 had been passed, allowing the entry of middle-class women to areas of public life from which they were previously excluded. It provided for the appointment of women as magistrates and jurors, as well as their entry to higher levels of the civil service and the expansion of their role in education, social services and government.

For the majority of ordinary women, however, whatever immediate benefits there were came primarily through the 1944 Constitution and its provision for universal adult suffrage. This gave all women a voice in the election of their political representatives, and vindicated the participation of ordinary working-class women in political parties like the People's National Party formed in 1938, or the Jamaican Labour Party established in 1943. Ironically, organized middle-class women did not support universal adult suffrage. This was in line with a middle-class view of the time, held by both males and females that the labouring class lacked the education to properly exercise the right to vote.

Changes after 1938 were not only determined by the policies of the British government as expressed by the Commission, but also influenced by the ongoing struggles of women. The Commission had failed to challenge the exclusion of married women from the civil service and teaching, and property laws by which the property of married women automatically became the property of their husbands. The struggles of women however led to the inclusion in the Sex Disqualification (Removal) Law of 1944 of provisions for married women to own property and to retain their jobs in the civil service and the teaching profession even after marriage.

Before the enactment of the law, these discriminatory practices had militated against women establishing their economic independence. Previously many women had been forced to choose between sexuality and/or motherhood, and a career. Many middle-class women chose to remain single. Amy Bailey, Edith Clarke and Una Marson were among those who apparently refused to trade financial independence for the satisfaction of home and family.

While in general the recommendations of the Commission and the measures arising from them favoured middle-class women, they too were adversely affected by the Commission's view, following the British model, of a woman's essential role as being that of a housewife. The professional roles recommended for them were thus limited to those considered suited to the housewifely temperament and abilities. As magistrates, they were expected to deal with young offenders, maintenance and other areas of 'family law'. As doctors they were to deal with venereal disease and maternity, and as nurses, with child care, and public health. As teachers they were to promote domestic science and related skills, such as sewing and other handicrafts. As social workers they would be working at the 'local' levels on committees which were largely unpaid, while men controlled the paid posts and the higher echelons of administration.

For middle-class women, as for poor working women, marriage was to be seen as life's primary responsibility and goal, though to somewhat different effect given their different circumstances. The report of the Commission specified marriage as the implicit aim of all female education: 'If there are to be happy marriages, girls must be able to be companions for their husbands and therefore need as wide a cultural education as possible.' The basic ingredient of this 'cultural education' was to be domestic science: 'Domestic science should of course form a part of the curriculum of all girls' schools.'[19]

Vocational education for girls was to consist of housecraft training, as was already being done in Guyana through the Carnegie Trade School for Girls. In Jamaica, all-male trade training centres, such as Dinthill and Holmwood, were eventually diversified to include domestic science for girls.

For girls of the lower classes, training in housecraft would be included in the elementary schools (beyond which few could advance). The stated aim was to equip them for employment as assistants in the infant play-centres which the Commission recommended be attached to schools. For this they 'might receive a small fee'. On this suggestion the Commission 'offered no comment', but felt that it 'would have to be decided in the light of local circumstances'. The bulk of these girls would, as we shall see in the statistics for the period, end up as domestics. In Jamaica, Amy Bailey's 'Housecraft Training Centre' attempted to offer these women more professional status as domestics.

On the surface the Commission's recommendations about social welfare seemed free of sex bias. They included, more of less in these words:

- an organized campaign to be undertaken against the social, moral and economic evils of promiscuity;
- an organization to be created and staff appointed, through the agency of which a well-defined social welfare programme can be planned and executed;
- social welfare workers to be trained for service in the West Indian Colonies;
- public funds to be used to supplement the voluntary subscriptions on which the creation of such agencies were expected to depend;
- the work of existing voluntary organizations to be extended by encouraging still more interest in that work from people of leisure who are in a position to help financially by subscribing to the cost of these activities and by personal service.

However, when the Council of Social Service was later proposed by T.S. Simey for the concrete realization of the recommendations, the proposal said that the Council was to be staffed by male officers who would work with the 'assistance' of three trained women social workers.[20] They would be supported by a host of voluntary social workers, most of whom were women. Up to at least 1947, trained social workers were mainly male, while the bulk of the voluntary social workers in the field were women. Males were predominant in the social welfare training courses organized by Professor Simey during his tenure as social welfare adviser. Women first outnumbered men in these courses in 1947 when Dora Ibberson took over from Professor Simey as social welfare adviser.[21]

The most extensive actions stemming from the Commission's recommendations were taken in the area of social welfare. Next came the appointment of a secretary for social welfare services to 'co-ordinate the welfare activities of official and non-official bodies'. 'Considerable assistance' had by then been given to Jamaica Welfare Limited, in the form of a grant under the Colonial Development and Welfare Act of 1940.

This assistance in effect shifted the focus of Jamaica Welfare away from the material issues of land settlement and income from agriculture, towards a social welfare approach based on conservation (living within your means), home improvement and family life. Jamaica Welfare, no longer in charge of its own policies, now had to act on government directives in line with the existing colonial policy. The new directions were based almost entirely on the free labour of women.

Activating the policy:
the Colonial Development and Welfare Acts

The Colonial Development and Welfare Act of 1940 was concerned primarily with social welfare, while the emphasis of the previous Act of 1929 had been on 'investment and finance'. Other such Acts passed between 1945 and 1959 revised the amounts allotted to social welfare in the 1940 Act and apportioned money specifically to 'research and enquiry'. These Acts were therefore the vehicles for implementing the social welfare recommendations of the Commission.

The 1940 Act contains explicit acceptance of the proposals of T.S. Simey concerning social welfare. Simey had recommended an extensive all-island network based on 'Village Community Associations'. To create the network, a Jamaica Council of Social Services was to be set up, which would coordinate

existing voluntary social work schemes, principal among them
Jamaica Welfare, but also the YWCA, the Church and others.

Simey's plan was based predominantly on the voluntary
labour of women in order to minimize public expenditure. The
village community associations could, moreover, 'discharge
some functions which are commonly in Jamaica thought to be
functions of government.'[22] Women were therefore expected
not only to take on for free the bulk of the work, but also to
subsidize with this free labour some of the work that the government was already paying for.

One of the main functions of these associations was 'educational'. The type of education had major implications for
women. To quote Simey:[23]

> Both men and women officers would find their practical
> functions best summed up in the phrase 'home-making'...
> The women should be competent house-keepers and be able
> to give instructions in the arts of child management.

However, the ideal family and home envisaged by these recommendations had little in common with the Jamaican reality.
The actual effect then was to increase by thousands the number of women who became domestics, even as they were being
encouraged to withdraw from visible agricultural labour and
confine their agricultural pursuits to the home, where they became subsumed under the women's role as housewives.

There were other ironic consequences. The Act of 1940 also
outlined a programme for land settlement and housing, which
favoured a nuclear family with a male head of the household
to whom the land was leased or sold. The preference for these
'proper families' meant that a female head of the household
stood less chance of getting her own land, and a wife, common-law or not, stood no chance at all. This did not go uncontested, and some women did manage to obtain land through
the programme.

In addition, the land settlement and housing programme
made the establishment of trade union laws and the facilita-
tion of trade union activity conditions for grants under the Act.
This development took place at a time when women were being ejected from key areas of the economy such as agriculture,

and relegated to unpaid or low-paid labour at home or in a small but growing manufacturing sector. As a result, unions became primarily male preserves.

Organizing home-makers: the Jamaica Federation of Women

The promotion of the 'ideal family model' was supported by the JFW, a huge mass organization developed with the support of the Colonial Office.

JFW was founded in 1944 by Lady Molly Huggins, wife of the Colonial Governor, who had arrived in the island in 1943. It was modelled on the Women's Institutes of Great Britain. The motto of the federation, 'For Our Homes and Our Country', was in essence the same as that of the institutes.

Women's Institutes had emerged first in Canada, and had been introduced into Great Britain in 1915 during World War I. They were rural bodies which organized farmers' wives and daughters to support the British war effort. They grew and preserved food to supplement supplies from overseas which were curtailed by war conditions. The women produced vegetables, small livestock, eggs, etc. which they sold to each other from village stalls. It was this level of subsistence agriculture which kept the country alive during the war years.

Many were managing their holdings alone since their men had been called up for military service. They were tackling for the first time 'jobs that their husbands used to do', and doing their housework at the same time. Their willingness to take on this double burden was seen as an admirable demonstration of their patriotism.

At the institute meetings there were talks on health, childcare, sessions on cooking, how to make preserves, sewing, knitting and the making of Christmas presents for the soldiers. The meetings also provided an opportunity to get out of the house for a reason acceptable to men. There were no subscriptions and no collections were allowed for any cause.

The institutes defined themselves as non-political, and drew members from all parties. They promoted civic education and made presentations to district and county councils from the rural housewife's point of view. It was not considered political to report on different matters to Parliament or to collect facts and suggest policy not yet adopted by any one of the parties.

In its focus on rural housewives and 'kitchen gardens', the social form and content of meetings and the 'non-political' claim of the organization, the Federation imitated the Women's Institutes, and similarly responded to the necessities of a war situation: in this case World War II.

In May and June of 1943, Una Marson, the Jamaican feminist and black nationalist, interviewed representatives of the Women's Institutes in a series of broadcasts from the BBC specifically for transmission to the West Indies. These broadcasts were published in written form in Barbados in 1944, by the Office of the Comptroller for Development and Welfare in the West Indies.

One of the representatives interviewed remarked, 'it seems only fitting that an organization of this nature, which was introduced into the Mother country during the last Great War, should spread to the West Indies during the present great struggle.' The formation of the JFW, then, had the official support of the British government, and seems to have been the result of an official initiative.

In patterning itself on the Women's Institutes, the JFW was establishing a link with the most conservative branch of British feminism at the time. After World War I, feminism in Britain had polarized into conservative and liberal factions. The liberal faction, with which Sylvia Pankhurst was associated, campaigned for reforms, welfare and equal pay.

On the conservative side, Emmeline and Christabel Pankhurst and their followers supported the war effort, and emphasized the importance of women's support for the preservation of the existing system. Women from this branch of feminists were admitted eventually to the Parliament they had previously opposed. This is the branch of feminism to which Molly Huggins belonged.

Among these feminists the image of women as housewives was strengthened, and the 'spinster' was seen as leading an unhealthy existence, though it was accepted that 'spinsters' could re-channel the sex instinct into creative vocations.

The JFW consciously sought to bring together the leadership of all the existing women's groups at the community level —teachers, nurses, postmistresses, parsons' wives, women of 'all classes'—under one umbrella organization. This was part of a concerted effort by Lady Huggins to draw in the black and brown middle-classes who were invited to be members of the Executive Committee of 20.

The Liberal Club, with its focus on the participation of women in politics and improvements in women's economic and social status, disbanded and its members joined the executive committee.

The aims of the JFW were in perfect harmony with the policy towards women as embodied in the recommendations of the West India Royal Commission of 1939 and the development and welfare programmes which followed.

The Civics Committee was defined as the organ of the Federation which campaigned for better family living. It encouraged marriage and 'parental responsibility', training in mothercraft (childcare), the establishment of basic schools and the promotion of voluntary effort. It was also the place where debate took place on issues of concern to women. By 1948 the Federation had a sizeable membership of 30,000 and about 400 projects.

The home-making focus of JFW and its promotion of the nuclear family were reflected in all its programmes. The organization had an annual Homemaker's Day, and a kitchen-garden competition. A Better Home campaign promoted the idea that it was an asset to have married parents. Mass weddings were initiated under the management of Mary Morris-Knibb, for which wedding rings were sold for ten shillings.

A total of 150 such mass marriages were organized, but they only marginally raised (by a mere 2 per cent) the percentage of the married population. This was despite a massive and expensive public campaign in which Lady Huggins marshalled the churches, schools, press, radio, welfare agencies and national associations.[24]

The organization's campaign for the registration of fathers started in 1945, ostensibly promoting child support, but betraying an intention to discourage illegitimacy by punishing fathers of illegitimate children. They were to be regarded as criminals and imprisoned if they failed to pay child support, regardless of their economic position.

There was no suggestion that fatherhood involved anything other than financial support, a subtle assumption of the 'male breadwinner/dependent housewife' ideology. Married men, on the other hand, could not be sued for child support as long as they remained in the matrimonial home—even if they were bringing in nothing and were being supported by their wives.

Nevertheless, this was to prove the most widely supported campaign of the organization. It gave poor women a chance to get some money from irresponsible men who joined them in creating children, then left them to mind them on their own.

However, there were important limitations which exist to this day: for example, the minimal amounts prescribed by law for child support, the onus placed on women to find their babies' fathers in order to get the court to pursue the matter, and most importantly, the failure to institute a public programme for child support through organized public contribution.

Over the years the membership of JFW declined drastically, from 30,000 in 1948 to 8,000 in 1984. An important factor was the challenge to its approach by the policies of the 1970s, which emphasized the economic rights of women, questioned their confinement to domestic roles and encouraged them to take on non-traditional work.

Effect on female labour

An examination of what was happening to female labour illustrates the far-reaching impact of the application of the 'male-breadwinner/dependent housewife' model on women's access to paid work.

Status of the Female Labour Force: 1921 and 1943

Year	Total Farm Labour	Total Agriculture Labour	Female Labour in Agriculture	Male Labour in Agriculture
1921	219,000	285,700	125,400	160,300
1943	163,000	228,600	45,600*	183,000

*Considered unreliable by this author.
Source: *Some Aspects of Jamaica's Politics, 1918–1938*, James Carnegie, Institute of Jamaica, 1973, p. 24.

According to these census figures, while in 1921, 71 per cent of the total labour force worked in agriculture, by 1943 this had declined to 57 per cent. In the same period, female involvement declined from 78 per cent to 25 per cent.

The explanation for the low figures recorded for female participation in agricultural labour in 1942, was the redefinition of women labourers into homemakers and domestics. The introduction to the 1953 Sample Survey of the population (Section 16: 64) states:

In 1943... women and children were thrown out of the labour force by the manner in which the definition of 'gainful occupation' was applied. The 1943 'gainfully occupied' concept was not closely comparable to the 'productive population' of earlier censuses.

The Labour Department Report of 1944 clearly describes the parameters of a redefined concept of 'gainful occupation':

For census purposes, a gainful occupation is one by which the person who pursues it earns money, performs a service or assists with the production of goods. Children working at home on general household duties or chores or at odd times at other work are not considered as being gainfully occupied. Similarly women doing housework in their own homes without salary or wages were returned as homemakers and not considered as being among the gainfully occupied.

This ejection of women from the labour force was, at least initially, more statistical than real. However, the ideology was by no means new, and had been gaining in strength over a period of time. Between 1891 and 1911, the ratio of females to males in the 'indefinite and non-productive' category had increased markedly.

By the mid-1930s, women agricultural labourers were mostly identified as unpaid family workers, 'homemakers' combining their housework with subsistence agricultural production along with some paid work on small mixed farms.

The 1943 census recognized only paid workers, and at the same time redefined 'mixed farms' to mean farms on which two cash crops together provided 50 per cent of the production value.

Previously, mixed farms grew food for the local market, as well as some cash crops and involved a majority of women farmers. By the new definition these farms were excluded from the statistics, and women who worked them were no longer defined as farmers.

Ratio of Females to Males in the 'Indefinite and Non-Productive' Category: 1891–1911

Age group	1891		1911	
	M	F	M	F
20+	1	3	1	5
25+	1	4	1	10
30+	1	5	1	10
35+	1	7	1	11
40+	1	4	1	10
45+	1	3	1	10

Source: Census of Jamaica, 1891 and 1911.

The labour of women therefore became more and more invisible. Women were, on the whole, not to be considered workers at all.

By 1944, women were struggling to retain their work on relief employment projects, while men sought to keep the jobs for themselves.

Ten years later, when Winnifred Hewitt was appointed assistant statistician in the Central Bureau of Statistics, and Sybil Francis became assistant secretary in the Ministry of Community Development, the *Civil Service Magazine* carried an article in which men questioned and criticized the appointment of women to these posts.

The article stated that 'men had better look to their laurels, as two women had been appointed to senior posts'. The overt anti-woman content of the statement was brought to the attention of the editors of the magazine by Hewitt, and a disclaimer of intent followed. This did not, however, change the fact that the sentiments expressed in the statement reflected a pervasive fear among the men.

Despite the negative impact of these measures on the material welfare of poor women, the social welfare thrust allowed middle-class women to break out of the confines of their own housewifely roles, and come into meaningful contact with the everyday lives of the poor.

This had a positive effect on the consciousness of some middle-class women, giving them a new perspective on the lives and problems of women of other classes. Similar opportunities were provided by their insertion into nursing, teaching, and other professions. In general, however, the class divide was retained.

Conclusion

Writers of Caribbean history to date have consistently failed to analyse the specific structure of women's integration into the socio-economic fabric, or the effect of historical processes on women as a group. Such an analysis forces a re-evaluation of these processes and can, as in the present case, bring into question certain assumptions about 'general societal progress'.

The implications are important, since ultimately policies that affect women, invariably have an impact on the entire population. Women's history is not a matter for women alone. It is critical to the understanding of historical processes in their fullness. It is even more critical for activists and those involved in determining directions for change and charting appropriate strategies.

While it is clear that the policies which are the subject of this chapter operated to undermine the material base and the overt power of women, it would be interesting to study the strategies of resistance which undoubtedly developed in response to these policies.

Simey's non-economic, 'social' approach was challenged and women did act in defence of their economic rights. They did this partly through the limited craft-oriented, income-generating programmes of both JFW and the social welfare movement, partly through measures to get men to honour their financial obligations to children and partly through other strategies still hidden under the veil of a gender-biased history.

Middle-class women were aware of and fought for their gender interests, and in the process conditions for all women were changed. The immediate gender interests of women from the masses were, however, addressed only to a very limited extent. For them direct access to material things continued to decline.

The problem remains. Quasheba's struggle continues.

NOTES

1. Lucille Mathurin, *The Rebel Woman in the British West Indies during Slavery*. Jamaica: Institute of Jamaica, 1975. p. 4.
2. Edward Long, quoted in Orlando Patterson, *The Sociology of Slavery*. Jamaica: Sangster's Book Stores, 1973. p. 163.
3. Lucille Mathurin, op. cit. p. 2.
4. 'A Conversation on Marriage,' Methodist Missionary Society Archives, quoted in Edward Kamau Brathwaite, *The Development of Creole Society in Jamaica, 1770–1820*. Oxford: Clarendon Press, 1978. p. 332.
5. Edith Clarke, *My Mother Who Fathered Me*. London: Allen & Unwin, 1966.
6. Ken Post, *Arise Ye Starvelings*. The Hague: Martinus Nijhoff, 1978. p. 44.
7. Ibid. p. 90.
8. Ibid.
9. *Plain Talk*, 20 February 1937.
10. Howard Johnson, 'The Political Uses of Commissions of Enquiry: The Forster and Moyne Commissions,' in: *Social and Economic Studies*, vol. 27 no. 3, September 1978. pp. 256–283.
11. Report of the West India Royal Commission (WIRC), 1939. p. 220.
12. Ibid. p. 221.
13. Ibid. p. 227.
14. Census of Jamaica, 1943.
15. Report of the WIRC, 1939. p. 221.
16. Ibid.
17. Report of the WIRC: Statement of Action on the Recommendations (WIRC-SA). p. 59.
18. Ibid. p. 22.
19. Report of the WIRC, 1939. pp. 130–131.

20. T.S. Simey, 'Proposals for Extending Social Welfare Work in Jamaica', Jamaica: Government Printer, 1941. p. 2.
21. D. Ibberson, 'Social Welfare Training Course (Fifty),' Report by the Dean and Social Welfare Advisor to the Comptroller for Development and Welfare in the West Indies. Mona, Jamaica, 1947.
22. T.S. Simey, op. cit.
23. Ibid.
24. M.G. Smith in Edith Clarke, op. cit.

7
An Experiment in Popular Theatre and Women's History:
Ida Revolt inna Jonkonnu Stylee

Honor Ford-Smith

Research by members of the Jamaican Sistren Theatre Collective on women's work and organizations between 1900 and 1944, unearthed a vast quantity of information about women in Jamaica. The work showed that the tradition of Caribbean feminism is one of the oldest in the region. The information, which had never before been collected and organized in a systematic manner, helped to open up a whole new area of discussion. But the researchers could not immediately solve the question of how to share these findings with the society or with women's groups.

This chapter looks at one experiment in making history available to our society through popular theatre. The approach requires different skills and resources and has an unusual relationship with both the subject and the audience. The Caribbean Popular Theatre Exchange (CPTE) was a five-week event involving members of Caribbean popular theatre groups in creating and presenting a play based on women's history.

Popular art

Most people all over the world see art as a kind of transcendental other-worldly autonomy. The artist likewise is viewed as a highly sensitive, individualistic being who is alienated from society. She exists in a kind of artificial social space in which she is permitted the luxury of behaviour usually considered socially unacceptable in others, provided this behaviour does not seriously affect the society in any adverse way. Expressing social or economic contentions directly in art is considered 'bad taste' and, in general, political art is dismissed as 'pamphleteering'.

This was not always the case. It is still not the case in many Third World countries and in many peasant communities. In the traditional arts of peasant societies, for example, we can still see how music, visual images and dance are closely linked to the social relations of the community in a functional way. Here there is no separation of pleasure from production or of enjoyment from learning. The arts exist as processes which influence one's daily life. They contrast with art products which can be consumed and offer instead a process which integrates various aspects of life through aesthetic experiences.

The experiment described here is based on a rejection of the view of the creative arts as something cordoned off from society, as something which projects a universal experience while ignoring what is social and specific to women's history in the Caribbean. If there is to be any universality it must come through this specificity.

In Jamaica, there exists a strong tradition of community dance and drama as an expression of social concern and social vision. This tradition has its roots in African retentions and the specific role of the creative arts during slavery. Caribbean society as a former colonial and now neo-colonial entity, has experienced processes of uprooting and violent migration. This has led to an intense degree of cultural penetration by colonial and imperialist powers.

Today, for example, in many islands (take the case of Dominica and the Bahamas) television is tied into United States satellite transmission. Radio programming is almost completely dominated by American music and announcers who imitate American disc jockeys. In Jamaica, this apparently extreme cultural domination has in turn created its opposite—a strong force of cultural resistance. This has established a base in areas where colonial penetration has been unable to fully control the society—both in terms of human experience and geography—in the mountains of the country and in the creative imagination of the people who live there.

Nettleford has argued the creative arts have acted as important reservoirs of resistance in the Caribbean. In particular, he cites dance as a strong force in the fight against slavery:[1]

> As a foremost creative activity serving Jamaican cultural resistance—not only throughout the periods of slavery and colonialism, but also following independence—dance was a primary instrument of survival. First, it is a skill that depends on the physical and mental capacities of the survivor. One's body belongs only to oneself, despite the laws governing chattel slavery in the English-speaking Caribbean, which until 1834 allowed a person to be the 'property' of another. Second, the language by which the body expresses itself does not have to be any one else's language, least of all the master's; even when there are borrowings which are inescapable in a multi-cultural environment, they can be given shape and form, on the borrower's own terms. These strategies are crucial in a situation of pervasive dependency where all influences are dictated by the overlord.

The commitment to define one's identity as different from the dominant capitalist and European-derived culture does not always emerge in an obvious way. Nor is the use of the creative arts as a means by which to do this always constant and consistent. At the present moment, for instance, it appears dormant. During the 1970s however, it demonstrated the extent to which it could inspire and influence the society. The influence and impact of the reggae artist and poet, Bob Marley, was probably greater than that of a pop musician in any other country in the world. How often has a religion been spread internationally almost solely through popular music? And how often, for instance, is a pop-singer given the highest national honours and a State funeral?

Yet, while many have argued for a revaluing and legitimizing of our historical, cultural experience, few, if any, have been clear about the situation of women within cultural resistance and the specific cultural identity of Caribbean women within the movement of the creative arts. The popular tradition of folk songs, stories and other forms of oral literature has been contradictory in regard to women. The experiments we did, sought to address this issue. At the same time, it sought to pick up on earlier efforts to do the same thing. In particular, it attempted

to continue the tradition, exemplified in the work of early na-
tionalist-feminist writers Louise Bennett and Una Marson. Both
these women have struggled in their writing to come to terms
with their experiences as black Jamaican women. Both documented and gave perspective to the concerns, experiences, fears
and courage of women. Both strived to build a dramatic movement which would reflect the voices of the working class. Their
work also gave a literary dimension and legitimacy to the Jamaican language, thus making it possible for working class Jamaican women to speak out and be heard in their own words.

The tradition of women's participation in and leadership of
community drama activities is still strong. Today, the annual
national festival of the performing arts is dominated by women
who make up about 80 per cent of the participants. They are
often organizers and directors of the events. Since the 1960s
this work has been carried out by women on a voluntary basis
and has done much to enrich rural life and to provide basic
training in group work and organization. Work in drama usually brings out women both as participants and audience and
can achieve a high level of mobilization and inspiration.

The experiment discussed here also aimed to create theatre
which integrated entertainment and education and was a conscious search for new ways of communicating and a recognition that newly unearthed historical material about women
could not be structured according to old dramatic formulae.
The experiment, therefore, was a quest for a new dramatic language, even if it meant breaking the barriers of what is considered theatre. In so doing, it drew on specific popular traditions
of the region which are older than bourgeois traditions.

In a sense, this was a recognition of the fact that the form
itself is determined by the viewpoint of a particular class. Form
often determined perspective and even choice of content. Many
of these traditional popular forms are linked to production processes. Some are work songs, some celebrate the harvest or other
moments in the cycle of cultivation. Others are rites of passage—
rituals connected to birth, adolescence or death. Whatever their
specific characteristics, they have each been tied to a special
social purpose. They have been performed for a reason. The
experiment which we discuss here tried to establish theatre
which was equally purposeful.

We aimed to devise structures which, whether they functioned as a process or product, involved participation by the community in the history of Caribbean women and of women in general. In particular, the dramatic process aimed to create structures through which the arts could intervene in daily life.

Within some of the traditional rites, a process of social negotiation takes place. For example, in the Kumina rituals in Jamaica, dance becomes the language of communication with the gods, the ancestors and the community. Through it community problems are aired and sometimes resolved. These processes suggest ways of using elements such as metaphor, dance and character—codes which one finds in ritual and structures for reflection and action—which unify reflection and action. Our work tried to draw on this experience.

Finally, the experiment recognized that the question of audience was fundamental to what was created and the form used to express it. A dramatic piece addresses a specific group of people and has been created for gatherings in specific spaces. Women's experiences need to be communicated to women in the first instance. They also have to be communicated to mixed gatherings of men and women of different classes. The experiment sought to see how drama could be created to affect and act on different audiences with different emphases.

Ida Revolt inna Jonkonnu Stylee:
the Caribbean Popular Theatre Exchange

'There is a woman here among us who was in the 1938 uprising at Frome,' shouts the man dressed as the traditional character, Actor Boy. Around him and several other colourfully dressed actors, is a crowd of 800 who have gathered outside the Petersfield Secondary School, Westmoreland to watch participants from the first CPTE perform *Ida Revolt inna Jonkonnu Stylee*. The crowd waits quietly as Hortense Campbell, a retired sugar worker, makes her way to the platform. Her testimony is one of those which forms the basis for the play the audience has just seen. Now Campbell is about to re-affirm the play's message with her true story. 'Tell us your story,' shouts Actor Boy. In the dim light from one floodlamp, Campbell describes the conditions of the 1930s. 'Just di same as nowadays', says one woman in the audience. 'Tings worser now!' says another.

Campbell describes graphically the participation of women in the uprising—laying to rest the idea that women are docile and subservient and adding her words to the process of bringing out of the shadows the little known story of the activism of women in the 1930s. 'Is people like dem we need today', concludes an old lady as the actors applaud the audience, making the connection between the struggles of the past and the problems of the present.

This final performance, more than all others, fulfilled at least one of the specific objectives of the CPTE—to bring history to life. But the project had many other goals. It wanted to bring together theatre workers from around the Caribbean region and to expose them to a method of collective creation developed by a Cuban group working with the Caribbean masquerade tradition to create street theatre. Also, it aimed to create a piece of street theatre based on material derived from research into women's movements and organizations in Jamaica between 1900 and 1944. Lastly it intended to use the native traditions of Jamaica to structure the piece.

Sistren Theatre Collective initiated the effort, raised funds and collaborated with other groups working with popular theatre in Jamaica to organize the exchange. The Graduate Theatre Company, Jamaican School of Drama, Jamaica School of Dance, all offered space and personnel to the workshop.

Representatives came from six English-speaking Caribbean countries and two Spanish-speaking Caribbean islands (Cuba and Santo Domingo). There were 20 Jamaican participants involved in different aspects of the project and about 12 organizations were represented. Resource people came from a wide variety of disciplines and perspectives. Apart from the usual team of designers, directors, writers and actors, there were choreographers, musicians, a dance researcher in *Jonkonnu*, the history project researchers and translators.

Jonkonnu, a Jamaican masquerade

Jonkonnu was selected as the form through which the play's story would be told. It was chosen partly because of its flexibility and its suitability to the Jamaican streets. It was also chosen

because elements of *Jonkonnu* can be found all over the Caribbean. Symbols and images recur in different rites and festivals
across the region. The organizing committee felt that participants in the workshop would add their experiences of the form
to the Jamaican core, thus giving the piece a regional quality.
They also felt that the form would help to unite the workshop
by drawing upon shared non-verbal Caribbean language.

Jonkonnu emerged in Jamaican society around 1700. British
observers of the time describe a dance performed by a male or
female dancer, wearing a horned headdress. Later this was to
be interpreted by researchers as a symbol of power.

An outline of the masquerade tradition in the Caribbean
compiled for the CPTE concluded there are two main sources:
the African secret society tradition of *Jonkonnu* and the European Roman Catholic tradition of the carnival. During the nineteenth century, the two traditions merged to become the free
Creole style, with music, dance and masks as central to the form.
With its roots in the secret society rituals, *Jonkonnu* still invokes
spirits and aims at social control.

In the middle of the eighteenth century, women's participation apparently became confined to the parade of the Set Girls—
groups of women dressed in the colours of the British regiments
resident on the island. The colours worn by the women and
their position in the parade were related to the colour of their
skin and to their relationships with men in the regiments. Later,
Jonkonnu came to be performed exclusively by men, with female impersonation as an important element.

Over the years, *Jonkonnu* has demonstrated a remarkable
adaptability to historical circumstances. The characters in the
masquerade have changed and are still changing in response
to social changes. For example, after migrations from India at
the end of the nineteenth century, *Jonkonnu* bands from western Jamaica included a character called Babu—an Indian indentured worker. Mother Lundi—or Mother Moon—the fertil-
ity effigy which was common in some areas, is hardly seen any-
more. The core element in the form, however, is the horned mask
and although other aspects of the ritual may change, this remains constant. Patterson and others have suggested that the
root of *Jonkonnu* lies in the adaptation of elements of African
secret society rites, combined with the Yam festival celebration.

The tradition may have been related to Ga, Yoruba and Ibo rites.[2]

During slavery, *Jonkonnu* was performed in the Christmas season when slaves were given a short holiday. On some estates the form was tolerated, on others actively repressed, and in some cases, attempts were made to make it into entertainment for the whites. In certain manifestations of the tradition, therefore, *Jonkonnu* incorporated elements of British mime, and combined these with the earlier African form. At times, the masked bands under the guise of revelry even invaded the Great House (the residence of the governor) at Christmas, mocked the whites and took over the streets.

Jonkonnu in Jamaica has never been quite like the tradition of carnivals in the other islands of the eastern Caribbean. It never had a strong Roman Catholic influence; it was never confined to performance on set days, or involved such large numbers of the population of all classes in the masquerade. In Jamaica, only slaves, and later, members of the working class or peasantry, performed *Jonkonnu*.

While *Jonkonnu* is supposedly comic, it combines this humour with a threatening and rebellious potential. This ambiguity is central to the form: fear and delight intertwine. On the one hand it is a satirical form mocking the elite, on the other it is a religious ritual suggesting survival in the face of adversity. In St. Thomas, for example, performers sometimes sprinkle rum on the graves of ancestors before going out on to the streets.

As a street form, *Jonkonnu* depends to a some extent on the element of surprise. In a sense, it ambushes the audience and takes over their space. It is traditionally accompanied by a bamboo fife and a drum or two. It uses visual elements such as large masks and bright costumes to attract attention. One of its central images is that of journey and procession.

Jonkonnu is in many ways a metaphor for the history of the Caribbean people, but it is history told from the point of view of the men. Just as the form has gradually excluded the participation of women as performers, it has also excluded elements of female experience (such as Mother Moon). But there is nothing inherently anti-feminine about the form. It derives much of its comedy from violations of expectations about authority. It exposes the absurdity of gender behaviour by mocking sexual stereotypes and behaviour which is considered 'sexually appropriate'. For example, the devil frightens the ladies of quality. The whore gal makes sexually suggestive movements aimed at any and everybody. On the level of narrative, traditional sequences offer typically passive images of the 'good' woman. One of them, for instance, is a sequence called 'the capture of the Queen'. In this sequence, the actor dancer costumed as the Queen is captured by Sailor Boy with whom she dances for a while. She is then saved by Warrick (Warrior) and reinstated into the community. This image, typically ambiguous, can be interpreted in many ways. At all levels, the female is portrayed as passive. Part of our project then, was to reinterpret the masquerade so that the form could incorporate the points of view of the women who were now going to use it to tell their story.

The content

Our effort was to break the divide between artistic and scientific ways of working. The content of the play dealt with research findings which had been uncovered using a social science methodology. We now attempted to transform the findings using an artistic methodology.

The methodology of collective creation used required that a scenario be written before the workshop began. As I was writing the piece, I was asked to select from the research material which could form the outline of action for the improvisations. I selected one of the testimonies about the 1938 uprising, which had led to nationalist reform for Jamaica. The testimony chosen was that of a woman who had allegedly participated in the riot. Although the story line, as it was finally presented, included elements from other interviews, the main events were based a single testimony.

While doing the research, I went to Westmoreland—the parish where the uprising had begun—to interview people who had worked on the estate at the time of the uprising. When I arrived, people I spoke to kept talking about someone called 'Hilda Rioter', someone, they insisted, had thrown the first stone and had probably sparked off the riots.

I was taken to find this Hilda. When I met her, she told me what she tells everyone. She had nothing at all to do with the uprising. She was, she said, a decent, hardworking domestic 'with ambition'. She was the office maid for the management staff on the estate. Not only did she have nothing to do with the uprising, but she was in fact sleeping when it took place. 'I have never attended a political meeting in my life,' she said. She told me that there was a supervisor on the estate who wanted to have sexual relationship with her. She was not interested and so she turned him down. He wanted to punish her. After the uprising he was selected by the police to point out people who had been involved in the uprising. He identified her to the police as one of the 'troublemakers'. They arrested her and she was in due course re-named Hilda Rioter.

A popular version of the story describes how hundreds of workers from the parish of Westmoreland stood outside the pay office on the estate, more or less quietly, demanding wage increases. The authorities called out the army and the police who surrounded the workers. One of the policemen was an officious character who was christened by the people 'the Mawga Lion'. Hilda Rioter could not resist flinging a stone at him to tease him. The stone was thrown, the riot act read and the uprising began.

I do not know which of the stories is true. Nobody does. But one thing is clear. Try as hard as she will to convince people of the truth of her version, as far as popular opinion is concerned, Hilda Rioter will forever be the woman who threw the first stone of defiance.

The story was selected for two main reasons. First and most importantly, because it offered two contradictory images of women. On the one hand, the warrior woman unable to tolerate the officious Uncle Toms of the estate system, and on the other hand, the ideal domestic servant looking towards upward mobility in the system and thinking of herself as 'better' than them. The play was to explore where the two images came from and how they were created.

The second reason for choosing the story was that there are parallel stories in some of the other English-speaking islands. Often it is women who are seen as the initiators of uprisings which took place in the region in the 1930s. In St Vincent, a woman named Bertha Mutt organized 15 women armed with sticks to attack the court house in the capital. These women were shortly joined by 200 others. In Trinidad, Ethlyn Roberts is accused of setting fire to Charlie King, a much disliked policeman who attempted to arrest the popular Uriah Buzz Butler during the oil-field workers' strike in 1937. Roberts, like Miss Hilda, denied having been anywhere near the strike.[4] The story seemed a good choice because the image of women as the leaders of uprisings against colonial authority was common to many islands.

I had great difficulty translating the general findings from the language of the research into drama. The first draft of the research findings had been completed in June. The exchange began in August and I was still thinking in terms of concepts such as 'autonomy' and 'domestication'. I found it hard to invest 'autonomy' with character, environment, narrative and action.

In many ways, it would have been easier if the research had been done to create the play and not the play to illustrate the research. The questions asked of the interviewees might have been more specific. As it was, I had tremendous difficulty finding one theme from the research and focusing on the testimony through that theme. In addition it was a challenge to find ways of integrating the storyline with the *Jonkonnu* form. There were no guidelines to follow for any of these processes.

In the end, after a period of improvisation with the actors, the following storyline formed the basis of the play.

Mother Moon comes to present the story of Ida, the woman who threw the first stone in the 1938 uprising. Her story is interrupted by a second band led by Ole Pirate. He enters with his group and takes over the telling of the story. In his version Ida works in the field. She is dissatisfied because she is doing heavy work in the fields which is, according to Ole Pirate, unsuitable for women. With the help of intelligent male leadership, the estate owner is convinced that the solution to her problems is to give her more suitable work (in this case domestic work). She is taken out of the field and put to work in the home and after that everything is all right. Ida is happy.

Mother Moon regains control of the situation and continues with her story. Her version is that the estate owner wants to marry his daughter to a man from overseas. He drains the last drop of work out of the workers (most of whom are men) to create the splendour and display he wants for the wedding. The male workers become more and more exhausted. The women become even more frustrated. They either depend on the men for money or work with them as unofficial work partners on the estate, receiving a portion of the men's pay. Finally, Ida, on behalf of the women, goes to the estate owner and asks for more jobs for women and more money to buy food. He refuses, but offers her a job as a domestic servant. She accepts on the grounds that this will somehow lead to more improvement for the other women too. The situation continues unchanged.

On the day of the wedding, Ida can stand it no more. She interrupts the ceremony and reasserts her demand. She is asked to wait. While she and others wait, the wedding guests are eating their feast. Ida again interrupts to ask for food. The guests laugh at her. She decides to take the wedding cake. The policeman intervenes to stop her and other workers join her. The workers take over the wedding feast and the guests withdraw.

Ole Pirate attempts to interrupt the proceedings to give his perspective again but is unable to. The celebration of Ida's action continues, involving the audience.

The process

Collective creation acknowledges the social nature of theatre. It brings out into the open the methodology of realizing a theatrical concept. Traditionally, such a methodology was considered something mysterious and highly esoteric. The process of collective creation requires that the mystery be removed so that the community becomes central to the development of the work. The onus of responsibility, then, is removed from the individual creator and placed on the group. The process takes account of the ideas of the actors, designers, musicians and all other members of the company. This does not mean that all these elements are unified, but rather that within the realization of the piece various elements of the piece might be unified in contradiction with each other. Collective creation challenges the traditional hierarchy of artistic production, in which all processes become centralized in the director, who in advance resolves the problems of the production which the actor then has to put into action. It further challenges the traditional hierarchical divide between the brain and the hand, developing a method for uniting the two by making the actor a thinker. It challenges the notion that the play is a literary text created to be put on stage. Instead it defines the theatrical text as:

> a system of texts, of codes (visual and sound) which cannot be produced without the mediation of an audience which only exist in relation to that audience... we are talking about a text which we could call 'oral' in the sense that it is more in line with the tradition of the roving musician, troubadour and bards of the fair, than with the literary tradition.[4]

During the CPTE workshop, the process began with the creating of the outline by the writer. At the next stage, a directing team comprising director, designer, choreographer and musical director was created. The director then explained to the participants how the process of improvisation would work. Each day the directing team prepared and presented to the group an analysis of one unit of action from the outline. This analysis consisted of defining the essence of the unit in a core image, the title of which was given to the piece of action. The actions were then analysed in terms of the motivation and the forces in conflict. Characters were analysed in terms of how they contributed to and acted on social forces and not as individuals. Any specific element of the scene which the actors needed to consider was also noted.

For example, the opening unit of Ida was called *The Drum Calls to Action*. The forces in conflict were Mother Moon's band and Ole Pirate's band motivated by a desire to control the space. Specific elements were a procession in celebration of Caribbean identity. The analysis was discussed with actors who afterwards divided themselves into teams. The actors then went away and prepared improvisations based on the story. The idea behind this is that the analogy or metaphor is a device which distances the audience from the action. It helps them to reflect on the theme with greater clarity. It produces, in the audience, a kind of shock of recognition. It enables them to feel that as social beings, they can change or intervene in the history described by the piece. Each day the actors, teams of designers and musicians were given a few hours in separate rehearsal spaces to prepare. There were no formal leaders selected in this process. Each actor made a proposal if he or she had one.

In addition to participation in the process of collective creation, the actors and others participated in workshops on *Jonkonnu* movement and dance, lectures on collective creation and dramaturgy as well as music workshops.

The performances

The actors and musicians bumped around the island in a battered and noisy bus (which finally ran into my car and smashed it up). They visited seven communities, most of which were in rural areas. In each case, the community organizations had been mobilized to expect us and assist us with food and drink. The actors began each performance with a procession through the community to call the audience and to advertise the play. In one town, the troupe in full costume with music made a procession through the market. One woman, on seeing Ole Pirate, jumped up spontaneously and left her stall. She ran to the actor, took a two-dollar bill from her bosom and slapped it into his hand with a big smile of delight on her face. But by far the most successful performances were those in the parts of the country where there is a long history of sugar production. The most memorable was the presentation at the Petersfield Secondary School in Westmoreland, which I have already described, and where the exchange seemed to have achieved its objective and the process come full circle.

Participants' problems

In spite of all the excitement and the energy unleashed in the workshop, it was not an easy time. At the end of it, the participants were exhausted. Conflicts (as opposed to debates) within the directing team were great. This in turn caused problems among the actors and affected the process. Participants identified several problems I will try to summarize, although not necessarily in order of importance.

There were definite regional problems. Participants from the English-speaking islands (other than Jamaica) felt that the story should have included more of the specific experiences of their countries' masquerade traditions. The absence of enough research on this and the Cuban control of the workshop led to the feeling that in comparison to the 'larger islands', that is, Jamaica and Cuba, the Eastern Caribbean islands were viewed as underdeveloped and inferior.

Because of communication problems in the preparatory phase many of the participants had not received the background material on the workshop. Most participants who came knew nothing about what had been planned by the Jamaican team. In fact, some participants said they came expecting to discuss their own experiences and share exercises.

A related issue was that participants came from different levels of academic experience and approaches to theatre. They also came from different political schools of thought. Some could sympathize with the nationalist aims of the projects but not with the feminist. Others were squarely opposed to what they described as 'this woman lib thing'. Some, at the end, confessed to having serious problems with the whole concept of collective creation. Others tended in the opposite direction, believing that there was not enough collectivity, especially in regard to the writing of the piece. This last group felt that the content of the piece should have been determined collectively by the group. Ideologically, conflicts also translated into conflicts over the division of labour, roles and power.

An evaluation

In 1985, the performances had reached about 2,500 people, and the workshop was given wide media coverage. Two years later, reading and seeing follow-up activities of some of the participants in their islands, it is possible to distinguish that the exchange had a great deal of positive impact after all. Several groups are using elements of the methodology in their work. For example, in 1987 in Santo Domingo, *Las Esclavas del Fogon* (The Slaves of the Hearth), a women's cultural organization in La Romana, mounted a similar workshop to popularize research findings on the Dominican Peasant Woman.

In general, there was much to be learnt from the whole experience. The first lesson was that, given the time available and the resources which we had, the exchange attempted far too much in too short a space of time. If emphasis had been placed on teaching the methodology in relation to the historical material and nothing more, that would have been more than enough. To try to incorporate the aim of researching and utilizing the *Jonkonnu* form at the same time, and to embark on a programme of performances all over the island, all in five weeks, was far too much.

Secondly, at the level of planning and organization, it was clear that there needed to be far more groundwork done inter-religiously before the exchange began. More efficient exchange of information among popular theatre workers would have assisted the process greatly.

As far as the participation of the women went, far more basic organizational work needed to be done here and still needs to be done. First, there should have been regional support for the organization of women within the popular theatre groups. In a sense, without having had a chance to identify their personal stake in women's struggles, they had difficulty relating the play to the details of their own lives. Many women came to the workshop from a situation in which there were no women's organizations.

This issue needs to be addressed before another such workshop. Also, the tools of theatre production need to be put into the hands of the women so that they can examine their own personal experiences and say what they need to say about it, before dealing with the historical roots of those experiences. At the same time, popular theatre groups require greater exposure to feminist ideas.

The CPTE participants from outside of Jamaica were largely male. The women who came, with the exception of those from Sistren and the representative of *Las Esclavas del Fogon*, were thrown together in a situation which assumed that they had a commitment to a certain analysis. This, in fact, did not exist. Most of the material and the feminist perspective were unfamiliar. There was no time to come to terms with this. The result was that for the women, their own understanding of women's history was only marginally enriched if at all. For the audiences, at the final presentation too, the element of women's history was not sufficiently clear.

Despite the problems, the experience showed the importance

of linking between women's organizations and women in mixed organizations. It also showed the importance of concretely linking cultural work at an artistic level to political strategy and action at a social level. The popular theatre movement offers a space for women to organize. However, the traditional divide between the arts and politics means that the level of collaboration between the two has not been clearly worked out. If theatre is to work better in the service of the movement in the future, there should be clearer conceptualization of the relationship between the arts and the movement at a strategic level and in terms of the changing context in the Caribbean.

At the level of form, we needed an analysis of the *Jonkonnu* from a woman's perspective in a practical workshop format. Popular forms are not in themselves supportive of women's interests or even of popular interests. They are often expressions of latent social contradictions. To come to terms with these forms requires serious study of the images and symbols they portray from a feminist perspective.

Developing stock figures and personifications of social forces which represent aspects of women's history is a long process which cannot be accomplished in the short period of one workshop. Unfortunately, this kind of work is either way behind or has not yet begun, perhaps because the same economic bias which affects the allocation of national budgets and the valuing of female labour, also affects funding for feminist research into art forms and makes them very low priority.

At the level of content, the methodology failed to provide for the contribution of the actors to narrative and dialogue. In a contradictory way, it left the writer (me) in a very autonomous position. In our experience, actors' proposals on dialogue and plot have been just as important as their proposals at other levels. In fact, in Sistren's work, this has led to a widening of the range of Jamaican language portrayed on stage and therefore we think that the role of the actor needs to be re-examined in the future, in the process of producing text.

The text which was produced was only a preliminary draft. Many elements within it were unclear and too closely based on early improvisations. The conflict between the *Jonkonnu* structure and the original testimony was never fully resolved and the text never took on a dynamic of its own. To work better, the text would have needed more time—time for analysis and time for re-writing. However, the final portion of the text (Mother Moon's story) unified as it is by the image of the wedding, can stand on its own as a short piece with some more work.

The CPTE was a complicated project requiring a large budget, a wide variety of skills and resources. It can be divided into the process (the creation of the piece) and the product (the play). The play *Ida* used an 'ambush technique' to reach people who ordinarily might not be interested in theatre. It reached a wide cross-section and especially working-class people because it was a street form of entertainment. It involved its audience as participants in dance and procession. *Ida* shocked, enchanted, and confronted its audience with a hidden experience in a form which is also often forgotten in the present time. It stirred the collective memory through physical image.

The CPTE process threw up a great number of methodological and theoretical problems, such as the relationship between the theatrical process and the feminist political perspective, the arts and science, traditional cultural expression and women's history, Caribbean cultural similarities and differences. The 1985 workshop was merely the beginning of a long process. To draw clear conclusions from this effort, far more experimentation and analysis are needed at an interdisciplinary level. Perhaps the most important achievement of the project has been the way it has created the possibility of new forms of discourse through the juxtaposition of different disciplines and methodologies.

NOTES

1. Rex Nettleford, *Dance Jamaica*. New York: Grove Press, Inc., 1985. p. 20.
2. Orlando Patterson, *The Sociology of Slavery*. Jamaica: Sangster s Book Store, 1973. pp. 244–245.
3. Rhoda Reddock, 'Women's Labour and Struggle in Twentieth Century Trinidad 1898-1960.' Unpublished Ph.D. thesis for the University of Amsterdam, 1984. p. 443.
4. Enrique, und. Buenaventura, 'Essay on Collective Dramaturgy' (source unknown).

8
Somalia:
Poetry as Resistance against Colonialism and Patriarchy

Dahabo Farah Hassan
Amina H. Adan
Amina Mohamoud Warsame

When speaking of Somali women it is essential to look at them in the context of the general Somali society of which they are an inseparable and integral part. They share with the men all the problems and benefits of this society and all other particulars that make it distinct from all others. But as we shall see, they also suffer specific forms of gender subordination that are unknown to Somali men.

Most African countries had to contend with one colonial power. But in the Congress of Berlin in 1885 Somalia was colonized by and divided between France, Britain, Italy and Abyssinia under the Menelik dynasty. Somali resistance to the colonial forces was organized by various parties and groups, of which the Somali Youth League (SYL) and the Somali National League (SNL) were the most prominent. The present republic of Somalia became independent from colonial rule in 1960, when the former Italian Somaliland joined the Northern region of the country, a British protectorate since 1887.

Historically, Somali women were shaped and moulded by their roots in nomadic life, both in culture and thought. Today their lives are, to some extent, influenced by an Islamic environment, although they are not far removed in their daily existence from the rest of African peoples. The colonial rulers not only introduced new customs, they also codified Islam and made it more inflexible. A paid religious official, the qadi, was installed. Together with the European officials, various changes were introduced in especially the marriage system which increased women's dependence upon their husbands.

Tradition, as transmitted orally from generation to generation, has the force of law among the nomads. The distinctive characteristics of the Somali nomad are strong egalitarianism (that is, along class, but not along gender lines), political acumen and fierce traditional pride. Islam adds depth and coherence to these common elements. The patrilinear kinship system is the basis of the society. The social unit is defined by a husband's property and residence. Access to grazing lands and water depends on the strength of one's clan or family.

The country is semi-arid, its economy is predominantly pastoral, with camels, goats and sheep as the main livestock. There has been continuing migration to the cities. Although urbanization has not yet progressed very far, the traditional fabric of society is being eroded by recent developments. Many men migrate to oil-rich neighbouring countries; yet the remittances they send home, however important for the national economy, are often irregular. When men lose their jobs or stop sending money for other reasons women are left to fend for themselves. There is an increasing number of female-headed households in the country today.

Although men and women had different sets of work to attend to, the nature and environmental conditions of traditional nomadic life did not permit women to be confined only to household chores. They also made and produced all the components of their temporary homes such as ropes, strings, beams, mats, as well as all the containers and utensils of the household. In fact Somali women were required to possess two major qualities: industriousness, and charm and regal bearing. They were also responsible for the upbringing of children and feeding all members of the family, besides caring for small animals such as goats and sheep. When the men were away fighting battles or exploring new pastures, the women took over their chores as well. And added to all these, there were the natural disasters, such as famine and drought.

Somali women, whether nomadic or urban, have never been submissive, either to natural calamities or to social oppression. They expressed their grievances, hopes and philosophy through poetry handed from generation to generation, from grandmother to mother to daughter, 'bearers and transmitters' of the female cultural heritage.

In this chapter we will trace the various forms women used to protest against conditions they felt were unjust, with the focus on the poetry of nomad women. We will also look at the formal women's organizations as they came into existence in the wake of the struggle for independence.

Oral history

The Somali language did not achieve its written form until as late as 1972. Therefore, from the moment we undertook the project on the history of Somali women's resistance, we knew we would not be able to find many written sources to refer to. Even the few pieces written about women were mostly produced by men who wrote about how they viewed women but not what women's real lives were or how they themselves felt. However, in every society that does not have a written script, the past is transmitted to the new generation through oral traditions. By merging our abundant oral sources with the meagre written sources a lot has been discovered of the lives, struggles, movements and organizations of Somali women.

The main thrust of the research was to piece together whatever fragmented knowledge existed about women and document everything before it was too late. We also focused on women's responses to the specific kinds of oppression they faced in their nomadic life. The effect of later urbanization was also looked into.

Analysis of the findings led to many important revelations, including the fact that Somali feminism was no borrowed western ideology. It was indigenous to Somalia. We discovered that whereas the early feminists in the west expressed their dissatisfaction with gender oppression through writing books or journals, the early Somali nomad feminists expressed their protests with the means at their disposal—poetry, work songs, children's lullabies—and tried to change things by addressing both men and women. Sometimes, because of their strong faith in God, they addressed Him to do something about the oppression they were experiencing. While those in the west formed clubs, their nomad counterparts formed informal networks, kinship groups, work groups or religious associations to strengthen themselves and fight oppression.

As we wanted to represent both regions of the country, we chose areas from both the northern part or the former British colony and the southern or former Italian colony. We selected women from the coastal towns that were open to outside influences such as Mogadisho, the capital, and Berbera.

As mentioned earlier, the Somali script, a modified Roman script, was officially created in 1972. Before 1960, the administrative language was Italian in the south and English in the north. From 1960 to 1972, English became the administrative language of both regions of the Somali Republic. But whether Italian or English, only the few government employees could speak or write it and they formed a miniscule percentage of the population. The records of the vast majority of the Somalis depended on their memory—maintaining their history by passing information from one generation to another orally.

Poetry is important in Somali life. As Said put it: 'The Somalis are often described as a "nation of bards" whose poetic heritage is a living force intimately connected with the vicissitudes of everyday life.'[1] Yet you will never hear of a great woman poet in Somali history, while there have been many celebrated male poets, whose poems have been documented and memorized by a large number of people.

This, of course, does not mean there were no women poets; but the reality is that nobody, neither the foreigners who ruled the country nor the Somalis themselves, bothered to view women's literature and the themes they talked about as important enough to be recorded. Even the women themselves did not see their importance because they had internalized the idea that their culture was of less significance than men's. Whenever we tried to document the poems of specific women who were said to be talented, we mostly ended up with two lines or so of a whole poem. In the same way women's private lives escaped the few written records.

In her article 'Women and Words', Amina H. Adan wrote:[2]

The activities of Somali women have been neglected by most foreign writers and travellers. Richard Burton commented on Somali poetry, but being a male chauvinist from Victorian England, he absolutely overlooked women's literature, even though he had a keen eye for every passing beauty!

Even Margaret Lawrence, a woman herself, overlooked her sisters' talents and like her fellow countrymen paid tribute to male poets only.

Where women's lives have been ignored throughout the ages, oral history is a most suitable methodology to document women's experiences. Furthermore, when the interviewer is a woman who can socially and culturally relate herself with those she is interviewing, she can skilfully bring to light aspects of their lives that have been left unrecorded.

Through the process of interviewing, women become aware of the importance of their lives. One woman activist who took part in the liberation struggle put it this way: 'At last somebody remembered to ask us what we did in those years.'

Oral history can fill many gaps in mainstream Somalian history. A case in point is the accepted notion of the part that Somali women played in the struggle for independence. In history books one mostly comes across Somali women donating their jewellery for the liberation struggle, and a rare case or two of a woman killed while taking part in a demonstration. Until we talked about actual experiences of the women who lived through the independence movement, we had no idea of certain facts about women's contribution to the movement.

For example, we learnt how Somali women struggled to have their rights recognized within the broader movement; how they used the occasion to take part in public activities and break away from their seclusion. They fought to become party members, to have equal rights with men as citizens, and they fought with their husbands to break away from seclusion. Many of those experiences were related to us in poetry composed by the women themselves.

We found group interviewing to be the best method of documenting, raising the consciousness of women and reviving women's history while at the same time stimulating their struggle. This was because of two factors.

First, the Somali society is egalitarian, with few class distinctions and people mix together freely. Within one Somali family you may come across a senior academic and an illiterate, a successful businessman or woman and a small stall owner, a nomad and a city dweller, an ambassador or a highly placed government official and a non-governmental employee. It is common to find women from diverse economic backgrounds the best of friends, sharing experiences without feeling self-conscious about their differences.

Second, the nature of the information we sought, did not pose any threat to anybody. For example, one of the topics we found most suited to group interviews was the traditional network or solidarity groups women had. We would ask one of the women present to tell us about a specific traditional solidarity group she had heard about or was part of. When that woman finished, another would talk about a different group or the same group from a different point of view.

Somali women have their own poetic form, the *buraanbur*, through which they express their joys and sorrows. Their songs are a spontaneous response to their lives and realities. As part of the process, we not only recorded songs with the interviews, but also took photographs as we went along. Photographing nomadic people can be difficult, especially since some of them believe that making a paper image of a human being is attempting to imitate God's powers. One old woman told us bluntly that she has been photographed once already, and that was when God created her in her mother's womb.

Other constraints were the lack of transportation and the fuel shortage. We also encountered women who were not willing to talk. These were women who had internalized the idea of their work and life as less important than men's, and thought some of the things we asked too trivial to talk about.

We remember one day we were having an informal discussion with an old woman and we asked her to recite to us some of the women's poems she could remember. She laughed uproariously and asked some other women present to come and hear what we wanted. She then asked us why did we not go and ask the men to tell us their poems. 'Men's poems have more important themes; women's poems are only on simple common things,' she said.

The Somali women's movement

The women's movement in Somalia came into being in the form of organizations linked to the struggle for independence. But, even before it emerged there was a feminist consciousness well under way in the traditional nomadic life of ordinary women, where they had their own means of protesting and conscientizing other women through songs and poems. It is safe to say that this consciousness was carried over to their urban life and their later participation in the struggle for independence.

During the 1940s, Somali masses actively organized themselves against foreign domination. Somali women participated in large numbers in this struggle. From the oral accounts of women such as Halimo Yusuf Godane, Kaha Ahmed and the gifted poetess Hawo Jibril, it appears that women from all ranks of life joined the struggle, although it is difficult to ascertain how far the rural women were involved.[3]

Later, within this broad struggle, they began to feel increasingly conscious of their subordinate position in the society and at home. As a result, they began a struggle against their oppression as women within their own political environments. After some time women felt the need to form their own separate organizations and in 1959 the first women's organization, the Somali Women's Association (SWA), was set up. The leadership was composed of wives of the leaders of the political parties and although SWA voiced women's rights, most of its activities were in the area of social welfare.

In 1960, Somalia attained independence. The new leaders did little to improve the condition of women in the country. A period of disillusionment followed, in which tribalism, nepotism, corruption, inefficiency and mismanagement were rampant. Women's aspirations, such as equal access to education and employment, and political participation, were not fulfilled. Many oppressive traditional customs were retained. As before, Somali women expressed their grievances in poems, such as this one by Hawo Jibril:

> Sisters you sold your jewellery
> Depriving yourselves,
> Enriching the struggle.
>
> Sisters, you stayed as one,
> United, even when your brothers
> Divided and deceived our nation.

> Sisters, you joined the fight—
> Remember the beautiful one,
> Hawa—stabbed through the heart.
>
> But, sisters, we were forgotten!
> We did not taste the fruits of success
> Even the lowest positions
> Were not offered
> And our degrees were cast aside as dirt.
>
> Sisters, was this what we struggled for?

Out of those grievances in 1967, the Somali Women's Movement (SWM) was born. The SWM was founded by educated middle-class women and one of its major aims was to fight for the social, political, cultural and economic rights of Somali women. It was the most radical women's organization that Somalia was to know, but it was short-lived.

In 1969, when the new revolutionary government came into power and General Mohammad Siad Barre became president, all political parties and social organizations were banned and what we could call the first phase of the women's movement was over. On the first anniversary of the new regime, Barre announced that henceforth the country would be guided by the principles of scientific socialism. Thus, as in some other African countries, socialism came into the country 'from above'.[4] To the majority of the population, Islam rather than scientific socialism remained the guiding principle in their lives.

For women, however, socialism was an instrument in their struggle for equal rights. In that same year, in 1970, a women's section was founded under the Political Office in the Presidency of the Supreme Revolutionary Council (SRC). Most of the members of this section were recruited from the banned SWM. This women's section established a committee in each village, district and region of the republic. Among its other tasks were mobilizing women and raising their political consciousness and cultural level, training cadres and expanding leadership in women's groups and the community, and establishing priorities in the process of change. Also, they set achievable goals for each women's group, raising their image of themselves and their image before society and inspiring, motivating and stimulating them to action.[5]

When the new revolutionary government called for equality, women were the first to respond. They actively participated in all the national goals for action.

It was not surprising, therefore, that in 1977, the important role played by Somali women was acknowledged by the government and the Somali Women's Democratic Organization (SWDO) was founded. At the moment SWDO is the only national women's organization.[6] If we reflect on the activities of SWDO and its contribution to the present women's movement, we find that a lot has been done within its present scope under the wing of the ruling party. Under the banner of equality and social justice, SWDO has indeed a lot of room to manoeuvre. In many cases SWDO, as the sole agent for voicing women's rights, promotes women's issues and inspires their awareness.

SWDO makes use of the government machinery in matters that the State advocates and which are also in the interest of women. The organization has became a vehicle of women's equality and a voice of justice. Ordinary women come to the organization and ask the leaders of the organization to intervene on their behalf where the court or an employer has proven unfair. Also, in all the government ministries, SWDO has a representation whose sole responsibility is to safeguard and watch women's rights and see that no discrimination is practised.

SWDO's aim of fighting against genital mutilation also coincides with government objectives. Somalia has of old known the most severe form of genital mutilation, the pharaonic circumcision, whereby female genitals are excised and infibulated. SWDO tries to break the taboos and secrecy surrounding this issue by using education programmes on radio and film, organizing seminars and involving religious leaders and medical personnel. The campaign is nationwide and is supported both by the ministries of health and education and by local voluntary groups.

These are a few major examples of how a women's organization can benefit from issues which coincide with the aims of a socialist government advocating social equality and which can be taken up without fearing conflicts with the State.

But, what about the other side of the coin? When women

want to struggle on their own lines and on issues they consider to be their priority as women, then the need to be autonomous is felt more and more. An example is the issue of polygamy which Somali women unanimously think of as a degradation. A majority of Somali women would like to see the institution abolished.[7] It is a grievance frequently mentioned in women's poetry. Yet, SWDO is not able to take it up. In the Family Law, the issue is tackled in a vague and ambiguous manner. In cases where this law would provide some protection for women, SWDO is not able to defend them: if for example high level Somali men take secondary wives without the consent of their first wives. Also, fundamentalist pressure to allow polygamy is rising. At present, with the civil war, it is uncertain whether SWDO will ever be able to campaign effectively for the abolition of polygamy.

Somali women's poetry

Poetry is the country's most popular form of expression. Generally speaking, in Somali society poets are the traditional spokesmen of their groups and have a powerful voice in inter-clan politics. In the old days poetry had the power to start wars and forge peace.[8]

Poetry in Somalia is generally classified into eight categories and the *buraanbur* is the highest of women's literary genre. Other female minor literary forms are the *hobeeyo* (lullaby) and the *hoyal* or work songs. *Gabay*, the highest of all poetic forms, is considered male territory and women are discouraged to participate in its composition. A Somali saying goes: three qualities that are considered a virtue for men, are considered vice for women: bravery, generosity and eloquence. The explanation is that if a woman is courageous she would be likely to fight her husband, if she is generous she might give away her husband's property which is entrusted to her and if she is eloquent she will defy him, this diminishing his prestige among his clan.

So women developed their own poetic forms of expression which belongs to them only: *buraanbur* and its sub-categories of which the *hoobeeyo*, the *hoyal* and the *sitaat* (religious song) are the main ones. The following songs are an indication of how women reflect on their lives through this literature. The importance of the work songs is not only that they break the monotony of the work; usually they convey messages in which people express their daily problems, desires and aspirations, grievances and protests against any form of oppression and subjugation:

> Once the colour of a date had I
> I was destined for a wicked one,
> Of each other nothing knowing.
> We went far in deepening our relations,
> Like the woolly-humped camels by a lion killed
> Before noon my cry was heard.
> Weep with me fellow women
> If to our alliance you belong.

Women always feel the necessity of aligning with other women folk since they are all subject to the intimidation and whims of their male counterparts.

The poem below is an illustration of a mother alerting and preparing her young daughter about the heavy load of work and hardships of life awaiting her as she grows into womanhood. The mother is graphically demonstrating the various tasks the young daughter is expected to perform simultaneously without help, mercy, or gratitude.

> After a journey so long
> and tiring indeed,
> Like a fully loaded camel,
> tired as you are under the load,
> You at last set a camp,
> beside a hamlet with no blood ties to you,
> Your livestock will need,
> to be always kept in sight,
> Your beast of burden will need
> to be tied to their tethers.
> The newly born baby sheep
> have to be taken out to graze.
> The house will always need
> to be tidy and in shape.

Your children will always need
your comforting care and love.
Your husband will call for
your service in different ways.
And may at times scold you
for services poorly done.
And may at times beat you
for no apparent reason.
So stop whimpering
and perform as best you possibly can
The responsibilities and the duties
set out for you to do.

The birth of a boy is an occasion for festivities and happiness. However, the birth of a girl causes unhappiness and grief to the mother. In the following song the mother expresses her historically denigrated role.

Why were you born?
Why did you arrive at dusk?
In your place a boy
would have been welcome.
Sweet dates would have
been my reward.
The clan would be
rejoicing,
A lamb would have been
slaughtered
For the occasion,
And I would have
been glorified!

This song is a *hoobeeyo*. Women improvise new lullabies according to the situation. Like all songs, these verses were not composed only to entertain a child: there is another level of meaning. The mother or the singer is always addressing someone else as well. On some occasions this could be a husband, on others a mother-in-law, a co-wife or men in general. Thus a lullaby could also be a complaint about a heavy-handed husband or a bad drought.

Here is another example:

> Oh my daughter, men have wronged us
> For in a dwelling where women are not present
> No camels are milked
> Nor saddled horses mounted.

The child and her mother are equally victims here. The mother feels and illustrates their unity in being women together. She is not only addressing her child, but also fellow women who have suffered the same indignities as she has.

In Somali society horses and camels are bride prices paid to a woman's family by her suitor. Thus the mother is asserting herself and declaring autonomy because prestigious family property comes through the female members.

There are also religious and healing songs, almost all of them with a double meaning. Even though they are primarily for religious purposes, equally important is the underlying voice of protest. Even the short, metered work song, *salsal* (the song of loading and unloading camels), becomes a platform for women's protest:

> For the polygamous man, lovely camel
> Worrying and nagging are his companion.

The *hoobeeyo*, which has represented for the Somali women their own history, gives us a glimpse of the nation's history as well for the last two hundred years:

> It is your trouble
> The inconveniences of the dowry
> Ceremonies and your constant whimpering cries
> And your 'the husband has beaten me'
>   complaints.
> Have I given birth to you to discomfort me?
> If only I didn't I might have saved myself
>   these troubles.

This is a mother's lament describing the state of all women. When a young girl marries, she is entitled to many gifts from her parents—the dowry which can drain their finances. Of course the bride price balances the scales. The dowry and bride price are important political features in a nomadic economy where a marriage is often a political alliance between different clans.

Another theme embodied in the song is that of the battered wife. Historically the court that protected women was a strong family. Where there was no family there was always the clan or the chieftains.

Men's literature about women

Even though women hold a prominent role in nomadic pastoral society, the oral traditions and legends give of them a distorted image. The legend of Queen Araweelo is a case in point. Araweelo was a fearsome ruler, who was supposed to have castrated males in her attempt to keep them from dethroning her.

The legend not only bears witness to the fact that women actually ruled the land sometime in the past, but it also illustrates the way men have traditionally looked upon powerful women.

The picture that Somali male poets give of women is not very different from that in the west. Women are expected to be passive and obedient. A woman who would stand up to a man is seen as uncontrollable and a deviant:

> Better an obedient woman
> Than one who is intemperate
> or intelligent from a better family.

There is a Somali proverb which goes: the breast that contains milk cannot contain intelligence. This crude statement demonstrates the measure of disrespect offered to women. The following poem leaves the reader in no doubt:

> My death will bring ruin upon the family;
> Your death, camel, will bring
> Empty vessels and starvation;
> But a woman's death brings
> Fresh groomings and remarriage.

Nomad men hold camels in high esteem. They use them in marriage for the bride price and their finest poetry is very often about their camels.

Women's poetry on independence

> I warn you, Somalis
> Disarm yourselves
> Leave each other in peace!
> Your women mourn every spring, while the
> vultures feast
> On their flesh
> I warn you, Somalis
> Leave each other in peace!

This poem is by Kadija Muse Mattan, one of the pioneers who supported the political parties morally, politically and materially. Her support was most vivid in her verses. She loathed tribalism, factionalism and described the fragmentation which was a consequence of tribal wars and their aftermath of orphans and widows in white mourning clothes.

Raha Ayanle was another woman poet who supported the struggle for independence with her witty verses. Somali literature is full compositions by women poets using their medium as a weapon to combat colonialism.

A verse by an unknown woman poet addresses Abdullaahi Essa Mohamoud, a prominent leader of the struggle for national freedom and former Prime Minister of the first independent Somali government. The verse was composed on the eve of Mohamoud's departure to participate in the UN General Assembly, with the aim of voicing the cause of the Somali nation:

> Since you are leaving oh Abdullaahi
> Permit me to recommend you that,
> If we are not slain by bomb or
> Other lethal weapons,
> Our fighting will never stop
> till the final victory!

One might well ask how did Somali women of the 1940s,

without education or specific formal organization of their own, come to participate in the struggle for independence with such vigour and determination? Especially since in the cultural and religious context, women's involvement in political decision making was extremely limited, if it existed at all. The answer, paradoxically, is to be found within the very culture, which while appearing to an outsider to be extremely limiting, did contain the necessary elements that allowed future political development for women.

Women saw in the struggle for independence not only a chance to achieve general improvement in Somalia's socio-economic situation, but more specifically, an opportunity to bring about a dramatic change in their own situation. Women were oppressed by the tribal nature of society, since tribalism is an institution which consolidates men's dominant role, based as it is on male pride and aggression. In there effort to join the national struggle, they drew on a weapon they had been using for ages, their poetry.

We conclude with two poems. The first one is by Hawo Jibril:

> We wanted to break away from our seclusion.
> We wanted to have the responsibility
> to express our feelings and our views.
> We wanted to show our concern for our country.

The last one is by Dahabo Elina Muse. It depicts more generally the conditions under which Somali women live, and against which Somali feminists rebel:

> Pharaoh, who was cursed by God
> Who did not listen to the preaching of Moses
> Who had strayed from the good word of Torah
> Hell was his reward!
> Drowning was his fate!
> The style of their circumcision—butchering,
> Bleeding, veins dripping with blood!
> Cutting, sewing and tailoring the flesh!
> This loathsome act never cited by the Prophet
> Nor acknowledged by the Hadith!
> Non-existent in Hureera...

No Muslim ever practised it!
Past or present the Koran never preached it.
When the spouse decides to break the good tie,
When he concludes divorce and desertion,
I retire with my wounds.
And if I may speak of my wedding night—
Awaiting me with caresses, sweet
Kisses, hugs and love.
No, never!
Awaiting me was pain, suffering and sadness.
In my wedding bed I lay groaning, grovelling
like a wounded animal.
Victim was I of feminine pain.
At dawn awaits me ridicule. My mother announces
Yes, she is a virgin.
When fear gets hold of me
When anger seizes my body
When hatred becomes my companion
I get feminine advice,
Because it is only feminine pain,
And I was told feminine pain perishes
Like all feminine things!
The journey continues or the struggle continues
As modern historians say!
As the good tie of marriage matures
As I submit and sorrows subside
My belly becomes like a balloon
A glimpse of happiness shows
A hope, a new baby, a new life!
Ah a new life endangers my life
A baby's birth is death and destruction for me!
It is what my grandmother called the three
feminine sorrows and if I may recall or record
Grandmother said the day of circumcision
The wedding night and the birth
Of a baby are the triple feminine sorrows,
As the birth bursts and I cry for help
The battered flesh tears.
No mercy, push they say!
It is only feminine pain!

And now, appeal!
Appeal for love lost,
Appeal for dreams broken
Appeal for the right to live as a whole
Appeal to Aidos.
And all peace loving people
Protect, support give a hand
To innocent little girls, who do no harm,
Obedient to their parents, elders
And all they know is only smiles.
Initiate them to the world of love
Not to the world of feminine sorrow![9]

NOTES

1. S. Samatar Said, *Oral Poetry and Somali Nationalism, the case of Sayyid Mahammad Abdilla Hasan*. Cambridge: Cambridge University Press, 1982.
2. Amina H. Adan, 'Women and Words', in: *Ufahamu Journal*, vol. 10, no. 3, University of California, 1981. p. 140.
3. Raquia H. Dualeh, Fadumaa Ahmed Alim, Dahabo Farah Hasan, Amina Warsamoud Warsame, Maryan Farah Warsame and Amina H. Adan, 'Women's Movements, Organizations and Strategies in a Historical Perspective: Somalia Case Study,' research report. The Hague: ISS, 1987. p. 30.
4. B. Munslow, *Africa: Problems in the Transition to Socialism*. London: Zed Press, 1986.
5. Raquia H. Dualeh, et al, op. cit. p. 37.
6. This chapter was written when the civil war which was to completely destroy Somalia had not yet reached Mogadisho or other vital parts of the country. By 1992, one of the authors of this article was in refuge in Sweden. The whereabouts of the other authors and members of the team are still unknown. Mogadisho, the university, the documentation and research centre started by this project are in ruins. –Editor's note.
7. Saida Awad Musse, 'State Ideology and Women's Emancipation, Conditions and Limitations: the case of Somalia.' Unpublished MA thesis. The Hague: ISS, 1988.
8. M.J. Cawl Faarax, *Ignorance is the Enemy of Love*. London: Zed Press, 1982. See also S. Samatar Said, op. cit.
9. Translated by Amina H. Adan.

9
The State and the Sudanese Women's Union, 1971–1983: A Case Study

Tomadur Ahmed Khalid

This chapter is an examination of the relationship between the State and women's organizations in Sudan. It is limited in its scope to the second period of the May Revolution (1971–1985).[1] After the failed Communist coup in 1971, all political parties were banned except the State's own Sudanese Socialist Union (SSU). The Sudanese Communist Party (SCP) and the Women's Union (WU) which was affiliated to that party, went underground. Some elements of WU joined the newly established government organization known as the Sudan Women's Union (SWU). This organization was a branch of SSU, which became the ruling party.

Not surprisingly, this period in the history of the Sudanese women's movement witnessed many fundamental changes in political, social, and economic relations which more or less reflected State ideology.

Nimeiry's 1969 May Revolution had seen radical changes in Sudanese political system. It ended a democratically elected but unstable parliamentary system, replacing it with a one-party State. In the beginning, the revolution strongly believed that a radical transformation in the government system would act as a preface to the easy application of its new policies and programmes. These programmes of action were supported by the Communists and other broad left elements who believed in the necessity of change in Sudanese society.

The government of Sudan, following a socialist path, wanted to redirect its economy through major reforms, to follow an anti-colonial foreign policy, and to set up SSU to encourage popular participation. It also wanted to 'settle' the southern problem through a scheme of regionalization.[2]

Because of ideological disagreements between SCP and the government, SCP was dissolved in 1971 after an attempted coup, although it continued to function underground. The State took a rightist turn and abandoned its former plan of action which had attracted so much popular support. The economy assumed a capitalist colour, leading to major changes in the class structure of Sudanese society.

At this juncture new political players appeared and established themselves by supporting government policies. The Muslim Brothers came to play an important role in the struggle for power, especially after 1983. They were the only political group who consistently supported the State, therefore they were given the right of political expression within SSU.

Given the fact that Sudan had become in effect a one-party nation, Islam proved to be particularly attractive for Sudanese women. The Muslim Brothers appeared to have the ability to financially support the people and presented themselves as the only alternative means of political expression.

The change from a socialist government to a rightist one after 1971, and to an Islamic State after 1983, had far-reaching consequences for the women's movement. After WU was banned, SWU became the only representative of Sudanese women. The power relations within the leadership were viewed in terms of 'independent' elements representing SSU versus the 'Muslim Sisters' who supported the Muslim Brotherhood. In reality, SWU was prevented from taking an independent political stand or from criticizing the government about policies and laws that affected women.

The Sudan Women's Union (SWU)

Membership of SWU was virtually compulsory, as every Sudanese woma was automatically a member of the local division in the area where she lived. It served as the only political, social and cultural organization for women, and all its activities were addressed through specialized offices of the government.

Its aims were formulated in the following way:
- To raise the standard of Sudanese women socially, economically and politically in order for them to participate in the process of development.

- To use women as the defending force for the people's gains by executing the revolutionary policies.
- To support women's issues and seek to fulfil social justice and achieve peace in the world.
- To create and enforce links between Sudanese women and women of the world.

The aims were a reflection of the revolutionary slogans raised earlier on by the government. To achieve these aims, SWU was to adopt certain measures which were at least initially based on mass support. The measures were:

- to show concern for family, childhood and motherhood through comprehensive social care;
- to preserve Sudanese heritage and values through good spiritual upbringing and education;
- to fight against all harmful traditions and customs;
- to develop and raise the standard of rural women by encouraging them to participate in national action;
- to fight illiteracy; and
- to concern itself with issues of work and female workers.

Since SWU worked and functioned as a branch of SSU, any formulation of objectives, or any action to be taken, could not be allowed to deviate from the general framework of SSU. In addition to this, SWU was structured according to the hierarchical set up of SSU. The SWU executive powers were vested in an Executive Bureau, composed of 21 members, supported by a Central Committee with 75 members.

Membership of the organization was officially open to all Sudanese women above 16 years of age, regardless of educational background. Membership was encouraged by the granting of incentives to those who were given recognition as 'protectors' of the Revolution. According to estimates by the Secretary General in January 1984, membership had reached a total of 750,000 throughout Sudan. However, the numbers do not differentiate between active and inactive memberships.

Financially SWU was dependent on SSU, the mother organization, in addition to assistance from international organizations such as UNICEF. The leadership was nominated out of SSU supporters. In the process, all opposition was silenced and many progressive women preferred to stay away rather than join the organization.

However, SWU did not represent a single political stand. The Muslim Brothers, who had always supported the government, in an attempt to increase their influence within SWU, pressurized the political leadership to nominate a Muslim Sister as a leader. This constituted a real threat for the women of SWU.

The Sudanese women's movement is a good example of how the ideology of political parties and the State can influence women's organizations. The ideological stand of SWU moved from the left to the right, and in the last stages of the May Revolution it was actually dominated by the Islamic group. At this point SWU was portrayed as the defender of the revolution against all enemies, especially the Communists.

At one of the women's conferences during these years of turmoil, the Sudanese president stressed that working women should wear modest clothes, that is, clothes that thoroughly covered their bodies, and SWU publicly approved the statement. Obviously, Sudanese women were no longer free to run their own lives. They were now subject to the opinions and demands of the Muslim Brothers. Women who did not dress in the approved way, did not have a wide choice of jobs. The operative word was *muhtashim,* with its emphasis on motherhood and being a good housewife. The Women's College, which was established as a faculty of the University of Omdurman, demanded absolute obedience to the Muslim dress code.

The programmes the Muslim Brothers tried to impose were based on fundamentalist Islamic interpretations of women's position in society. They succeeded to some extent in attracting girls in secondary schools and universities to the Muslim Brothers' cause, especially in the absence of an alternative to SWU.

SSU and SWU

SSU was created to be a popular organization in the sense that other social forces were expected to work from within that body. Thus the task of organizing and representing any social group was given to SSU as its main task. In theory, SSU directly controlled SWU through the 'democratic representation' of women at different levels of SSU, in villages, towns, cities and regions.

The expected task of a representative was to provide a clear description of women's demands, to suggest solutions to the policy-making body at the national level, and in turn gather the membership's opinions about these solutions. In most cases this did not occur. Right from the grassroots level, SSU had the upper hand in choosing candidates for the election. Any one with a political stand other than SSU's would not be allowed to challenge an SSU member. This effectively meant that all women would serve SSU interests first and women's issues would take a second place. Women who were labelled 'radical' or 'progressive', representing a political position different from that of SSU, did not even have the opportunity to stand for election, since SSU candidates had full political and economic support, not to mention the blessing of President Nimeiry.

Another problem was that women voting for the nominated candidates were mostly illiterate. Among them were many housewives and women who worked in small factories or in the agricultural sector. Others were teachers or nurses, professions that were considered low in status. The majority of these groups had no clear political views. They sometimes voted for women whose names they did not even know, rather than voting for a woman who might genuinely represent them.

Even though the system appeared to be democratic, its sole purpose was to legitimize the powers of SSU. The fact that SWU was represented at every level of SSU, from the grassroots Basic Unit to the Central Committee at the national level, clearly demonstrated the influence of SSU on the organization. When 25 per cent of the seats on the local government councils were kept aside for women, they were still controlled by SSU. In any case, there were never enough women for the full quota.

The top posts for women in the political pyramid of SSU were under the direct control of the SSU president, who was also head of State. For example, of the 20 seats on the Political Bureau, one was reserved for an SWU member. This post was not, however, open to *any* SWU member, but only to those who were highly committed to support the May Revolution. During the life of SSU, only two women held the post, which meant that the job kept rotating between the two. At the same time, one of them monopolized the presidency of SWU for eight years.

The system of choosing the general secretary of SWU ensured that women at the top basically remained unchallenged. A 1979 issue of *Sudanow* reported:

A single central committee member put forward a nomination, another member seconded it and the successful candidate was announced to the assembled delegates who responded with deafening applause. The nomination was then approved by President Nimeiry and thus Dr. Fatma Abdel Mahmoud, who is also head of the SSU Women's Committee, began her second three-year term of office.

The situation clearly did not allow members to participate effectively in SWU matters, since contact between them and the leadership was not possible. The latter were afraid of losing their highly important posts. Therefore, the membership, which appeared to be impressive in numbers, counted for no more than a signature for many of the activities. A 1978 issue of *Sudanow* described their predicament thus:

They just participate with ink, and no paper, which is absolutely unacceptable', complained the national assistant secretary Ms. Nafisa Kamil, who extended her criticism to mention that some of the 30 Central Committee members 'don't even attend meetings, let alone do any work.

There are various reasons for this lack of enthusiasm. First, political commitment to the goals of the May Revolution was a condition of joining SWU, and every member had to commit herself in writing. In a *Sudanow* interview the same year, one of the SWU leaders explained: 'When the Union was first formed, some women were afraid to do that [make a political commitment] particularly in the West of Sudan where other ideologies dominate. In a part of Khartoum, for instance, we used to need police protection when we were going around informing people about the Union.'

Many women felt that housework deserved more attention than joining SWU, as work with the Union meant only sessions and meetings that took up a lot of time, but in which they were not even allowed to actively participate.

There were other practical problems, particularly that of transportation during the rainy season. Many headquarters and villages were isolated, leading to a lack of communication and information between the centre and regions.

Finally, therefore, SWU could not become a truly representative body for the bulk of Sudanese women. Instead, it became a leadership without a base, with leaders who belonged to a privileged class. However, only a few women actually reached the top of the political pyramid, such as the former Minister of Social Affairs, Dr Fatma Abdul Mahmoud, and the 12 women who were representatives in the People's Assembly, among them the prominent figure of Nafissa Ahmed El Amin, who held the SWU leadership on a virtually permanent basis.

As to how this affected the perceptions of SWU, in a *Sudanow* interview in 1979, one of the 'leaders' argued: 'As discrimination has gradually disappeared from the statute book, so the Union has ceased to be a political pressure group and has concerned itself with activities and services for women such as literacy classes and community services.' The interesting thing about the statement is that the so-called 'leader' believed there is no discrimination against women outside the statute book.

Having seats reserved for women on the local councils did not have much effect. SWU was unable to provide the right women for such posts, in addition the ideological factor of 'protecting Sudanese values' did not permit many women to participate in the public arena. Conservatives, as well as the Muslim Brothers, saw such women as a challenge to male authority and men's sphere of influence.

A study conducted in Omdurman in 1978 reported complaints of women councillors that their male counterparts were using certain tactics to keep them out of council affairs and politics. Women councillors who wanted to vote on certain issues were always urged to vote on the basis of family, ethnicity or the political allegiances of male relatives.[3]

There were several reasons for this. Firstl, there was an implicit assumption on the part of men that only disreputable women entered the political arena, an attitude that discouraged many conservative women from taking part in politics and adversely affected the social standing of those who did. Also, the local government's general reputation of being corrupt proved a disincentive for many, especially the women.

On the other hand, some women were not even fully aware of the opportunities offered by the system, and underestimated their influence on the decision-making process. Thus, issues such as the placing of water pumps or health facilities—of vital concern to women—were decided in terms of men's needs and all the women could do was complain among themselves.

Obviously, if there had been systematic coordination and consciousness among the SWU membership, women in such cases would have been able to raise their voices and be heard.

SWU support for the government was rationalized by pointing to the many gains achieved during Nimeiry's government. However, most of those gains were a result of the struggle of the women's movement since independence, some of which could be enumerated as follows:

- According to the Public Service Ordinance of 1973, Sudanese women became entitled to full measure of equality with men regarding wages, pensionable services, inheritable pension and all back-service benefits.
- Working women were entitled to a four-year leave without pay when accompanying their husbands abroad or on a national mission.
- Maternity leave with full pay extending to two months was accorded to all working women.
- Working women were entitled to one hour per day for baby care.[4]

What were the factors that inhibited the implementation of these rights earlier? The previous parliamentary party system did not deal with women's issues separately at all. Thus nothing was done, although the women fought hard for their rights, especially since before 1969 the women activists were highly committed Communists. The nature of the post-1971 women's organization, on the other hand, with its lack of commitment, control by the State and the opportunistic slant of some of the leadership did not create an environment conducive to implementing rights that would benefit all women.

When Nimeiry's government came to power in 1969, the women's organization was a major constituent in the process of mobilizing and gaining the support of the masses. Nimeiry decided to focus on what the previous government had missed, and that included the implementation of women's rights. The point was, however, that those who joined the government had to be in line with the prevailing State ideology. Therefore, the seats available for women were filled by those who represented the president's interests and not that of Sudanese women.

Not surprisingly, the gains were confined to working women in the 'modern' sector, that is, government offices and factories, although a majority of Sudanese women still work in the agricultural and informal sectors. Thus, not only the government but also the leadership of SWU did nothing to deal with issues confronting the majority of women, instead they limited themselves to the interests of women from the middle class, to which most women leaders belonged.

Moreover, after 1977, when the influence of the Muslim Brothers was becoming an unbearable burden for many, internal conflicts arose within SWU. Islamization of the country had affected both the leadership and the members of the organization. In 1983, before the women's committee of SSU (*Aminat al-Mara*) was dissolved, the ideological differences within the leadership came to the surface. Both groups—the Socialist Unionists of SSU and the Muslim Sisters—were fighting for political recognition.[5] I personally believe the dissolution of the committee was a political solution to satisfy the different interest groups, of which the Muslim Brothers were a major force. To avoid any ideological conflict, Nimeiry issued a decree dissolving the women's committee at a time of many other ministerial reshuffles.

In 1984 another incident took place which highlights this internal rift. Secretary General Nafissa A. El Amin was challenged by a Muslim Sister for her post, backed by the Brotherhood. Amin won only because of the support of President Nimeiry and of a broad coalition of women who voted more in opposition to a fanatic Muslim Sister than in her favour.

Nimeiry initiated Islamization after severe economic problems led him to open discussions with the Brotherhood. He needed their financial support, and by making them part of the government, he thought he would be able to control them. Meanwhile, the Muslim Brothers were aiming to overthrow Nimeiry by corroding his popularity. Aware of these undercurrents, Nimeiry continued to support Amin and other women loyalists. This gained him the name of the 'Guardian of the Women's Movement', although it is difficult to take seriously a 'movement' whose every expression was controlled by the State.

All this did not prevent the underground movement from taking tangible action in varying forms. WU had been officially banned in 1971. Its leader, Fatma Ahmed Ibrahim, who had organized and led women since 1952, felt the necessity of reorganizing the Union, incorporating a number of educated and progressive women who were isolated by State policy.

SWU, therefore, faced two major forces, internal and external. The Muslim Sisters were the major internal challenge, supported by the Muslim Brothers and the ideology of Islam. Externally the challenge came from WU, a mobilizing force for women, working underground with the support of progressive forces such as the Communists. Each group had its potentialities, yet SWU remained the major body of State representation until the April revolt of 1985 in which Nimeiry was overthrown.

By creating hierarchical structures within SWU, the State had actually weakened the position of the organization itself. It was seen as a middle-class organization working solely for the interests of that class. Given all the facilities and budgetary resources allocated to the organization, ordinary Sudanese women could have benefitted a great deal if SWU had reached out to rural as well as urban women. Instead, an atmosphere of antagonism was created among women who felt the need to join or be represented by this organization.

A research note

Women's lives and the history of their struggle have never been as visible in historical research as men's lives and *their* struggles. In both the First and Third Worlds, therefore, there exists an acute need for material on women. Male bias in Sudanese historiography is strong. For example, Hasan, in his work on the history of modern Sudan, makes no mention of women at all.[6] Also, women's studies in Sudan is yet to develop into a major area of academics.[7] Thus we felt a great need for the historical analysis of women's struggles and organizations.

Our research team was formed of four women who had shown active participation and interest in women's issues— two senior researchers who were staff members of the Department of Sociology, University of Khartoum, and two research assistants. We concentrated on formal women's organizations because in Sudan such organizations still exist, and have had a profound impact on the women's movement and the general situation of women in the country. Our focus was on the urban areas within a recent time frame, as the women's movement, like any other movement for social change in Sudan, has been an urban phenomenon led by the urban middle class.

We felt that with our research efforts we might help to improve the deteriorating position of Sudanese women by making them aware of our own history. Our main assumption was that women's participation in politics declined markedly during the last 13 years of the Nimeiry regime, in comparison with the decades of the 1950s and 1960s. A major theme we investigated was the control of the women's organization by the State.

Thus our primary aim was to gain an understanding of aspects of women's history which would shed some light on their status in contemporary Sudan. We rejected the traditional positivist methodology and its value neutrality, objectivity and non-commitment. We felt that these were impossible positions to maintain, especially given the situation in which we were living, one of political repression in which women's organizations were used as part of the government apparatus to rationalize and reproduce that repression.[8] The study was conducted between January 1984 and September 1985 when political unrest had reached a peak, instigated by the introduction of Islamic laws in 1983 and the general atmosphere that resulted from those laws.

Our main research technique was intensive interviews with women for the collection of oral history. However, we also did archival research, collected a lot of published material and observed what was happening in the media and society with regard to women. We also observed the changes taking place in our own private lives. With Oakley[9] we rejected the paradigms of traditional interviewing which relegate interviewees to the role of objectified data and which perceive the interviewing process as one-directional. In fact both the researchers and the researched changed through the interviewing process.

The women interviewed came from different social backgrounds and educational levels and their experiences as leaders and members varied enormously. This had an impact on their willingness to discuss all the topics that came up during the interviews. Some were very helpful and open, while others had their reservations. As researchers, we felt the degree of openness and freedom was high in women who did not belong to SWU. Those who had been active members of that organization were generally reluctant to share even the common problems of daily lives.

We concentrated on certain core information, leaving the specifics to develop spontaneously during interviews that varied in length from two to six or eight hours spread across many visits. Most interviews were conducted in the homes of the interviewees. In all, we met about 40 women, of whom 26 had been actively involved in women's organizations since 1940. The rest were interviewed specifically to measure the impact of the slideshow we had prepared.

Questions generally focused on social backgrounds of the interviewees, personal information, history of involvement in the women's movement and their analysis of the movement. To cross-check the information, we had thought of group interviewing, but that proved very difficult for several reasons. Unfortunately we also did not have access to much of archival material.

In general most of the women were helpful, hospitable, and enthusiastic. Yet we also experienced some problems. In my first interview, one of the leaders of the early women's organizations, Fatima Talib, first questioned me closely to satisfy herself about my commitment and knowledge, before answering any of my queries, which she ultimately did very willingly.

We had another interesting interview with one of the pioneering women of Sudan, Al Sayda Sara Badri. She belonged to the first batch of educated Sudanese women. When we interviewed her, she was about 80 years old. Yet her memory was strong and she was fond of poems, songs and stories. At first, when we introduced ourselves, she could not relate to us, as we belonged to families she did not know.

Badri was the first trained midwife in Sudan in 1923. Her work had shaped her personality. She was assertive, strong, brave and tough. As a midwife she had had to walk or ride a donkey for miles, regardless of the heat, cold or rain, or Nature's other dangers such as snakes, scorpions and men. She also faced much adversity within her family and society. Finally, she joined the Midwives' Training School in Omdurman.

Badri is exactly the opposite of what a Sudanese woman is expected to be. I felt it important to make that comparison and went to great lengths to set up the interview. She proved very hard to talk to, partly because of her age and her unique experiences. She provoked and attacked me verbally. At first I was embarrassed. Then I was angry that I could not pay her back in kind for her rudeness, because she was an old woman and because I needed to interview her.

The only way to deal with the situation was to be 'insensitive' to her lack of consideration. I also reminded myself that throughout her life she had showed great commitment to her work and to women. She taught as a voluntary lecturer in the Midwife Training School at the age of 80. She was one of the few women of her generation who were vocal against female circumcision. Finally we managed to come to some sort of understanding and the interview could continue.

I had another difficult experience with one of the active members of SWU. Because she was a president of one of the committees and a well-known member of the ruling party, she was reluctant to talk about her experiences in the women's organization which had now been dissolved. Her 'political commitment' to SWU shaped and coloured the conversation, often distorting the truth. She also tried to check my political commitment and how far I believed in Nimeiry's May Revolution. I knew I could not give an answer that would satisfy her and had to pretend to be too busy with my studies to involve myself in politics. I kept a low profile in order to get as much information as I could from her, not openly disagreeing with her even on issues that definitely did not appeal to me, such as the effectiveness of SWU and the leading role of president Nimeiry towards women.

There were other situations in which the research team found itself in a defensive and uneasy position. For example, for our interview with one of the Muslim Sisters, we had to abide by the Islamic dress codes before she would agree to see us.

The group interviews proved practically impossible, although several women we interviewed were enthusiastic about the idea. But then these were women who had never belonged to SWU, while others refused for political reasons. In any case, fuel shortages and general communication problems finally prevented us from organizing group interviews.

The only women interviewed in a group were from the informal sector, the market women whom we interviewed for our slideshow. The marketplace of Omdurman is the most crowded and traditional part of the city. The women we met were about 50 years and above, mostly uneducated migrants, and heads of households. Because of our clothes and the equipment we carried, they concluded we came from the town council to solve their problems. Before we could start interviewing we had to clarify our positions and our limited abilities: that we had no authority to get them back to the central place in the market from where they had been removed; and that we could not provide services to them such as good shelters.

Research problems: external and internal

It would have been very useful if we had been allowed to use the official archives. We did get to see some material on the pre-independence period, that is, before 1956, and after 1969, that is, the May Revolution under Nimeiry. The period between these two dates was classified information, because, according to government sources, 'the files were being reviewed'.

The fact was that the State claimed that the women's movement began in 1969 with the May Revolution. As women's organizations prior to 1969 had strong links with SCP, their very existence was denied by the Nimeiry government. But in reality, the officially recognized SWU actually materialized only after the attempted Communist coup of 1971.

Our access to other forms of published material was also limited. Very little has been written about women by women in Sudan. Some of the literature was banned after 1972 and some was lost or burnt. The available resources are written by men, and are full of male biases, so that we had to take care in analysing them.

Within the research team, the atmosphere was tense and formal in the beginning because of the hierarchy existing between lecturers and research assistants. It took us some time to work this out. However, our major problem was the political repression at the time of the research. It was dangerous for the team to investigate the history of the women's movement when official wisdom dictated that the movement started in 1969, and only with SWU.

Some of the women who were members of the banned women's organization were under continuous detainment and it was extremely risky to go and interview them. Many women were reluctant to speak about certain issues and reveal facts or release documents. WU had gone underground in 1971. We could only try to trace its activities, and many areas still remain to be covered.

Women who were currently leaders in SWU, were reluctant to talk about their roles in WU in the 1950s and 1960s. Their sensitive political position in the new regime created further insecurity for them. They were suspicious of our intentions, some plainly identifying us with opposition to the regime.

We also faced the problem of being women researchers in an Islamic, underdeveloped, urban context. In a society where housework, children and social obligations are the total responsibility of women, we had to constantly maintain a balance between our public and private lives. At the same time there were continuing external pressures of shortages that affected the entire economy. All this naturally had an impact on our research, but we felt the context reflected rather effectively the reality of Sudanese women.

Conclusion

In the end we did manage to fulfil our major objective—women's history, neglected, buried or hidden for so long, is now accessible. Many struggles of Sudanese women have been finally documented. At the local level, public lectures have been presented by some of the researchers about possible ways of organizing women under situations of complete State control, such as that under Nimeiry. Articles have been published locally and internationally, and several papers were presented at local, regional and international conferences which revolved round the issue of Sudanese women's history. The slideshow that was made about market and rural women, is a valuable asset in the consciousness raising work we are doing today, as well as for teaching purposes.

Our long-term objective is to use the present documentation as well as new research to help change the lives of Sudanese women. We hope an awareness of women's history in Sudan will be a process of learning and empowerment for all of us.

NOTES

1. In May 1969, Colonel Nimeiry initiated the so-called May Revolution which was to last until 1985, when his government was overthrown after a period of popular protest. Until 1971, Nimeiry's policies can be characterized as relatively socialist; but after an abortive Communist coup that year, the government took a definitely right-wing turn.
2. In the southern part of Sudan, the Sudan People's Liberation Army (SPLA), under Colonel John Garang, is fighting for the autonomy of this primarily Christian region. This war, which started around national independence and more or less came to a standstill in 1972, was sparked off again by the imposition of Islamic laws in September 1983, with full-scale implementation of punishments such as amputation of limbs and flogging. —Editor's note.
3. S.M. Kenyan, 'Women and the Urban Process: A Case Study from El Gala, Sennar.' Development Studies and Research Centre Seminar Paper #46.
4. 'Sudan Report, Women's Movements, Organization and Strategies in a Historical Perspective.' The Hague: ISS, 1987. p. 150.
5. Ibid. p. 148.
6. Fadl Yusuf Hassan, 'Some aspects of the writing of history in modern Sudan,' occasional paper. Khartoum: Institute of African and Asian Studies, University of Khartoum, 1978.
7. Zeinab el Bakri, et al. 'The State of Women Studies in Sudan', *Review of African Political Economy*, Double Issue, nos. 27 and 28, 1984. pp. 130–137. See also Zeinab el Bakri on E.M. Kamir (forthcoming, in Arabic) 'Women's Studies in Sudan: A critical view,' at Nustaqbal al. Arabi.
8. 'Sudan Report,' op. cit. p. 8.
9. Ann Oakley, 'Interviewing women: a contradiction in terms,' in: Helen Roberts (ed.), *Doing Feminist Research*. London: Routledge and Kegan Paul, 1981.

10
The Crisis in the Sudanese Women's Movement

Zeinab Bashir El Bakri

The April 1985 popular uprising in Sudan (commonly called *al-intifadha*) which resulted in the overthrow of the 16-year-old military regime of Colonel Nimeiry was expected to have far-reaching effects on Sudanese society. The aim of this chapter is to present and analyse the impact of the uprising on women and to attempt to explain the contemporary status of the Sudanese women's movement.

Many Sudanese women had hoped that a return to the path of democracy would signal the resurgence of a strong and popular women's movement which would squarely confront problems faced by women, especially during the years of military rule. Why this has not occurred to date and what is the future of the movement will form an important part of the present discussion.

We start with the premise that the present situation can only be described as a crisis, to be analysed, understood and possibly acted upon in relation to a critical comprehension of aspects of the history of the Sudanese women's movement and some major developments in Sudanese political economy.

There are many important indicators of this 'crisis':

- The absence of a voice (individual or collective) raising women's issues whether in the mass media, in government or in other political institutions, except in situations where certain political forces stand to gain.
- The majority of women remain outside both women's organizations and general political organizations.
- Government plans and policies do not give adequate consideration to gender issues, with the result that women are bearing the brunt of the economic crisis and poverty is becoming increasingly feminized.
- The rising tide of fundamentalism and its appeal to young

urban women calls for serious consideration.
- The most serious indicator of all is the inability of the existing women's organizations to deal with women's problems or attract enough women and transform them into a critical political force in society.

The April 1985 uprising and its aftermath

The uprising of April 1985 had been in the making for several years, primarily because of the evident inability of the military regime to sustain any kind of development in the country, causing severe economic deterioration and leading to the imposition Islamic laws since September 1983, along with rampant political oppression. Added to this was the development of a strong armed movement in the southern part of the country which the government was unable to control.

The uprising was led mostly by what has been labelled the 'modern forces', notably the salaried professionals, the urban proletariat and lumpen proletariat under the leadership of the National Alliance for Salvation. This Alliance was constituted of several political parties and many major trade unions. Members of the alliance signed a charter which outlined a minimum number of demands upon which these groups had all agreed.

The actual events included widespread demonstrations and a general strike. To prevent any bloodshed (the movement had been comparatively violence-free to date), the army intervened on the 'side of the people'. A Council of Ministers and a Transitional Military Council (made of the army's top brass) assumed power and promised to hold elections following a one-year interim period, during which time the various political parties would be allowed to organize and prepare for the elections.

Women's participation during this period essentially covered three different areas. Women as part of professional unions took part in meetings and preparations for the general strike. Several women trade unionists were arrested. Many women took part in demonstrations, several of them led by housewives—an interesting phenomenon on which there is very little available information. Finally, as part of the traditional family structure, women allowed secret meetings in their homes, and helped to protect the people attending the meetings.

Not one of these women raised gender issues, as they were viewed to be of secondary importance at that time.

The year of transition witnessed a defeat of some of the slogans raised by the popular uprising. No radical economic reforms were in sight; inflation continued to skyrocket; worse still, consumer goods shortages were accompanied by a flourishing black market. Islamic and other repressive laws (such as the State Security Act) continued in full force. The state of emergency was not lifted. There was no end in sight to the armed struggle in the south as no serious negotiations with the resistance movement took place.

The 'modern forces' which had actually paved the way for the uprising were isolated from the process of decision-making which rested in a conservative Council of Ministers and an even more conservative and clearly more powerful Military Council. A principal reason for this development was the intervention of the army at a particular point in the uprising, which helped to prematurely arrest the conflict and tilt the balance in favour of conservative forces which ended up participating in the Military Council and Council of Ministers.

Women were specifically affected in the following ways:

- They were not represented in the Council of Ministers; in fact there was severe opposition to this idea especially from the Minister of Health and the then Prime Minister.
- Nor were women represented in the National Alliance, the rationale being that they did not constitute a political party, neither did they compose a separate trade union and that they were already represented within the existing trade union structure. Of course, no one took into consideration the fact that a majority of Sudanese women were not part of the trade unions at all.
- A move (whose motives were suspect) to reserve special seats for women in Parliament was defeated on the strange rationale that this would be 'undemocratic', and might necessitate reserving seats for workers, farmers, etc.
- As mentioned earlier, the 1983 Islamic laws which specified severe restrictions on women's legal status were not abrogated.
- Instead, a new decree specified that married women working in the government would be entitled to two-thirds of

the male officials' housing allowance. This was primarily based on the assumption that married women have reduced financial responsibilities since they have a husband who is the primary bread-winner.

- A Women's Committee was instituted at the department of passports and immigration, the aim of which was to enforce restrictions on the travel of women abroad when not being accompanied by male relatives (this rule already existed since 1980). The pretext for this was to curtail the travel abroad of women who were going 'for reasons of prostitution to the various oil-rich Arab countries and were causing serious damage to Sudan's reputation abroad.'
- The vast majority of women remained outside formal politics. Only five were candidates in the April 1986 Parliamentary elections. The only two who managed to enter Parliament turned out to be members of the National Islamic Front. It is crucial to note that this in no way constitutes a measure of the popularity of the Muslim Brothers. It merely demonstrates the manoeuvring of electoral procedures and laws by conservatives in such a way as to make it exceedingly difficult for progressive forces to enter Parliament.

How did such a situation develop in relation to women in Sudan? There was, of course the macro context—the typical features of Sudanese political scene and social structure. But there is a second, more specific explanation for the phenomenon, which necessitates examining the various women's organizations and their ability to deal with the present crisis.

Political scene and social structure

The main features of the Sudanese political economy have evolved as a result of two spans of foreign occupation. The first by the Turko-Egyptians, during the nineteenth century and the second with the setting up of the British colonial State in 1898. Colonialism, together with the features of indigenous Sudanese society, resulted in a specific economic, political and class structure, the main features of which can be summarized as follows:

- A dominant bourgeois class (made up of a small industrial bourgeoisie and a larger commercial and agricultural bourgeoisie). The development of a parasitic sector of this class has been a phenomenon of the past twenty years, during which time, they have enriched themselves through corrupt practices, as well as gained power and influence in the political sphere.

- A small professional middle-class.
- The urban proletariat and lumpen proletariat.
- Small farmers and agricultural workers.

Although the struggle for independence was waged by the small middle-class, subsequently politics have been dominated by the traditional parties (namely the Umma Party, the Democratic Unionist Party and the National Islamic Front). Although exhibiting minor differences in ideology, these parties clearly represent the interests of the bourgeoisie.

The country has undergone two periods of military rule: 1958–1964 and 1969–1985. The second period was especially severe on the people as it led to widespread political oppression. During the final years of this so-called May Revolution regime, the government relied on heavy political and financial support from Muslim fundamentalists. As a last resort, under pressure from the Muslim Brothers, the regime agreed to impose Islamic laws on the country (the infamous 1983 laws).

The April 1985 uprising was able to overthrow this regime. Although the 'modern forces' had posed a serious challenge to the hegemony of the bourgeoisie, this challenge proved short-lived. The April 1986 elections brought to power a coalition government made up of the Umma and National Democratic Parties, the two major traditional parties representing bourgeois interests. The National Islamic Front, although it did well in the elections, did not enter the government.

The crucial issue has become that of power-sharing between the different factions of the bourgeoisie, none of whom have a solid economic base on which to lean. With political survival the immediate priority, women's issues and interests are pushed aside, while women themselves remain largely outside the formal political struggle.

It is even more aggravating that all these developments are taking place in a context of extreme economic disarray. The economic policies followed by the military regime since 1971 (and reproduced by the 'democratic' post-April 1985 government) have practically resulted in the destruction of the economic base of Sudan. It is interesting to note that it is women who must carry on the endless search for consumer goods, signifying severe restrictions on their time. At the same time, it is they who must continue with informal economic activities to pay the blackmarket prices of essential commodities.

Obviously, a combination of factors has led to a situation where women have become increasingly inward-looking, with their activities totally limited to the private sphere of the family. In addition, the defunct military regime's restrictions on political action and organization had already forcibly removed a whole generation of women from the realm of politics.

> Therefore, among women, as in many other segments of the society, an attitude was engendered by expecting everything from the State and not having to engage in any social activity to improve their condition. This pattern of special interaction between the State and women that was formed during the single-party regime continued after the transition to the multi-party democracy.[1]

In this context, it is imperative to examine the role of the extended family as it relates to women's situation. Although as an institution it has undergone changes (the nature of these changes must be seen in relation to class and regional differences), it remains among the most dominant in Sudanese society. Within it, sharp role distinctions between women and men continue to exist. Most social life and activities revolve around the family and these are primarily the domain of women. Births, deaths, marriages, circumcisions are the most important celebrations and women have to attend, contribute (either financially or by providing labour) and spend time, or else they will be subjected to ridicule and lose some of the family support upon which they all depend, especially the working women.

The point that needs to be emphasized is that the extended family in Sudan is not only a locus of women's oppression (as witnessed by the reproduction of gender roles, gender role typing in the socialization process, the repressive role of in-laws, etc.), but also one of support. We believe the extended family has fulfilled many important needs for women in Sudan which had to be fulfilled for women in the west by the feminist movement. However, in no way does that imply that the extended family has replaced the need for women's organizations. It is merely an aspect of the Sudanese social structure which requires extensive research and analysis.

Women's organizations

The Sudanese women's movement can trace its origins to the 1940s together with the growth of the nationalist movement—a recurrent pattern in many developing countries. It has mirrored larger political developments in various phases of Sudan's history, and was supported by the nationalist movement at large.[2] The nationalist forces saw in it a means of placing pressure on the colonial state as an additional proof of their worthiness for independence. Like the nationalist movement, the women's movement was essentially urban and middle-class. Rural women remained at the extreme periphery of the movement. The movement had several forums, the largest and most active being the Women Union's (WU), although several other organizations existed, reflecting different and mostly reactionary viewpoints regarding women. WU was most active during the 1960s when women gained their right to vote and right of equal pay for equal work. The first woman to enter Parliament was the president of WU.

The late 1960s witnessed a severe political crisis: the traditional forces through their political parties, which were in power at the time, were trying to silence popular resistance to their reactionary policies. Communist members were expelled from Parliament, there was an attempt to pass an Islamic constitution and the war in the south escalated. In this tense atmosphere, a military coup took place in May 1969. The coup, led by a group of young and progressive military officers, was supported by a section of the Communist Party and other broad left elements, all of whom believed in the need for radical change.

However, persistent disagreements with a section of the Communist Party culminated in an abortive Communist-backed coup two years later. The coup, which lasted only 72 hours, proved to be a crucial turning point for Sudanese society, since the State immediately took a rightist turn and abandoned its progressive plan of action, which had attracted so much popular support in the beginning.

The May regime had come at a time when WU was facing internal problems concerning strategies and means of action, and the extent to which the Communist Party should intervene in the Union's affairs.

WU was among the first organizations to support the regime in May 1969. As problems between the Communist Party and the regime grew in 1970, so did the tension between WU and the regime, leading to the dissolution of the Union by decree in May 1971, leaving a void in a critical moment of the women's movement.

Significantly, whereas previous conflicts within the Union, especially in its earlier days, had been between the progressives and the reactionary elements (especially Muslim Brothers), during this short period (1969–1971) the conflict was between different factions of the progressive elements themselves. Earlier conflicts had been over issues such as whether women were to be granted political rights, whether such rights were un-Islamic, etc. The new conflict did not relate to the women's movement or its role in Sudanese society. It was concerned with larger ideological issues, relating to the extent of support to be given to the May regime. The conflict was damaging to both the women's movement and the left in general, since it allowed the regime to abandon its former plan of action and simply take a directly rightist turn, dealing a near fatal blow to democratic and progressive elements in Sudanese society and consequently to the democratic women's movement in the country.

Sudan Women's Union (SWU), set up in November 1971 under the auspices of the Sudanese Socialist Union (SSU), the sole political party in the country, was portrayed as the defender of the 'revolution' against all enemies, especially the Communists.

The principal effects of the creation of SWU on the Sudanese women's movement were the following:

- An official and legitimate monopoly over women's affairs was created, since by law SWU was the only legitimate women's organization.
- Its intimate, dependent and subordinate relation with SSU and the government, effectively prevented it from taking

independent political stands or criticizing a regime whose policies were contributing to the deteriorating position of women.

- In the process it isolated most educated, progressive and committed women, who did not wish to be involved in a structure inhibiting democratic expression and perpetuating the existing status quo.
- In its hurry to spread to all parts of the country, the organization filled its positions with opportunist women with political ambitions. Like other State organs, the SWU became a hotbed of corruption.

Thus, during the 16 years of military rule, few forums were open for women. WU continued to exist, but as an underground organization, thus signifying a severe curtailment on the range of its activities and membership.

With the rise to power of the Muslim Brothers, and with the consolidation of that power after the passing of the September 1983 laws, there was an attempt to set up their own women's organizations. The most important of these was called *Raidat al-Nahda* which was registered as a charity organization.

The programme for these organizations was based on a fundamentalist reading of women's position, emphasizing and reinforcing women's familial and household roles. The movement tried to attract girls in secondary schools and universities. In the absence of viable alternatives to SWU, this organization was indeed able to attract many women, especially younger ones who had had no experience of the pre-1969 women's movement. However, it remained an urban phenomenon, and was not able to reach all parts of the country.

The April 1985 uprising overthrew military rule, and with it, SWU. Its leaders were temporarily jailed together with other leaders of the May regime. In the aftermath, the principal challenge faced by WU was that of how to transform itself from an underground secret organization into a public one.

It had been the expectation of a lot of progressive women (even those who had not been members when the Union was underground) that WU would act as the rallying point for their many demands and problems, become a vanguard for the women's movement and wipe out all the wrongs perpetrated by 16 years of military rule.

In actual fact, WU closed into itself and became very selective in accepting members, reducing its membership to those women who were in the Communist Party, or those who were guaranteed to be not against the party line, thus isolating once more many energetic and committed women. Publicly, the leadership of WU announced that any woman regardless of her political colouring could be a member provided she did not have a 'bad reputation' and had not been involved in the previous regime.

During the early days of the popular movement of 1985, the activities of the Union were limited to holding public talks, in which the main speaker was the leader of the Union, Fatma Ahmad Ibrahim. The talks, which were well attended, concentrated on general issues such as underdevelopment, the nature of democracy, criticism of the transitional government, etc. rather than upon specific women's issues.

Some aspects of the ideology adopted by WU contained ambiguous positions on women's status in society.

Women's problems were seen as part of the general problems of society, to be solved by following the socialist path. It was assumed that all problems were caused by economic underdevelopment, imperialism, etc. and could be dealt with by conquering illiteracy, providing adequate health services and non-discriminatory labour legislation, etc.

The Union saw the family as the most important institution in society. That it was also a focus of women's oppression was ignored. Problems relating to the family were identified as 'evil habits' which the Union would fight and eradicate. An example of this was the *zar* ceremony. Issues relating to the family such as domestic labour, were not dealt with at all. In a television interview the president of the Union stated, as the attitudes of the Sudanese male were a consequence of years of conditioning, it was perhaps too early to bring up controversial issues such as women and domestic labour.

Their position on religion was that essentially the Union was not against religion, specifically Islam, but that an enlightened interpretation of Islam was what women in Sudan needed, especially regarding personal laws. It is interesting to note that WU (like the Communist Party) is very sensitive about religion. Members are afraid of being branded as atheists, especially

when a lot of debate already exists concerning relations between
religion and the State. In media appearances, the president of
the Union always covers her head and a large part of her face
in accordance with conservative Islamic custom.

The Union's position is anti-feminist: it wants to have nothing to do with relations between men and women, or even those
between women and society. Disapproving of the international
feminist movement (its only close relations are with the
Women's International Democratic Federation), the Union con-
siders discussing women's position a 'bourgeois diversion',
deflecting attention from 'real problems'.[3] In an interview conducted by the Union's magazine with Nawal el-Saadawi, the
renowned Egyptian feminist, the bias was evident. The interviewer seemed intent on demonstrating that the feminist position was essentially a 'rightist' one, that the call for women's
solidarity signified a retraction from class analysis, etc. The
readers were not allowed to judge for themselves the worth of
Saadawi's ideas.

Given WU's concentration on class analysis, issues related
to marriage, sexuality and virginity—of great importance to
young Sudanese women subject to far-reaching social control—
are not raised at all. Meanwhile, their activities have remained
the same in the last 30 years: holding charity fetes, mobilizing
women during elections, organizing talks on international
women's day, etc.

Since 1985, the Union has not held a general congress which
would have provided the opportunity for discussing these problems. This also means that the leadership of the Union has not
changed in all these years. The absence of any theoretical debate within the Union has kept it frozen in time, ignorant of
issues which are significant to contemporary Sudanese women.

The National Women's Front

The counterpoint to WU is the National Women's Front (NWF),
which is closely associated with the Muslim Brothers, currently
known as the National Islamic Front. The nucleus of this organization was formed in the late 1950s by two Muslim Sisters
who had defected from WU over the issue of whether granting
women political rights was against Islam. The organization

continued to exist although more as a charity organization and under different guises.

The extreme ideological oppression during the final years of military rule, plus the financial strength of the Muslim Brothers (backed by Islamic banks and companies), all helped to make this organization an influential one. After the popular uprising in April 1985, NWF emerged as one of the strongest and most well-funded groups.

Their ideological position is unequivocally the same as that of the Muslim Brothers. Their aim is to spread Islam and establish an Islamic nation. They vigorously propagate images of the ideal Muslim woman and family, especially through the mass media.

The principal strategy which NWF (together with other organizations of the Muslim Brothers) utilizes is to reach different groups of women by fair means or foul, even if this necessitates the use of slogans generally raised by non-traditional organizations such as WU. Two recent activities which demonstrate this trend are described below.

After the government came to an agreement with the IMF and carried out some harsh economic measures, NWF was the only women's organization to head a women's demonstration to the Prime Minister's office, where a statement protesting the IMF agreement was handed in. Needless to say the demonstration received a lot of media coverage.

Recently, the Front created a voluntary organization, the League of Working Women. Recommendations passed at the first meeting included: working to fight sex discrimination in employment, calling for the extension of maternity leave to six months with full pay, urging employers to provide transport for female employees, organizing women in the informal sector of employment, etc.

The Umma Party

The Umma Party, the ruling party after 1986, also tried to set up a women's organization. The women's wing of the party first presented its ideas in a press statement in November 1985, in which it was mentioned that some organizations were claiming to speak on behalf of Sudanese women, whereas actually they represented narrow partisan interests (the reference was to WU and its connection with the Communist Party).

As an alternative, the Umma women proposed the creation of a National Alliance of Women which would have within it representatives from all women's organizations and women's wings of political parties. It was envisaged, that this alliance would constitute the official voice of Sudanese women in both national and international forums. It would also coordinate with the National Alliance of Parties and Trade Unions on issues of national significance.

Specific objectives of the alliance included the creation of special women's constituencies in the upcoming April 1986 elections. Several meetings were held between the Umma women and women from other organizations. The meetings were fraught with disagreements, especially concerning the set of basic demands which would be acceptable to all organizations. The alliance never saw the light of day. Interestingly, once the Umma Party had established its new image as the defender of women's rights, guaranteeing the vote for women, the debate about women's constituencies died a natural death, as did the call for a national alliance of Sudanese women. The only concession made was to have a woman as Minister of Social Welfare, which was not much of a concession, considering the same thing had happened during the years of military rule.

Conclusion

Evidently, the women's movement in Sudan is in the middle of a serious crisis, which none of the women's organizations have been able to deal with adequately. The Sudanese political scene, with its instability and its current domination by traditional bourgeois parties after 16 years of military rule, is not conducive to women's participation in activities outside the family and the home. Together with economic hardships, this has led women to become more and more confined within their private spheres. The extended family itself, despite the numerous changes it has undergone, and despite providing a lot of support for women, has encouraged this process of isolation.

None of the existing women's groups have become true representatives of Sudanese women, since a majority of the female population, even the urban educated, have stayed outside the organizations.

One way of drawing more women into the movement is to organize around specific issues, such as consumer goods shortages, day-care for children, legal advice, etc. WU has made such attempts in the past and an evaluation of that experience would help to shape a new strategy.

At the same time, existing women's organizations should re-assess their relations with larger political organizations and the degree of autonomy to be maintained should be decided upon.

Introducing gender issues in education should help in the generation of a society-wide debate regarding women's rights, turning it into a political question, rather than merely a question of social welfare.

Unfortunately, the present political environment would not allow any of these strategies. The requirement, clearly, is for widespread change, with a radical restructuring of the entire political economy—a grand scheme not exactly feasible right now. However, on a smaller scale, the women's organizations could strengthen the movement by honestly reassessing their own roles in Sudanese society, and by taking some basic steps towards building solidarity among women.

NOTES

1. Sirin Tekeli, 'Emergence of the Feminist Movement in Turkey,' in: Drude Dahlerup (ed.), *The new Women's Movement: Feminism and Political Power in Europe and the USA*. London: Sage, 1986.
2. In 1947, the first women's association was formed by two educated young women. Its membership was restricted to educated women. There were great differences within the leadership. The president was a leftist activist who devoted a large part of her energy to the anti-colonial struggle. The secretary belonged to conservative circles. She later joined the Muslim Brotherhood. The association was short-lived, but these differences still colour the Sudanese women's movement. —Editor's note.
3. Fatma Ahmad Ibrahim, *al-mar'a al-'Arabiyya wal taghyir al-ijtima'i, al-Markaz al Tiba'i*, 1986.

11
Masses of Women, but Where Is the Movement? A Case Study of the Anti Price Rise Movement in Bombay, 1972–1975

Nandita Gandhi

Protests, and mass movements have been a part of Indian life, except for a brief interruption of 19 months, when Prime Minister India Gandhi declared a state of emergency in the country, suspending all civil rights in 1975.

In the rural areas, the Communist Party of India, later split into the Communist Party of India (CPI) and the Communist Party of India (Marxist) (CPM), led mass land grab campaigns which involved almost half a million people in different parts of the country. Regional parties like the Lal Nishan Party in Maharashtra, autonomous Marxist groups like the Shramik Sanghatana in Shahada (Maharashtra) and independent tribal leaders received tremendous response from the dalits,[1] people of Scheduled Castes and Tribes, and landless labourers on issues like price rise and unemployment. The Naxalites—radical, underground Maoist groups—in West Bengal, Bihar, Andhra and Kerala, spread their own areas of influence.

Independent of party structures, students in Gujarat spearheaded an agitation against high prices which was supported by a coalition of farmers, political parties, and concerned individuals (the Navnirman movement, 1973). Students in Bihar drew inspiration from this movement which succeeded in toppling the ruling state government, and invited the Sarvodaya leader Jayaprakash Narayan to shape and lead a Bihar-based grassroots movement in 1974, aimed at economic and social upliftment.

In urban centres, strikes, demonstrations and agitations had become regular occurrences. Maharashtra recorded the maximum number of disputes and closures in those restless years of the early 1970s and Bombay as its foremost industrial city took the lead.[2]

What was significant in all this was the willingness of different political organizations to work together for a common cause. Secondly, coalitions formed independent of political organizations brought into the political arena sections of the people who had never been vocal before. Thirdly, most of the struggles were directed against state governments, rather than the government at the centre. The Bihar movement went on to outline an alternative political and organizational ideology.

Women were in the forefront of most of these agitations which swept the country in the period between 1967 and 1975. Documentation of this period often reveals the surprise of party cadres at the militancy of the women and their eagerness to join the protest movements in large numbers.[3] Landless women working in famine relief programmes willingly participated in protest marches and demands for land. Women from the organized sector joined the self-employed, casual workers and lower middle-class housewives for a common show of strength against unemployment and rising prices. Probably for the first time after the Maoist student groupings, young women students in Bihar and Gujarat from peasant or small trading, middle-class families joined their colleagues to face a baton charge by the police.

What become popularly known as the *Mahagai Pratikar Samyukta Mahila Andolan* or the Anti Price Rise Movement of Bombay (APRM) was one of the many struggles against inflation, where women played a key role.

In 1972, women leaders of the two Communist Parties and the Socialist Party routinely met to discuss the possibility of joint action against rising prices. The objective of the joint front was to pressurize the government to check the price rise and ensure an adequate quota of subsidized essential commodities through the public distribution system. Sporadically, but faithfully, through a period of three years, middle-class and working-class women—young, old, housebound mothers, members of innocuous 'women's clubs', women working at home, or as domestic servants—about everyone joined the demonstrations, marched in public brandishing rolling pins, plates and spoons as their weapons, and confronted officials and state ministers.

Widely publicized by the media, these events created a ripple effect in different parts of Maharashtra and in neighbouring Gujarat. The *Latni Morcha* or the Rolling Pin Demonstration attracted nearly 20,000 women. Its surprised leaders hailed it as a 'new women's movement', and as the beginnings of a 'people's movement'. The APRM came to an abrupt halt with the arrest of most of its leaders during the Emergency in 1975.

Although reams of paper have been filled about 'the darkest period in the history of free India', conspicuously little has been written about the women who participated in the movements of the time. The APRM too, except for some newspaper articles, has not been comprehensively documented. This is consistent with a general trend in history where women appear only in flashes through centuries of oral and written material.

At the same time, in a span of 15 years, the APRM participants themselves seem to have forgotten their movement and slipped back into a routine with barely any change in their lives. I noticed this when I first attempted to meet and talk to some of them. In 1983 the same leaders were eager to revive the movement, as they once again confronted high prices, a falling standard of living, unemployment, etc. I attended their first mobilizing meetings. But their efforts met with little success outside the circle of their regular activists and party members.

These observations raise two questions: why has women's political participation been neglected by the social sciences? And can all women's mobilization be classified as women's movements? The APRM (1972–1975) is a good case for study as it stands midway between a fast disappearing past and a present that is yet to be documented. Secondly, it was exclusively a women's campaign, peopled only by women, which was perceived as a part of the women's movement as well as linked to a general struggle.

Women's political participation: some theoretical considerations

The women's movement has given visibility to women's oppression as well as to their contribution in all spheres of life.

Western feminist academicians like Mies[4] and Stanley and Wise[5] have criticized the social sciences for their male bias or androcentrism. The fact that social sciences happen to be male preserves is only one reason for this bias. More important and subtle is the conceptual framework and methodology of social science research which has excluded a range of experiences, perceptions and contributions to society.

One of the most obvious reasons why women's political participation has gone unrecorded is the traditional academic emphasis on collective statistics. Evidence of political participation has been gleaned from membership of political parties, attendance at meetings, participation in campaigning or some 'official' contact with the political process. Reasons for women's lack of participation in these activities are not difficult to locate. Their domestic responsibilities and lack of education, leisure, mobility, resources, or organizational experience, prevent them from joining formal politics.

Women have more readily joined in direct, one-time actions, or played supportive roles in long-term struggles. Such actions usually do not require regularity, attendance, debate, organizational functioning and official responsibility. Women's political participation has been predominant in price protests, food riots, land issues, crisis related work/wages issues like famine relief, housing and rent issues, alcoholism and corruption.

The emergence of the so-called 'new social movements' of the 1970s, like the human rights movement, science, ecology, anti-nuclear and neighbourhood associations movements, has provoked a political and theoretical debate. Laclau and Mouffe are critical of the traditional leftist conceptualizing of social conflicts which links the social agents, peasants, bourgeoisie, etc. with the economic or the 'objective', as in the transition from feudalism to capitalism.[6] But it is getting increasingly difficult to identify social agents as coming from one specific economic or social grouping. Consequently their interests and demands are not necessarily specific to their economic and social relations.

What becomes evident is that social movements emerge and develop from complex, fluid relationships between the State and society, the character and ideology of the dominant political institutions, the form of the economy and the 'culture' of political participation. To hunt solely for a material basis for movements reduces the emergence of a movement to the linear and the simplistic.

The history of the APRM

'Was it called the Anti Price Rise Movement? I only remember the big *latni morcha* (rolling pin demonstration), we waved our *latnis* like swords and felt strong enough to fight mountains. Of course, the prices did not come down, but we got some rations. Then the *latni* went back to the kitchen and now I have only a red flag for remembrance,' said Saraswatibai, 55-year-old domestic servant from Bombay.

In August 1972, Meenaxi Sane, president of the Maharashtra state branch of the Communist Party of India's (CPI) women's wing, appealed to some 280 women's organizations and individuals to come together for a discussion on the price issue. A small meeting of nine women decided to call themselves the *Mahagai Pratikar Samyukta Mahila Samiti* (the Anti Price Rise Joint Women's Front) and initiate a signature campaign and prepare a scheme for controlling inflation to be submitted to the government.

The rationale for such collective action was not formally discussed at the first meeting. All of them shared a history of joint action and politics. It was understood that, prices affected women the most severely because all of them regardless of class looked after the family.

A formal committee with office bearers was considered necessary for organizational efficiency and representation. The distribution of office, usually a touchy subject, was speedily dealt with on the basis of electoral success. Mrinal Gore, the only state Legislative Assembly member, was nominated president because as an opposition party member in the legislature she had some standing with the government. All the city level municipal corporators were recommended as vice presidents. The composition of the *Samiti* underwent some minor changes in the course of its three years of life, but for most of its active period it retained the same office bearers.

The objective of the Front was to pressurize the government to control the prices and provide adequate foodgrains through the public distribution system.[7] Small demonstrations were to be held to register the discontent of women. Then a public meeting was organized in September 1972, which attracted hundreds of women. This unexpected success and a sympathetic press coverage encouraged the Front to plan a sit down strike for the next month. The well attended and colourful strike staged in the congested commercial area of Bombay established the identity of the Front.

The Front functioned informally, its members meeting at different members' homes, taking on-the-spot decisions, and dividing responsibilities between themselves. No records were maintained. Money was raised when the occasion demanded through donations. Front members kept in touch with each other over the phone and each of them in turn informed the women they had mobilized. Individual Front members decided whether to involve the Front in a particular action or take it up by herself. Mrinal Gore, for instance, took out a procession at a milk dairy in Goregaon under her own banner in January 1973.

The Front did not bring out any literature or position papers outside of memos or press statements. Its demands were verbally articulated by the members of the *Bhartiya Mahila Sabha* (BMF) at a public meeting:

- All illegal money should be taken out of circulation.
- Trade in essential commodities should be nationalized.
- All essential commodities should be distributed through fair price shops.
- The government's policy of deficit financing and indirect taxation should be halted.
- Hoarders, food adulterers, blackmarketeers and income tax evaders should be severely punished.[8]

The emphasis of the Front was primarily on action and mobilization. It solicited complaints about the availability and prices of foodgrains and other essential commodities. A delegation of women would meet the official in charge. If they were unsatisfied with official replies, a meeting would be organized to highlight the problem. At times, the entire Front would pitch in to organize a rally. One of the first intensive campaigns was on the price of milk. In January 1973, the press published excerpts from correspondence between the state government and a large local milk dairy which revealed that not only was the price of milk about to be increased but its fat content was to be reduced. And this was to be done without informing the consumers. The Front swung into action with a delegation of women going to meet S.B. Chavan, a state cabinet minister, and virtually holding him prisoner until he escaped the enraged women on the pretext of going to the toilet!

The women soon perfected the art of dramatic confrontation. Complaints of dirt and pebbles in foodgrains prompted a demonstration. Women were asked to collect all the dirt found in the grain distributed by the fair price shops and bring it to a demonstration. Hundreds of women in April 1974 watched an effigy of the Chief Minister being weighed against the collected dirt. The old, traditional practice of the king weighing himself against gold to be given in charity had been creatively modified to suit the times.

In February 1974, a cut in the quota of rations available at the fair price shops provoked strong public resentment. The Front announced a *ghanta vadan*, or 'ringing of bells'. Women were asked to come out of their homes at an appointed hour of the night on to the street and beat empty plates with spoons. Hopefully, said the leaders, the noise will reach our rulers' ears.

In August, 1974, a scarcity of kerosene disturbed even those women who might have so far remained aloof, because now they were forced to use coal or even cow dung cakes as fuel. A group of women entered the state secretariat, surreptitiously made their way to the cabinet meeting room, whipped out several empty kerosene tins with which they made a deafening noise until they were arrested.

Behind all the eye-catching, ear-splitting symbolism was the hard labour of mobilization. Each Front member we spoke to, claimed to have mobilized the largest number of women for the movement—it was undoubtedly a sign of status as well as strength. The momentum of the APRM was maintained by interspersing marches with representations, debates in the legislature and direct confrontations.

The campaign spread on its own accord to other parts of Maharashtra. Thousands of women took part in protest marches in Nagpur, in Pusad, the chief minister's stronghold. The campaign reached its peak with the now famous Rolling Pin March in October, 1973. The astonished and jubilant Front leaders, now began referring to it in more exalted terms. A 'new women's movement', said Mrinal Gore of Socialist Women's Wing; a 'popular consumer movement', said Pramila Dandavate of Samajwadi Mahila Sabha; and Sushila Gokhale of Bharatiya Mahila Federation saw in it the dawn of a 'people's movement'.

The Front declared 26 November 1973 Anti Price Rise Day. It collaborated with political parties and trade unions in organizing the protest activities. A black flag demonstration against Prime Minister Indira Gandhi, provoked the Bharatiya Mahila Federation to withdraw from the Front. The rest of the Front continued functioning until the declaration of emergency when they went underground and their activists abandoned the movement to protest against the emergency. The APRM could proceed on its three year course without much dispute and theoretical hairsplitting because the members of the Front shared a more or less common ideology on women's oppression.

All the leaders came from middle-class, upper-caste backgrounds, were well-educated and were roughly between the ages of 48 to 78 years. They had been drawn into politics during the 1930s, a period dominated by Mahatma Gandhi, and the tremendous idealism generated by the nationalist movement. They had all participated in the struggle for independence, but a deepening disillusionment with the leaders of the movement led to a shift towards the left. After joining the Communist and socialist parties, the Front leaders, as part of their political work, joined the All India Women's Conference.

The AIWC had been set up by women sympathetic to the Congress Party as a non-political body for the propagation of women's education and welfare. The Front leaders set up AIWC branches in different working class areas, worked on its magazine, *Roshni*, and captured key posts to make policy changes in favour of toiling women. After many years of power tussle with women members of the Congress Party, the largest nationalist party in the country, they left to set up a parallel mass women's organization called the National Federation of Indian Women (NFIW) in 1954. The younger socialists soon followed with the *Samajwadi Mahila Sabha* in 1956.

The Front members shared a common understanding of women's oppression. They felt that women suffer a great deal of oppression because they lack the self-confidence to fight back.

According to them, the roots of this mental slavery lie in the attitudes and customs derived from the ancient scriptures. They quoted examples of concepts like *kanyadaan,* or donating a daughter to her husband, and *patidev,* or the 'husband god'.

It was the cumulative experiences of their political beliefs and personal lives which helped crystallize their perceptions. All of them struggled to live their politics: wearing the home-spun *khadi,*[9] opposing their parents by going through dowryless, intercaste or interregional marriages, and working to support their political husbands. They all felt strongly that women should get involved with politics, to assert their rights.

Their own lives outline a portrait of brave, unconventional, dedicated women with a zest for life and politics who had managed to combine their family and political roles in a rational and harmonious way. Their perceptions were in essence no different from the official position of the NFIW which states that its objective is 'to struggle by the side of the exploited people with our menfolk to build common actions which will change society into an egalitarian one.' The problems may be presented from the women's point of view, but the effort should be to support issues that affect everyone. Through the years, NFIW has taken up such issues as women's right to work, upliftment of peasant and agricultural women workers, amendment to marriage, inheritance and dowry laws, literacy programmes, prices, children's rights, and world peace.

The socialist women's organization, the Samajwadi Mahila Sabha, was visualized as a non-political body with the objective of creating an awareness among women of their national, social, and political rights and to give women a social democratic outlook. The organization believed that patriarchy had done grave injustice to women, and that it was time for both men and women to work together to rid society of this oppressive environment. The organization has mainly concentrated on issues related to women's rights, prices, employment, service programmes, study circles and income generation schemes.

Organizing women

How did most women get mobilized? They came in contact with political parties through male local leaders and male cadres.

Interestingly, the wife of the local leader or cadre who maintained links with the women and the party did not have a similar position as her husband. The male worker or leader was in a position of power because of the services he provided to the people, the party and to industry. His female counterpart had no such power but commanded the trust of the women in the area, who came to her in times of need, and when intervention of the party was required. Such was the role of the local mobilizers for the APRM.

Most of them belonged to lower middle-class backgrounds. They saw themselves as the important link between the leadership and the women from the grassroots. Their earliest political tasks were at the behest and advice of their men. They joined the APRM when the women leaders spoke to their husbands about it. And not all their initial experiences were exciting, especially when they had to sit through study circle sessions, listening to high profile women leaders talk about capitalism and struggle in languages they could hardly understand.

However, most of the men's support stopped at encouragement. Women were expected to complete all their domestic work and then engage in politics. Young mothers and unmarried girls were automatically excluded. At Chinchpokli, a working-class suburb of Bombay, women point to Tawdebai as the most active member of the movement because she is a widow and, 'has no one to bother her or prevent her from going to the rallies.'

The attitude of the local mobilizers towards their leaders was one of admiration and personal loyalty. Most of the local leaders had understood the causes for the price rises and the necessity of organizing, through their dialogues with the leaders. Because of the personal style of discussion, the local mobilizers usually also picked up the tone and rhetoric of their leaders.

All the local mobilizers vividly remembered the movement and all its actions. Women are not easily drawn out of their homes. They had to be cajoled into attending meetings and rallies. The local mobilizers developed their own methods of mobilizing women to participate in political actions, talking in a language the poor urban woman would understand, pointing out the daily deprivations and practically and directly linking them with the government's failures. Sometimes, they held street corner meetings to explain the necessity of organizing or invited the leaders to speak in their areas.

A large number of women responded to the call of the local mobilizers. At the peak of the movement there were as many as 10,000 to 20,000 women marching down the streets with rolling pins in the hands, shouting slogans and waving flags and banners. The bulk of them came from the slums and tenements of the city.

Mrinal Gore, the President of the APRM committee had been working in the Goregaon area of Bombay for 30 years taking up such issues like water supply, housing and corruption. Ahiliya Ragnekar, the vice president, was active in the Communist Party trade unions in Bombay for most of her career. Manju Gandhi, another vice president and Prema Purav, the treasurer, had both been active in the textile mills and the Communist Party women's programmes. A scattering of middleclass women from voluntary organizations and local women's groups lent the movement 'respectability'.

The patron-client relationship between the leaders and the cadre is strongest among women because of their utter inexperience and bewilderment with anything official. The most obvious consequence is that the women's first loyalty is to their local male/female leader and not to the party. Women with a common identity like workers or slum dwellers remain divided on issues of caste and region instead of forming a homogeneous group. For the party, it is an organizational weakness not to have direct contact with the people except through an intermediary. The fortunes of the party in a particular area often rest in the hands of local leaders. There has been little attempt to change that situation.

Parliamentary politics demands the investment of innumerable hours and efforts in electioneering which detracts from building networks. The two-tier system provides an easier and more expedient access to clusters of people. Also, this system works on pay-offs. The local leaders need the party as much as it needs them.

During the movement's lifetime, slum committees in contact with the movement or their parties, had promised to mobilize women. Each family sent one member, either the wife or the daughter-in-law, to the rallies. The underlying feeling was, if we do our bit then the leaders can do something at their end. Although the leaders spent endless hours speaking to women at street corner meetings, it was not enough time to acquaint them with the concept of collective bargaining, the official channels of food distribution, political awareness and their rights. But repeatedly going to rallies did bring the women confidence, a sense of euphoria and a feeling of collective strength.

On the other hand, the local mobilizers had a close relationship with the leaders, based on their unquestioning allegiance. But a sense of awe, and loyalty, however strong it may be, are not conducive to any real debate or exchange of ideas. If differences cropped up, the local mobilizers simply dropped out, rather than face their leaders' ire, polished oratory, class and education. It is not surprising, then, that none of them emerged as leaders later on.

The two-tier relationship encouraged and maintained vertical linkages, of women to leader to party, rather than horizontal ones between women. One of the main advantages of this was that the organizing committee could mobilize different castes and classes. The APRM was unique in bringing middle- and working-class women together. It demonstrated how party-affiliated organizations with their network of contacts can build up collective strength which can threaten state power.

Horizontal linkages are difficult to establish. There was little time or space for getting to know the women. By and large they walked into the rallies as passive participants. They remember the novelty of the experience, the excitement, and a sense of collective strength. But it was not 'their' movement. There was no feeling of owning the movement. The local mobilizers on the other hand had formed strong relations with each other on the basis of a common socio-economic background, involvement in politics, and their common ties with the leaders. Their feelings of solidarity, sense of empowerment so changed the routine course of their lives that they could recall incidents and details of the movement with pride and excitement.

The APRM ideology

It appears that the Front leaders drew upon a blend of two ideological frameworks—Gandhism and Marxism—in formulating their understanding of women's oppression and their strategy. They basically defined themselves and all women as 'housewives', whose 'natural' work is procreation, child rearing and maintaining the home. They believed that there was a 'natural' sexual division of labour as a result of human physiology. These beliefs must have been reinforced by Gandhi's views. He saw the male and female biological differences and their active/ passive characteristics determining human lives and work. 'In trying to ride the horse that man rides, she brings herself and him down,' he had written.[10] This concept of man and woman as complementary to each other, actually places women firmly under patriarchal wings, where they may lead glorified, vicarious and parasitic existences as 'queens in their own homes'.

Both the women leaders and Gandhi held 'social tyranny', the ancient scriptures, tradition and customs, unjust laws and practices responsible for the subordination of women. Therefore, to some extent men were responsible for the present state of affairs and should feel responsible for women's education and dignity—thus setting a trend in Indian politics of male patronage for women's progress and entry into public life.

Women were also responsible for their own subordination as they had accepted being prisoners in golden cages. Their liberation rested in their ability to shake off their mental shackles. Women's struggles were thus to be fought with men and at an individual level on the moral, social and psychological plane without the necessity of any changes in relationships within the family, in public production or society.[11] The strategy for change would then be persuasion and a social work approach rather than active, militant, self-motivated struggle.

With their leftward shift, the Front leaders jettisoned that part of Gandhism which contradicted a class analysis. They also deviated from the Gandhian non-acceptance of women's wage work. Marxism saw the infinite degradation of women as part of the general oppression in society. Engels describes 'the historic defeat of the female sex' as the result of the appropriation and control of surplus by male hunters and cattle tenders who then began asserting their authority within the family and tribe. The first class division is between man and woman at home. He then concludes that men and women can be free individuals with the abolition of private property and class society.

But it was the organizational genius of Lenin which had a much greater impact on the Communist members of the Front. Lenin considered feminism a movement without class character, concerned only with women's rights within a bourgeois framework. Only the proletarian revolution could lay the foundation, among other things, for the necessary revision of material and sexual relations.[12]

Thorny issues within this ideological framework, like the tacit Marxist acceptance of the male-female biological difference, or the primacy given to capitalist relations and the theoretical invisibility of the linkage of reproduction to production, were never debated. The concept of patriarchy was accepted only as understood and described by Engels, that is, as an outcome of private property and class society which ignores the fact that even in propertyless, working-class and landless labourer families, the wife and children remain the property of the husband. And even if this were to be dismissed as remnants of feudalism it does not explain its persistence through time. Nor does it explain why there is still male domination in the socialist countries with all its the structural changes. Or why in spite of women's remarkable progress they are still to be found at the bottom rungs of skill and income.

Both Gandhian and Communist thought have had a special concern for women and have contributed much to the women's movement. But both have an inbuilt structure of reasoning which theoretically marginalizes women, attributes to them limited capacities, or keeps them at the periphery of exploitative relationships. Both ideologies, with their immense differences, have attempted to change and revolutionize women without allowing women in their turn to influence and transform them. Both ideologies arrived at the conclusion that women by participating in the broader struggles could attain their emancipation. Following the same mode of thought, the Front leaders failed to realize the potential of a massive uprising of women.

Throughout its three-year course, the APRM consciously limited itself to the issue of prices and the alleviation of the housewife's hardships. By doing so, it accepted the sexual division of labour and women's unequal and disadvantaged position within the family. All women were defined as housewives, brandishing rolling pins and carrying bags of dirt and pebbles found in foodgrains. Yet the majority of them were engaged in some income generating labour.

The impact of the price rise provided the opportunity of raising the complementary issue of domestic labour, its relations with the production process and capital and with men and the family. It could have been politicized by demanding a recognition of domestic labour, legislation for compulsory creches and subsidized eating places, and emphasizing men's responsibility for sharing housework. Women's work, both inside and outside the home was unimportant in their own eyes. The movement could well have become the medium for projecting women as workers. However this vital shift from women's practical interests to their strategic interests, to use Molyneux' terminology,[13] or their politicization and transformation was not attempted by the APRM. The overall oppression of women and the necessity of revolutionary change was never given serious consideration in the movement.

Conclusion

The APRM was deliberately maintained as a one-issue campaign by its leaders because it was part of a broader struggle against the ruling government. Its structureless functioning was designed to mobilize the maximum number of women. Its anti-government agitational approach was meant to politicize women by educating them about the parliamentary and administrative framework of the government. Its drawbacks and wrong policies would then be rejected by these political and conscious voters. And without any doubt, the Front leaders were successful in raising an anti-government consciousness. But did it advance women's strategic interests?

A women's movement not only specifically takes up women's issues but links them with other issues and systematically questions basic premises and assumptions regarding women's lives and work. It attempts to develop an understanding of women's oppression and builds strategies for the transformation of unequal relationships between women and men. It develops a vision of change.

Unfortunately, the only vision the APRM had was to bring down the state government of the time. Perhaps it would have

developed into a movement had it not been so abruptly termi-
nated by the declaration of emergency. Perhaps the militancy
and enthusiasm of the women would have eventually transformed the agitation into a dynamic movement, giving a new
identity, pride and place to women in the making of a truly
egalitarian society.

NOTES

1. Literally, 'the downtrodden', a name adopted by militant
    members of the 'untouchable' community.
2. *Indian Labour Journal*, 1974.
3. G. Omvedt, *We Will Smash This Prison*. Delhi: Orient Longman,
    1979.
4. M. Mies, 'Towards a Methodology of Women's Studies,' ISS
    occasional papers, ISS, The Hague: ISS, 1979.
5. L. Stanley, and S. Wise, *Breaking Out, Feminist Consciousness and
    Feminist Research*. London: Routledge and Kegan Paul, 1984.
6. Ernesto Laclau and Chantal Mouffe, *Hegemony and Socialist
    Strategy, towards a radical democratic politics*. London: Verso,
    1985.
7. The fair price shops were set up as outlets for the public
    distribution system, where essential provisions are sold at
    subsidized, lower than market rates.
8. R. Gavankar, Political Mobilization in Maharashtra, unpub-
    lished thesis in Marathi, 1982.
9. Clothes made of rough, homespun cotton, called *khadi*, were
    promoted by M.K. Gandhi as a symbol of resistance to the
    imposition of British mill produced cotton in Indian markets,
    which had a disastrous effect on the indigenous weavers and
    the Indian handloom industry.
10. M.K. Gandhi, *Women and Social Injustice*. Ahmedabad:
    Navjeevan Publishing House.
11. M. Kishwar, 'Gandhi on Women,' in: *Economic and Political
    Weekly*, vol. XX, no. 40, 1985.
12. V.I. Lenin, *On Emancipation of Women*. Moscow: Progress
    Publishers.
13. Molyneux, Maxine, 1985, 'Mobilization without Emancipation?
    Women's Interests, State and Revolution in Nicaragua,' in: D.
    Slater (ed.), op. cit.

12
Deterrents in Organizing Women Tobacco Workers in Nipani

Chhaya Datar

Many of us in India became feminists through our own experiences at home as well as in our political lives. Our exposure to women at the grassroots level helped us to understand the potential of women, in their daily productive activity, as well as in their struggles. Our own experiences of deprivation and subjugation were juxtaposed with the strength manifested by women from the masses when they participated in class struggles.

We soon realized that women workers cannot have only a single identity as members of an exploited class. They are also experiencing specific forms of oppression as women, as members of the exploited gender. We also realized their participation in class struggles is awakening them to aspirations for justice and equality as women. We discovered that while documenting these struggles, historians have paid very little attention to the special experiences of organizing women workers. Women's participation in struggles has been assessed by the same criteria as those used for men, such as actions in the streets, speeches at rallies, fighting court battles, negotiations with employers. The usual reason cited for low participation of women, quantitatively and qualitatively, is that they have not yet achieved class consciousness to the same extent as men.

Against this background, I felt it was essential to study women workers, if possible in action, within their own organization, and reveal their special features as women. I approached an organization of women tobacco workers in Nipani, a town in western India. The *Chikodi Taluka Kamgar Mahasangh* (Chikodi Block Workers Federation) had a strong following of 5000 workers, all women.

My original study posed many questions, such as the methodology of organizing, the structure of the organization, the leadership pattern, etc. It also documented the history of the tobacco industry in the area and that of organizing women workers, both in the tobacco and *bidi*[1] industries. This chapter will concentrate on the process of unionization and investigate the deterrents experienced while organizing the women workers.

Women tobacco workers in Nipani

With a population of 40,000, Nipani is a town ruled by tobacco merchants who wield more power than the government. Located at the border of Karnataka and Maharashtra, it is famous for its special aromatic *bidi* tobacco. In the last 50 years, the town has risen to the status of a major commercial centre entirely through its tobacco trade.[2]

Nipani has two types of women workers. The *bidi* rollers who bring home the raw material to roll *bidis;* and the tobacco processing workers who go to the factories and process the *bidi* tobacco.

There is a strong aroma of tobacco wherever you go in Nipani, just as there are women busily rushing to and from the *bidi* factories. In the middle of the morning the home-based workers join the crowd, carrying their load of rolled *bidi* to their employers or taking home the raw material for another day's labour. Shopkeepers in Nipani will tell you, 'Men in Nipani are impotent—their women have to work and feed them.' It is true that few men have regular employment in Nipani, since there is no other industry except one small household utensils factory. Some work as coolies in the factories. Some are masons or plumbers who work as contract labour. Many others have already migrated to the cities. A large number of women are single—some are widows, some have been deserted by their men, and others are *devdasis* who by custom are not allowed to marry.[3]

At present 13 *bidi* factories offer women raw material to take home. This is called the *gharkhep* system. These factories produce labelled *bidis*, pay minimum wages and offer benefits prescribed by the government. There are a few small factories which produce unlabelled *bidis* and do not have to pay excise duty on their product. They pay lower than mandatory wages. Officially there are 2190 *bidi* workers in Nipani, most of them women. In reality there are many more. In addition, children regularly assist their mothers at home, but are not counted as labour. On an average a woman is supposed to roll 1000 *bidis* in eight hours, but without the help of her children this target would be impossible to reach.

There are 79 *bidi* processing factories in Nipani, out of which 35 employ 20 to 400 workers. There are at least 5000 women workers working in these factories. A similar number must be working in the factories located in 21 small villages in the Nipani tract. The factories in Nipani town work almost the whole year round, except for a few days in the rainy season. The factories in the countryside are mostly seasonal, and are generally owned by the same tobacco traders who already have factories in the town, to circumvent problems arising out of union activities there.

The *bidi* processing industry has been in Nipani for more than a century, but the methods of operation have undergone a lot of transformation with mechanization during the last ten years. *Bidi* rolling too has been carried on for more than fifty years and has moved from the factory to the home. But very few mechanical changes have occurred in *bidi* rolling. There is a history of union activities from 1942 till 1962, although the old union of *bidi* workers has become defunct. At present both sections of workers, those in tobacco processing and those in *bidi* rolling, are organized under the same leadership. It is also interesting to note that male coolies who work in the same industry, are not daily wage workers, nor are not organized. Most of them are the husbands of these women workers.

Transformation from the informal to the formal sector

The *bidi* industry is going through a process of transformation from an informal sector industry (Harrod 1980) to a formal one.[4] Women workers in the tobacco industry remained largely invisible until 1980, when they started organizing in Nipani. There was no law of minimum wages for tobacco workers until they got organized. *Bidi* rollers, on the other hand, are organized all over India and officially recognized as home-based labour eligible for welfare, such as medical facilities, scholarships for children and housing loans.

No clear statistics are available about the *bidi* tobacco factories. Officially they have been subsumed under the *bidi* industry, without getting the benefits provided under the law. The important difference between the two groups is that the one group works at home and the other in factories. This reality influences the composition of the workforce as well as their attitudes and consciousness about organizing. Although the *bidi* tobacco workers in Nipani have a longer history of organizing, the present union was started by the *bidi* rollers. Even so, it is the tobacco workers who have provided impetus for the union activities and given the character of a mass movement to the union.

Bidi tobacco processing work is an extension of agricultural operations which are done in the field itself. Women are involved at various stages, such as transplanting, weeding, plucking and curing the tobacco in the sun. Later on the cured, crushed leaves are brought to the godowns or factories. The processing, which includes pounding, grading, sieving, winnowing, powdering of stems and stalks, is performed mainly by women. These are all traditional skills of women and so women workers form the backbone of the industry.

All these operations were performed manually until 1976, when the first machine appeared on the scene. Until then, the processing work used to be more or less seasonal, with a long break during the monsoons. The workers used to work in the fields during the monsoon. Some of them had their own land and many worked as agricultural labourers. Gradually, with tobacco acquiring the status of a cash crop, more and more small land holders sold out and came to live in Nipani. Also, with inheritance dividing and redividing the land, the process of pauperization started. The women became full-time workers.

Machines made it possible to process tobacco even in wet weather. Cutting, grading and grinding machines replaced the operations of beating the tobacco leaves, manual sieving and grading and pounding of stems and stalks. This semi-mechanized process provided longer and sustained employment for a few workers, and displaced many. It also imposed its own rhythm on the work, which women were not used to.

Thus, apart from their appalling work conditions, these changes had a destabilizing effect on the women and they felt the need for organizing. Today they face the threat of further mechanization; already a completely automatic machine has been installed in one of the factories in Nipani which has increased the productive capacity of the women workers 30 times compared to the manual method of work.

If two more machines are installed and run in three shifts, the number of women in all the factories will be reduced to 250. Also, the women will have no place in the second and third shift according to the existing laws. The government of Karnataka has already

sanctioned cheap loans to buy a very costly machine, which processes one ton of tobacco per day.

Socio-economic composition of women workers

It is unusual to find women workers concentrated in such large
numbers in one small town. The men of Nipani, the shopkeepers
and tobacco traders, acknowledge the industriousness of the
women, but also resent their freedom and economic independence.
Free women in their terms also imply 'loose women'. Many women
have migrated to Nipani from the neighbouring villages, sometimes with their families, sometimes without, rebelling against
oppressive husbands or families.

The 1981 census confirmed the existence of a larger number of
women workers in Nipani, compared to any other town of similar
size. My own micro survey showed almost 50 per cent of these
women contributed more than 50 per cent of the household income. Although many of these are poor households, the role of
women in the household economy is a vital one.

The process of unionization

The *bidi* industry's entry into the formal sector is being pushed by
the process of unionization. The first demands of the union were
about the formalization of the status of women workers, such as
providing them with an employment card, a provident fund, leave
wages, festival wages, etc. Later on the demand for a bonus, negotiable each year, gave an edge to its activities. Along with these
demands, the union also asked for lay-off compensation and filed
suits in the court and won them.

The owners, feeling threatened, are trying to create a common
front. Some units closed after strike calls. Mechanization is helping the owners, allowing owners of closed factories to get their
tobacco processed on a job-work basis from the new mechanized
factories.

The union had a lot of victories to its credit at the early stage,
but increasing number of disputes pending in the courts and the
staggering cost of the court proceedings took their toll. At present
the union has taken up the mechanization issue seriously and has
started collaborating with the workers in Gujarat, a neighbouring

state, who form 80 per cent of the total work force in this industry. Pressure is also being increased to stop further mechanization by imposing fiscal measures such as prohibitive excise duties on machine processed tobacco.

At this stage the Nipani union needs to re-evaluate its strategies in the light of new developments, not only in this industry, but in many others from which women workers are being systematically displaced. If women's demands are subsumed in the broader trade union demands, a well-organized base of 7000 women will disintegrate.

Structure of the union

The union for tobacco processing workers, The *Chikodi Taluka Kamgar Mahasangh*, (Chikodi Taluka Workers' Federation), was founded in 1980. Although much the impetus came from the women themselves, the leader of the movement is a man. There are four full-timers in the union who look after administrative matters, one of them a woman worker victimized by her employers because of her involvement with the struggle. Almost all the women members are illiterate. The full-timers, and their leader Subhash Joshi, a lecturer in a local college, constitute the executive body of the union. They are assisted by a consultative body elected from among the workers. Union activities are mostly funded through nominal membership fees.

There are various informal structures which come into play. The office of the union is in Joshi's home. It is open from seven in the morning till midnight and his wife Sunita has been drawn into many of the union activities. She runs a 'consumer society' with the workers. Her father who lives in a nearby village is always ready to supply bail for arrested workers.

The organizing efforts of women have developed multiple dimensions. A Multi-Purpose Women's Cooperative provides cheap and good grain and kerosene to the women. It has a small savings scheme for advancing loans and relieving workers from the clutches of money-lenders. A creche has been started for the workers' children. A transitional women's home is being set up, which will offer facilities to rehabilitate *devdasis* and other women with family problems. Non-traditional marriages and informal counselling are already taking place within the union structure. Also, medical help with a critical understanding of the system of medical care is being provided.

Thus, multifarious activities undertaken by the union are gradually increasing the women's sense of power. Most of the workers, are not yet involved in the daily running of the union, but are enthusiastic participants in public action.

The process of culturization

Experiences at Nipani make it clear that in order to reach women workers effectively, a trade union needs to be involved in many other activities, such as individual counselling, marriage counselling, educational activities, cultural activities and so forth. Other studies too have found this to be true. Based on his experiences in Kerala, a coastal state in the south-east of India, Matthew suggests that taking up social issues within the communities where these workers live, encourages them and helps build their confidence in themselves.[5] One way of doing this is by voicing their grievances through a cultural programme in the community. The SISTREN theatre collective in Jamaica for instance, is trying to use theatre workshops to sensitize workers working in free trade zones (see Ford-Smith in this collection). Matthew calls this a process of 'culturization'.

In a sense then, the women workers' trade union does not strictly remain a trade union, but becomes a women's organization too. This implies that it not only takes up the challenge of economic oppression, but also starts changing the personal lives of women, sensitizing them against the patriarchal value system.

Deterrents to unity

In this context, it is important for organizers to be conscious of the most obvious barriers to the unity of women workers: strife between women of different castes and religious communities; contradiction between urban and rural women workers; and patriarchal values about gender relations.

Bidi and tobacco workers belong to two religious communities, Hindu and Muslim. *Bidi* workers who belong to the Muslim community are referred in a derogatory manner by the Hindus. Not surprisingly, the union has less Muslim members among the *bidi* workers, although previously many Muslim men and women had taken leading roles in the struggle, among them the Malabaris (from the Malabar district of the state of Kerala). In Nipani the poor Muslim women do not wear *purdah*, which has remained a symbol for the upper class Muslims.

Muslim women workers are generally at a greater disadvantage with a Muslim employer because of the stranglehold of patriarchy in the community. Hindu women understand this, but nevertheless refuse to be sympathetic. The pressures exerted by the community on the women are a major reason why Muslim women remain unorganized.

Hindu women workers are themselves divided mainly between the caste and casteless communities. Casteless Hindus are the 'untouchables', the poorest of the poor, and the most oppressed in society. Untouchable women comprise only 12 per cent of the *bidi* workers. Since *bidi* rolling is done at home, caste Hindu women and untouchable women hardly ever have to meet socially. All women of higher castes whom I interviewed said they would not like to eat in the home of an untouchable or be related to her by marriage. Nevertheless, one change was definitely noticeable. They were ready to serve food to an untouchable person in their own homes, something which was previously not sanctioned.

About 50 per cent of the women tobacco workers are untouchables. Almost all the factories used to have separate pitchers of drinking water for untouchables and high caste women. Slowly, the union is making a dent in this custom. Many a time they sit separately for lunch. They do not exchange food. Untouchable women on the whole accept these practices and do not want to make an issue of it. But the prejudice against the lower castes can often be extremely humiliating and cause serious internal strife among the women.

Some 30 per cent of the women tobacco workers come from nearby villages. These women have a different relationship with the union. In a hurry to return home, they are unable to attend many public meetings which start after work and sometimes continue till 9 o'clock at night. Those who possess a piece of land or a milch animal, are not solely dependent on factory work and their interests in the activities of the union are secondary. The result is women in Nipani feel that the village women cannot be relied upon for consistent support. This alienates the rural workers who also face stricter patriarchal control within their own communities.

The rural women fight back by assuming that women in the town are far too careless of their morals, and in the process unintentionally reinforce their own subservience to patriarchy.

I have noticed that patriarchal values internalized by the women have an even more damaging effect than caste and urban-rural divisions. The most important factor in terms of her status within the patriarchal value system is the kind of sexual relations a woman has with a man. One only needs to study the abuses women humiliate each other with. I came across five of them.

The ideal women is called *sati*, or *soubhagyawati*, or *patrivrata*, that is, one who is fortunate enough to be married and remains an obedient wife, however badly beaten or ill-treated she may be. Any woman failing to meet this ideal is a bad woman. A variety of terms is used to describe a woman's bad behaviour, once again according to the kind of relation she has with a man.

She may be called *rand*, meaning widow—unclaimed by any man, without a heritage or a protector, and thus free to lead a sexually immoral existence. She may be called *undagi* or *uthaval*, that is, the disobedient one who defies her husband and starts living independently. The assumption is that such a woman would be sleeping around with other men. It is not important that she may be rebelling against a cruel and oppressive husband. She may be called *chawchal*—a woman who sings with a roving troupe and is without concern or regard for her family. She may be called *bajarbasavi*, a prostitute. A woman who leaves her husband and lives with another man, will be seen as a prostitute, irrespective of whether she ran away from an abusive relationship to a better and more equal one. And finally, a woman may be called *kunwar*, that is, a virgin—a spinster to be looked down upon.

Under patriarchal ideological influences, women view other women through the eyes of men. An important component in their judgement of a woman is her chastity, something that is never applicable to men. There were a number of examples of conflict among women in the union, where a sexually derogatory comment became a bigger issue, diffusing the real trouble underneath—that caused by an exploitative work environment.

Ideology lags behind practice and becomes a hindrance in the path of unity. But then, the situation of Nipani women is definitely unusual to say the least. The proportion of single women is very high here. Similarly, instances of sexual freedom are also on the high side.

Pauperization and alienation from the land is driving many families to the breaking point. Men behave irresponsibly and migrate, leaving the children with their wives. The women migrate to nearby areas in search of jobs. In the villages, very little possibility of paid work exists. Also, women want to get out of the clutches of their in-laws. Nipani offers them job opportunities for which traditional skills are required. Having to work only with women also provides them with a sense of camaraderie as well as security. This is a unique situation, with the town offering an atmosphere of freedom unthinkable in the village.

But it is not only sexual freedom which is involved here. There is also the factor of economic compulsion. In Nipani too they do not get proper wages and have to supplement their income by other means. Nipani being a trading centre, there are many regular visitors who like to have a second home at this place. There are also some small traders and drivers in Nipani who keep a second house and a mistress. Thus there are always men who do not mind being partial providers to these single women. I came across two cases where the husband had encouraged his wife to have extramarital relations so that some source of income was assured. A few women also engaged in partial prostitution whenever the need arose. Nipani being a commercial place, customers are easily available. Women help each other in this activity, such as providing a house for a short period.

Cases of sexual harassment by owners and clerks were common among those brought before the union. That is one reason why there are very few young women in the tobacco factories. In many homes the mother-in-law works in the factory but the daughter-in-law stays at home and rolls *bidis*. That is a more 'respectable' occupation for the young.

The kind of sexual relations which exist in the villages are different. Married to a physically abusive cripple, Guna is rescued and coaxed by her brother-in-law into a relationship which is sanctioned by her parents because it is financially expedient and even by her sister whose co-wife she is to be. Everybody in the neighbourhood knows about the relationship and accepts it as a traditional solution. Guna, therefore, thinks she is morally superior to her women colleagues who are guilty of choosing to live with a man other than their husband. The divide, evidently, can be at multiple levels of complexity.

Patriarchal ideology has always divided women into 'good' and 'bad'. In Nipani, it has given religious sanction to the function of being 'bad' through the institution of the *devdasis*. But for other women the rules remain strict and divisions based on women's sexual relations with men continue to create strife among women.

Within her own community, the *devdasi* is respected and accepted. She is even in an envious position: with the sexual freedom she is allowed, she can choose her man, or drop him. She is accepted as a shopfloor leader. No social boycott exists in her case. Thus the presence of a *devdasi* can become an important factor influencing the behaviour of many women. Occasional prostitution, living as a mistress, deserting the husband, none of these invoke a strong sense of guilt among the women of Nipani. The *devdasi* system may be keeping the legacy of the matrilinear past alive in their subconscious.

However, there is a discrepancy between what the women practice and what they believe. The ideal is still the properly married, well-off housewife. Though all the women have been workers and know that they can dictate better terms at home because they have an income of their own, yet they keep on aspiring for a nice providing husband. Although they see many marriages broken, men battering and deserting wives, they marry off their daughters as early as possible to men they know nothing about. They even prefer boy children who abuse them when they grow up, although experience shows that daughters are more useful and caring.

Uniting idea with practice

That economic necessities force people to change their value systems and adopt new values has been a theory accepted by many progressive people for a long time. But our experience shows that practice does not necessarily change the ideas, the world view. It does not automatically create a vision of a new world with different social or gender relations. At the same time, there is no doubt that developing new visions does give a new strength to the movement. Striving for a new society gives passion. It is important for revolutionary politics to change its ideology along with practice—create a justification for the practice and make women perceive themselves with the help of the new ideology. Otherwise this conflict between theory and practice may create more deterrents than liberating forces.

In Nipani the women's class identity has been reinforced by the struggles they underwent together against their employers. The union has given them a sense of solidarity and attempted to change their self-perception. Despite this, there prevails so much internal strife that the fibre of their class identity is torn apart. Whenever some struggle is on, these personal quarrels subside, but as soon as a lull prevails the clashes re-emerge, and are expressed in terms of patriarchal accusations based on the ideal of feminine chastity.

Feminists assert that chastity is no longer valid in a situation of scarcity and poverty, where the institution of marriage is in a state of collapse. Also, hypocrisy is rife where chastity is expected only from women, and not from men. It is a concept born out of the ownership of a woman by a man. Once women workers start seeing the behaviour of their colleagues from this viewpoint, the divisions among them will be reduced. To forge long lasting class unity the contradictions within the class need to be dealt with through the induction of a feminist value system. This is possible in Nipani, where the union belongs to women.

NOTE

1. Tobacco rolled in *tendu* leaves is the indigenous version of the western cigarette—the *bidi*.
2. See also Anil Awachat, 'Report on Bidi and Tobacco workers in Nipani,' in: *Purogami Satya Shodhak*, Pune, vol. 1, March 1978.
3. *Devdasis*, literally the servants of God, are women dedicated to goddess Yellamma and ritually married to the god Jamdagni, Yellamma's husband. See also Chhaya Datar, *Waging Change, Women Tobacco Workers in Nipani Organize*. Delhi: Kali for Women, 1989. p. 75.
4. J. Harrod, 'Informal Sector and Urban Masses: a Social Relations of Production Approach,' mimeo. The Hague: ISS, 1980.
5. P.M. Matthew, 'Organizing Workers in the Informal Sector,' in: *Economic and Political Weekly*, 20 Dec., Bombay, 1986.

13
Matrilinearity and Women's Interests: the Minangkabau of Western Sumatra

Saskia Wieringa

The Minangkabau are the inhabitants of the highlands of Western Sumatra in Indonesia. They adhere to a matrilinear system of kinship and inheritance, and are staunch followers of Islam at the same time. With some six million people, half of whom have migrated to other parts of Indonesia, they are one of the largest matrilinear societies still in existence. The port of Padang is the largest city of the region, while the market town of Bukittinggi, situated in the central highland plateau, has of old been the centre of the region.

Far from being a static society, the region has gone through major historical changes of which the most important are the introduction of Islam, the imposition of colonial rule, the Japanese occupation, national independence, a regional uprising, a coup, modernization and development. This chapter attempts to discuss how far women's organizations in Minangkabau society have reflected these transformations and how they have been able to defend women's interests.

Although I find Molyneux's separation of practical and strategic gender interests not feasible, she is part of a surprisingly small group of feminist theoreticians who have at all attempted to define women's interests.[1] Usually the term is loosely used to denote what concerns women's share in particular circumstances. Cook and Fonow, in an article entitled 'Knowledge and Women's Interests',[2] completely ignore the issue of women's interests, instead concentrating on analysing the principles of feminist methodology. While in Marxist thought the existence of 'objective class interests' is hardly doubted, post-modernism with its insistence on fragmentation, subject-centeredness and positionality has made us aware of the fragility of once hardly contested categories such as 'interests'. It has become impossible to conceive of 'objective women's interests' which would be equally valid for all women of all classes and races and historical circumstances.

However, women have fought and are fighting for whatever they see as their interests. Jónasdóttir decides that the concept of interests may be useful, if redefined. Following Parks, she relates the concept of interests to processes which 'increase real possibilities to determine what values become the objects of choice and to see alternative choices clearly, free from distorted feelings and aided by adequate concepts and sufficient information.'[3] Apart from the difficulty of deciding what are 'distorted feelings' and 'adequate concepts', her definition is useful in that it points to subjective processes of determining what do become interests and the element of choice.

In an analysis of 'women's interests' thus two positions can be minimally distinguished: that of the women whose activities are being analysed and that of the researcher. In the case of contemporary Indonesia, another important actor is the State which defines women's interests for them.

Thus, instead of *a priori* categorizing women's gender interests, I will analyse how women active in women's organizations defined their interests and which issues they perceived as interests of such relevance that these formed the basis upon which certain activities were undertaken.

Minangkabau society until World War II

To start with, it is necessary to outline those elements of the *adat* system which are relevant to this chapter. The *adat* system is not a fixed, timeless structure, but a dynamic, flexible set of practices, based on an oral tradition—*pepatah pepitih*. Only with the arrival of Dutch administrators and scientists was the *adat* system 'frozen' in writing. Thus, 'the *adat* law', as we know it, is actually a construction of early Dutch colonial domination. Only relatively recently have Minangkabau experts such as Hamka[4], Hakimy[5] and Rasjid Manggis[6] translated their knowledge into writing. The major elements underlying matrilinear Minangkabau *adat* are a set of rules of descent and inheritance, communal property, a tradition of male migration (*rantau*) and a strong belief in democracy.

Descent

There is a wide variety of names for the various genealogical and residential units. Described below is a simplified system of what we encountered during our fieldwork in the rural areas around Bukittinggi. It conforms to Josselin de Jong's synthesis of the earlier material on the Minangkabau *adat*.[7]

The smallest residential and economic unit is the *parui*, the people living in the typical Minangkabau house, the *rumah gadang*, a long house with two or more 'horns', originally indicating the number of married women living there. Such a unit generally consisted of a woman with her married and unmarried daughters and her young sons, and the children of the married daughters. Husbands would visit their wives at night, but they would never actually live in their wives' homes. The female head of such a *parui* is called the *limpape*.[8] Ibu Jamilah Jambek, *limpape* of her *parui*, repeatedly stressed in our interviews with her that no decision on the communal property of the *parui* could be made without the consent of the *limpape*.

In a *kampung*, various *parui* live together. A cluster of *kampung* is called a *nagari*, the highest recognized authority. The main clans of the Minang kinship are called *suku*. The general marriage rule is *suku* exogamy and *nagari* endogamy. Descent and inheritance are organized through the maternal line.

Democracy

An egalitarian ideology and a strong belief in democracy are central to the Minangkabau *adat*. The Dutch general De Stuers wrote in 1825 that the Minangkabau had maintained 'an individual freedom so great that there was little discernible difference between a chief and his followers.'[9] Although men are the public representatives of the members of their lineage, no decision can be taken without the consent of the women who collectively own the communal property.

The *mamak*, or mother's brother, is responsible for the children of his sister(s), his *kamanakan*. The male *parui* head is called *penghulu;* the *penghulu kampung,* together with his advisors, is responsible for the affairs of a *kampung.* Another term for the *penghulu* is *datuk.* The *penghulu* possess no executive powers; their role is to bring the demands of their families to the attention of the other *penghulu.* Loeb noted that if such a lineage chief failed to act as a just representative of his family, his family might displace him.[10]

Traditionally, the *datuk* or *penghulu* were generally elected. The *penghulu* of the various *kampung* grouped together in one *nagari* made up a council which was the ultimate authority; no higher authority was recognized. Thus the Minangkabau society can be characterized as a *nagari* democracy with a high degree of regional autonomy.

Communal property

Adat rules recognized two kinds of property relations. The *harta pusaka,* mainly land and houses, fell under the collective ownership of the women of the matriclans and was inherited according to the matrilinear rules. The *harta pencarian* was individually-owned property, that which had been acquired by a man during his lifetime. Eventually this type of property also became *pusaka,* as it too was inherited along matrilinear lines, that is, via the daughters of a man's sisters—especially if it were newly opened rice fields. There was always the possibility of making a formal gift of the *pencarian* to a man's own children, via the Islamic practice of *hibah.* According to Kato,[11] the *hibah* became more common in course of the nineteenth century.

Traditionally, *pusaka* land could not be sold or pledged by individual clan members. The only reason why land could be pawned was when money was needed to meet an *adat* requirement, such as the burial of a member of the family, the marriage of a young girl, repairs to the *rumah gadang,* or the installation of a lineage chief.

Male migration

Women's duties lay in the home and the fields surrounding it. They were hardly permitted to leave their mother's home and fields. Men on the other hand were encouraged to go off and seek prestige and wealth in the *rantau,* a loose term originally meaning the lands not belonging to the Minangkabau heartland. The wealth so obtained would accrue to the lineage property. Graves[12] observes that especially in the poorer villages, men romanticized about going on *rantau,* and ridiculed those who stayed at home. Thus, the *rantau* was meant to be temporary, and was linked to the moral and social obligations of a man to care for the welfare of the members of the extended family back home. Yet, as has been noted by Naim,[13] this kind of migration laid the basis for the emergence of the nuclear family, as the social relations in the *rantau* were not based on agriculture but on the individual capacities of the men concerned.

Women's power according to adat

Although the extent to which women wielded power in this society is difficult to estimate, most ethnographers agree that they had considerable influence mainly due to their economic position. Both Willinck[14] and Korn[15] mention women's power due to their possession of the rice fields and their control over the income derived from it. Korn adds that especially older women participated actively in the family councils, aided by the fact that they were usually the mothers of the male lineage chiefs. We have already noted the power of the *limpape.* As far as the process of decision-making is concerned, it should be noted that women not only participated in the deliberations, they were also the ones who had to implement the decisions taken by unanimous consent. Men could only validate the decisions taken. If there was no male *mamak* available, women could also be appointed in that position.[16]

Contrasted with this considerable economic and political power of older women is the way the sexuality of younger women was controlled. The marriage of a young girl was entirely arranged by her elders. She was supposed to be a virgin until that time, whereas boys were encouraged to go off and seek 'experience'. If the couple were ill-matched, the husband could find an easy way out in polygamy, or he could simply go to the *rantau* and stay away. He could also divorce his wife according to Islamic rule. Women who committed adultery were heavily punished. The male *adat* chiefs were responsible for the appropriate sexual behaviour of the women of their lineages.[17] Both Manggis[18] and Hakimy[19] give long lists of appropriate codes of behaviour for women.

But once married, women also had their ways to control their own lives. Loeb writes that according to Minangkabau *adat* 'a man neither gains possession of a woman by marriage nor a woman a man.... The Minangkabau man has no rights over his wife other than to demand that she remain faithful to him.'[20] He further observes that if a woman wanted a divorce, she would simply change her sleeping quarters. The husband would thus know that he was no longer wanted and would disappear. Many informants told us about this practice, stressing that in earlier days it was much easier for a woman to force a husband to leave her. Many Minangkabau people, men and women, stated emphatically that rape and wife-beating were unheard of in the old days, and even now are extremely rare.

Relationships between related women were strong. Not only did they collectively own their property (although fields were allocated to a woman upon her marriage for her individual use), they also performed many tasks together.

The introduction of Islam

Islam was probably introduced into the animistic and partly Hinduized Minangkabau region around the beginning of the sixteenth century. It did not spread very fast. Well into that century Minangkabau was still reported to be 'largely heathen'.[21] Well into the eighteenth century, Islam was characterized by strong mystic influences. Rather than changing the regulations of *adat*, Islam provided a new system of meaning.[22]

By the end of the eighteenth century, zealous Muslim reformers, the Padri, some of them returned from a pilgrimage to Mecca, started a militant campaign to purify Islam. In 1821, some *adat* chiefs called upon the Dutch to intervene. From then on, the war of religious purification turned into a war of independence. Dobbin has shown that one of the factors which gave rise to the Padri war was the desire to give more force to Islamic law in inheritance and other property affairs.[23] Thus the Padri war can be seen as one of the earliest examples in the Minangkabau of patrilinear Islam infringing upon matrilinear *adat*. The Padri war ended in 1830 in a Dutch victory.

By that time a delineation of power between Islam and *adat* had grown. The *penghulu* and other *adat* chiefs wielded political power, the religious leaders governed the spiritual realm. But this does not mean that the relationship between the *adat* and the *syaria* (Islamic law) was static. For the Minangkabau people the two belonged together, constructing the specific identity of Minangkabau society. The main saying concerning the relationship between these two systems is: *adat* is based on *syaria*, and *syaria* is based on *adat*. Thus, Islam in a sense legitimized the value of *adat*.

However, as Van Eerde remarked in 1901, 'in his heart every Malay (sic) has more affection for his own children than for his *kemanakan*, and this feeling is a powerful ally for Islam, which is slowly threatening to supplant the matriarchal *adat*.'[24] The relationship between *adat* and Islam is evidently complex and the historical development of both systems indicates that both *syaria* and the *adat* structure and the relationship between them have been constantly and still are being modified.

Colonial domination

After the end of the Padri war, the Dutch established control of the Minangkabau region. A system of forced cultivation of cash crops, mainly coffee, was introduced. The peasants were compelled to deliver their produce to the Dutch at low fixed prices. At the same time, a ban on the export of rice was imposed. The system was not so successful as the Dutch had hoped it would be, as many people evaded these restrictions.[25]

Despite promises never to introduce taxes, the Dutch did so after 1880, when the coffee cultivation did not yield enough revenue. A few tax revolts followed, which were suppressed. As the *mamak* were taxed (and not the women, which would have been more logical), men were forced to earn money now, and the traditional pattern of migration changed in character. Men now left the villages for longer periods of time. This development was stimulated by the fact that more opportunities for wage labour opened up for men outside of agriculture.

Politically, colonial rule had serious implications for the Minangkabau egalitarian and democratic system. The Dutch tried to influence local politics by strengthening the power of the *nagari* councils which were under their control. Their aim was to create a more 'rational', hierarchical and unicentric local government organization.[26] Thus the Dutch imposed a supra-*nagari* rule and at the same time tried to prevent the free working of traditional politics. Traditional *adat* institutions were rigidified as titles became more strictly vested in certain individuals and groups. Formerly, the method of selecting *penghulu* was based on family and lineage rivalry, which made it possible for persons from lower ranking families to move to the top. The Dutch effectively stopped this rotation of power. The only way upward for 'middle-class families' now became the new colonial civil service.[27]

In the meantime, a new political actor had appeared on the scene, the Communist Party. When the *Sarekat Islam* (SI) was founded in Java in 1912, it soon acquired a big following in Minangkabau. This Islamic revivalist movement, which was based on national trade interests, also contained progressive socio-economic ideas. The left wing of the SI was one of the founding groups of the Partai Komunis Indonesia (PKI) in 1922.

The PKI became strong in Western Sumatra by instigating protest meetings against the taxes imposed by the Dutch. Both the *adat* chiefs and the Dutch colonial administration were opposed to them. In 1926/27, the first Communist uprising took place. It was particularly strong in the Minangkabau, where PKI members attacked both the *adat* chiefs and native and Dutch officials.[28] The uprising was soon repressed, and many followers, including women, were sent to detention camps, such as Boven Digoel in what is now called Irian Jaya.

By the beginning of the twentieth century, the Dutch had introduced a system of formal education to train 'native' bureaucrats. According to Graves,[29] the Minangkabau responded more eagerly to these new opportunities for upward mobility than many other Indonesian ethnic groups. Two factors are of special importance here: the *rantau*, by which young men sought prestige outside the home, and the Minangkabau traditional family system, by which resources were pooled to help a member of the next generation. Young men who could no longer aspire to social mobility by traditional methods, looked to the school system as a way for their advancement.

At the same time, another Islamic reform movement started, the Kaum Muda (the Young Ones). The influential Datuk Sutan Maharadja was a proponent of a liberalized *adat* which was in line with a modernized Islam. He stressed the democratic foundations of both systems. His followers in the Kaum Muda stressed modernization, democracy and the importance of women's role in society. These reformists modernized the existing religious schools by introducing a classical system, a new curriculum and new teaching methods.[30] The graduates of these private religious schools formed the backbone of the opposition to the colonial system.

The significant changes caused by the imposition of colonial rule thus were in the political and socio-economic realm. Politically the traditional system of Minangkabau *nagari* democracy was undermined. Yet the Dutch did not fully succeed in their attempt to set up a more 'rational' hierarchical system of government.

The major effects of the socio-economic changes introduced by the Dutch were on land tenure and migration. After the 1930s, the migration pattern changed; men would sometimes take their families with them. Through their wage earnings, the importance of men's *harta pencarian* increased, and with it, the attempts of men to give this property to their own children, rather than to those of their sisters. The wives of successful men who followed their husbands lost their direct access to land, houses, and support from their relatives. For the first time a pattern of nuclear family residence was established.

The growing monetization of the Minangkabau economy with the introduction of the system of forced cultivation and taxation decreased the importance of the subsistence economy.

Gender relations and women's interests

The changes outlined above had critical consequences for women.

In the first place, women's workloads increased and the sexual division of labour changed. Formerly, men would divide their time between work on the fields of their wives and their sisters. With increased male migration, women had to step up their efforts to work in the fields and in some cases they also had to take over tasks which men used to do. Furthermore, the relative economic importance of the subsistence sector, in which women were mainly employed, decreased.

Secondly, the roles of men in general and that of the *mamak* in particular were strengthened. Women used to control the purse strings. Now the *mamak* were responsible for paying the taxes. In general, as the monetization of the economy increased, so did the status of those who had easier access to opportunities to earn money, that is, men.

Thirdly women were not given access to a new avenue to upward social mobility—education.

Fourthly, as the political system became more hierarchical, the role of women in decision making decreased. This development was strengthened by the fact that the power base of women, their control over the communal land, lost its importance in relation to the new socio-economic sectors.

Fifthly, although Minangkabau women could still divorce their husbands relatively easily, in some cases women were denied divorce. This occurrred particularly when a woman's claim for divorce was brought before the Dutch administrators, who referred to the religious officials, with the result that the claim was almost always rejected.[31]

Finally, increase in the number of nuclear families supported patrilinear patterns of inheritance.

The transformations outlined above and the consequences for gender relations were felt very unevenly. In the period before 1942, many of these processes had barely started. However, the trends have continued through the following years.

Women's organizations

As in other parts of Indonesia, women's organizations were formed in Minangkabau from the beginning of the twentieth century. The women's groups concerned themselves mainly with education for women, marriage reforms, political reforms and women's access to religious instruction.

One of the most well-known pioneers of the Minangkabau women's movement was Rohana Kudus. She was the daughter of Datuk Sutan Maharadja. He taught her how to read and write at home, in the village of Kota Gadang, near Bukittinggi. Born in 1884, she is reported to have started writing in 1899. In 1905 she established the first school for women, Amai Setia (the Faithful Woman). The topics taught included general knowledge and women's affairs. Between 1911 and 1924, she worked as the first Indonesian woman journalist, contributing articles to the periodicals run by her father (*Utusan Melayu*, Malayan Messenger) and her husband (*Tjaja Sumatera*, Sumatran Glow).

With the support of her father, she founded the first Indonesian women's paper, *Sunting Melayu* (Malayan Headdress). Her co-editor was Zubaidah Ratna Juwita. Together they wrote about issues such as the evil consequences of polygamy for women, religious education, colonial domination and beauty contests. Later she founded another women's periodical, *Suara Perempuan* (Women's Voice).

In an interview when she was already 82 years old, Rohana Kudus stated that for her the reason to work in journalism was her desire to safeguard the regulations of Islam and *adat* for women, which were changing fast: 'At that time many young Minangkabau men started to leave their homes to get scientific knowledge, while the girls were kept secluded.... If we want to get a healthy equilibrium between young men and young women, we women must get the same chances as the men to go out into the world to look for knowledge.'

Rohana Kudus also founded the major women's organization in Minangkabau, the Serikat Kaum Ibu Sumatera (SKIS) or the Union of Sumatran Women in 1911. It had its own periodical, called *Al Sjarq* (the East), which was later changed to *Suara Kaum Ibu Sumatera* (Voice of Sumatran Women). In 1925 Rohana Kudus had succeeded in bringing all women's groups under the umbrella of SKIS. By 1928 it had branches in seven cities in Minangkabau. Representatives of SKIS attended the first Indonesian women's congress which was held in Yogyakarta in 1928.

In 1911 Kudus's school became the Association of Keradjinan Amai Setia (Activity of the Faithful Woman) (KAS). It acquired legal status in 1915. Its curriculum included reading, writing and arithmetic, besides needlework and cooking. In principle, all woman of Kota Gadang were members of the Association. Its activities extended to the promotion and sale of handicrafts to supply the members with an income. In 1914 and 1919, lotteries were organized to pay for the school building and to purchase materials. In its statutes it is emphatically stated that the main purpose of KAS was to 'improve the position of Minangkabau women'.

The Kaum Muda movement inspired another woman, Rahmah El Yunusiya, to set up a women's koran school in Padang Panjang in 1923, the Sekolah Diniyah Putri (Religious School for Girls). This school tried to fulfil the growing desire of women to get religious education. It is still the largest school of its kind in Indonesia.

What did Minangkabau women see as their major interests in those days? It is clear that the desire for both secular and religious education was foremost in their minds. The Kaum Muda movement helped set the climate in which such demands could be voiced.

Another issue they were concerned with was polygamy and marriage reforms in general. Women's periodicals carried articles against polygamy, while SKIS advocated marriage reforms. Polygamy was an important social issue at the time. Various novels of the period depict the unhappy fate of women in polygamous marriages. Only Islamic women's organizations, such as Aisya, supported polygamy.

At a congress of Aisyah in Bukittinggi in 1932, representatives of SKIS spoke out against polygamy.[32] Polygamy was relatively widespread in Minangkabau. While the 1930 national census gives a figure of 1.9 per cent polygamous marriages for Jawa and Madura, the figure for Minangkabau is 8.7 per cent.[33] The fight against polygamy was one of the central issues of the Indonesian women's movement before World War II. Due to concerted efforts of the women's movement in the middle of the twentieth century, a *talik* was added to the *talak*, the formula a man should pronounce three times to divorce his wife. The *talik* specifies the conditions in a marriage contract under which a man is obliged to grant his wife a divorce.

Women were also politically active. SKIS advocated that women should have the right to vote and be elected in the municipal councils which had been set up by the Dutch.[34] But SKIS never allied itself to any political movement established before World War II. Increase of women's political power was perceived as women's interest, but women's organizations did not make any major impact on the formal power structure.

However, the fact that women's organizations were at all set up and that women spoke up in the political domain and in the major periodicals of their time, and even started their own journals, can be seen as important achievements in themselves.

The period between 1965 and 1985

After independence in 1950, President Soekarno put his considerable charisma and energy into building a nation and stressed the importance of the construction of Jakarta as a modern capital, the seat of government, and the main center of commerce and industry. The process of nation building obscured the regional and cultural differences among the many ethnic groups.

In Sumatra the first decade after independence was characterized by increasing disenchantment with national politics and growing tensions between Islamic and Communist groups. This culminated in a regional uprising between 1958 and 1962. The blood bath which followed the coup of October 1965 was very severe in western Sumatra.

Under the New Order of General Soeharto, all political activities have been curbed. Modernization and development are the key words, to be implemented via a centralized, hierarchical government dominated by military interests. The national bureaucracy has extended its grip on the traditional power structures to such an extent that the old system of *nagari* democracy has been destroyed and replaced by the hierarchical power structure, Javanese style. In 1982 the function of *nagari* chief was abolished.

The emphasis on modernization and development by the government has had two major consequences for the Minangkabau: the growth of new sectors in the Minangkabau economy such as industry, transport and communication and administration, and the decline of agriculture, especially in the subsistence sector.

Trade also increased in importance in the period between 1966 and 1980. In these 'modern' sectors mainly men are employed. The proportion of agriculture, traditionally considered women's domain, declined from 56 per cent in 1966 to 35 per cent in 1980. Whereas the proportion of industry, transport, trade and administration together increased from 34 per cent in 1966 to 55 per cent in 1980.

Economic Activities by Sector, between 1966 and 1980 (%)

	1966	1970	1980
Gross domestic regional product at constant 1975 prices MRP	107092	135135	279848
Agriculture	60213	66507	99137
	(56.2)	(49.2)	(35.4)
Farm food crops	36695	40358	56363
	(34.2)	(29.8)	(20.1)
Industry	7771	11821	35748
	(7.2)	(8.7)	(12.7)
Transport and communication	5787	7509	25748
	(5.4)	(5.5)	(9.2)
Wholesale and retail trade	18868	23509	70561
	(17.6)	(17.3)	(25.2)
Public administration and defence	4018	12115	23435
	(3.7)	(8.9)	(8.3)
Other sectors	10435	13647	25219
	(9.7)	(10.1)	(9.0)

Source: Based on *West Sumatra in Figures, 1982*, BAPPEDA and *Kantor Statistik*, Sumatera Barat.

In 1960, a national land reform law was promulgated. In it provisions were made for maximum land holdings. This law, based on the original Dutch concept of 'private property', ran counter to several principles of Minangkabau *adat* regulations. Under this law land was supposed to be registered, after which it could be sold or inherited. The major implication for the Minangkabau was that the rule that *pencarian* property eventually should become *pusaka* property was considerably weakened. Also, it meant that *pusaka* land might eventually fall under the jurisdiction of this law.

The first attempt at implementation of this law was made by the Barisan Tani Indonesia or Indonesia Farmers' Front (BTI), which was one of the mass organizations linked to the PKI. Their actions met with great resistance from the traditional *adat* chiefs.

After the coup of October 1965, attempts to implement the new law were temporarily halted. Researchers carrying out fieldwork in the 1970s present ambivalent data as to its effects. F. and K. von Benda-Beckmann report that 'knowledge of the law by Minang villagers is rare, and conversion of *adat* rights to the new rights of individual property is minimal so far.[35] Kahn observes that the rules of pledging have relaxed, in the sense that there are many cases in which cash obtained from pledging land is used for purposes of trade or of financing a craft.[36] Gura's research, carried out in the 1970s, indicates that more land has become individually owned and that inheritance rules are changing. She points to the increasing landlessness of women. In the four villages in which she carried out fieldwork, only 40 per cent of the women still held usufructuary rights to matrilineally inherited rice land.[37]

We ourselves carried out two surveys, one in the village of Baruah, near Bukittinggi, the other one in a quarter of Bukittinggi itself.[38] The experience we gained, led us to the following conclusions:

- There was great discrepancy in land rights between the town and the countryside. As could be expected, private ownership was much more common in Bukittinggi.
- Although many people voiced their disagreement with the new agrarian law and many women specifically said they refused to register their land, even in the village of Baruah several households stated emphatically that they considered their land to be 'private property' (*hak milik*).
- Half the households we interviewed in Baruah did not have any access to land at all.

Obviously, the system of land rights is undergoing a transformation in Minangkabau. Although the matrilinear communal ideology is still strong, communal land rights are gradually giving way to individual rights, and property relations are becoming monetized.

The motor behind this uneven, halting process is no longer the leftist Farmers' Union, but a government instrument, the Agrarian Office. According to officials at the Agrarian Office of Bukittinggi, mainly men ask for land certificates which they need as bank guarantees for purposes of trade or the purchase of cars.[39] The following tables show the increase in the number of certificates issued between 1979 and 1983 in Bukittinggi.

Land Registration in Bukittinggi

Year	M	B	P	H/C
1979/80	135	22	-	52
1980/81	126	43	4	118
1981/82	1112	74	6	132
1982/83	213	50	-	242
Total	1582	189	10	544

Source: *Bukittinggi Dalam Angka*, Kerjasama BAPPEDA, Bukittinggi, *Kantor Statistik, 1983*. M: private property, B: construction, P: official use, H/C: mortgage or credit.

Changes in Certification in Bukittinggi

Year	Private property	Construction
1979/80	171	26
1980/81	150	17
1981/82	265	16
1982/83	265	33
Total	842	92

Source: *Bukittinggi Dalam Angka*, Kerjasama BAPPEDA, Bukittinggi, *Kantor Statistik, 1983*.

The total population of Bukittinggi in 1982 was 70,000. Although the number of certificates was not large, it is evident that it was already an accepted practice to monetize land for purposes not indicated in *adat* regulations; and contrary to all *adat* provisions, land deeds were being given to individuals, in many cases to men.

The officials at the Agrarian Office were not able to tell us what percentage of the certificates issued was given to men, but they did indicate that that was indeed the most common practice.

Implications for gender relations and women's interests

The hierarchy imposed on Minangkabau society and the erosion of women's communal land rights have seriously weakened women's political and legal position. Women are hardly represented in the regional parliament and the local councils, and they have no access to the state courts. Thus, if women's communal land rights have been violated by their formal representatives, they are not able to sue them. If, for instance, a *mamak* registers clan land under his name and sells it (illegal under *adat* regulations), the women of the *kaum* have no legal ways to retrieve their land.[40]

Unification of the Indonesian law, therefore, implies that local *adat* traditions are being undermined. In Minangkabau this process entails a reduction of *pusaka* land, individual registration of *pencarian* land, an individualization of legal status to the detriment of clan rights, and a shift towards patrilinear inheritance patterns, based on the *syaria*.

Another process which encroaches upon women's traditional *adat* rights, is the hierarchical, male-oriented process of development based on national prerogatives. Gura[41] reports despite the fact that the majority of the rice fields is still under the control of women, male agricultural extension agents are dispensing seeds and fertilizers to men. And K. von Benda-Beckmann[42] observes that the whole direction of development is male-biased, with male administrators and male development project officers negotiating with the male lineage representatives, taking decisions which women have to carry out.

Men are seen as heads of 'their' families (that is, of their wives and children), exercising control over land their wives have rights to, land which does not belong to their own lineage. Men are given access to credit, not women.

In our fieldwork too we encountered numerous women who had similar complaints. In one case a man refused to allow his sisters to take the necessary steps to get credit for a tractor which they needed to plough their land as they were too old to do the work themselves. As a result the land remained fallow.

Minang identity rests on matrilineally inherited communally-owned land. The national government has started a concerted drive to introduce the land laws of 1960 which has grave implications for this system. Women do realize that. In Baruah many women refused to get their land registered. Men welcome the change. With a certificate, they can mortgage the land to buy a car. Thus these new regulations increase the tensions between the sexes.

If gender relations are becoming more skewed within agriculture, other socio-economic developments are aggravating this trend. I have already pointed to the decreasing importance of agriculture in relation to other, male-dominated sectors. Women do enter into these sectors, but in far smaller numbers and under more unfavourable conditions. As Naim notes, women workers in industry and the service sector are seen as 'second class citizens'. They generally work in low-paid, monotonous, mechanical jobs.[43]

Thus, women lose out both in the fields and in the cities. As men migrate from the villages, women are left behind to work on their rice fields. Baruah is inhabited by twice as many women than men. They complained that there is not enough male labour available to carry out the tasks traditionally assigned to men, such as ploughing and digging. Rich women solve this problem by hiring male labourers. Poorer women try to do this work themselves.

Another problem is that the exchange rate between the cities and the countryside is changing. The price of rice is controlled, as the government tries to keep the cost of living in the cities down. As a consequence, women receive proportionally less for their labour. 'Formerly', they say, 'you could sell one kg of rice on the market and eat well from the proceeds. Now you have to sell at least 5 kg of rice for one proper meal.' Apart from that, their expenses have risen. Especially, the cost of educating their children. Children are still supposed to be their mothers' responsibility and men contribute reluctantly to their education. They say that formerly you were rich if you had access to many rice fields. Now it is almost impossible to send your children to school if you have to live off your land.

The monetization of society and the fact that men have much

easier access to money have considerably strengthened men's position *vis-à-vis* their women. Wives and sisters compete for their money and men are able to demand more in return. There is a particularly sexist saying which is heard more and more: 'Women have to take good care of three spaces—the room, which has to be clean and smell nice, their mouths, that is, they have to be able to cook delicious dishes, and "below", to perform well while sleeping with their husbands.'

Women who used to control the purse strings through their control of the products from the land, now find themselves responsible for domestic labour and dependent upon the money income of men. The erosion of women's legal and socio-economic rights is reflected in an increasing male control over women's sexuality and in changing marriage relations.

As we noted above, divorce used to be relatively easy for both men and women. Today it remains easy for men, while women are dissuaded in several ways. The word *janda* (widow or divorced woman) has acquired a negative connotation. There are also strong economic reasons not to get divorced from a disagreeable husband: children who used to be economic assets, are now an economic burden. Divorced men rarely contribute to the education of their children.

Although the strict *adat* rules for marriage have been relaxed, and young people seem to be freer in the choice of a spouse, many women said that polygamy among men actually seems on the increase. In our fieldwork we were confronted with a significant number of polygamous marriages by men. We counted eight cases among the 20 interviewed households of Baruah, and seven out of the 30 in Panorama, where the neighbourhood head denied to us that there were any polygamous marriages. They did not show up in his statistics either, as polygamy is prohibited under the new marriage law.

Women are caught in a vicious circle. They have to be very careful to keep their husbands. To do so they have to consent to have many children. Having many children proves that a man is sexually and economically powerful. In the process, a woman is manoeuvred into a dependent position.

The issues mentioned here are not the only problems Minang women face. As Indonesian women they share the concerns of other women in their society. In their preparatory paper for the

1985 Nairobi NGO Forum, Kowani, the national umbrella women's organization, cautiously reminds the readers that although the Indonesian constitution guarantees equal rights for women, there are still certain shortcomings. The paper indicates that women are lagging behind men in education, employment, political representation; that there is still a high level of maternal mortality; and that the family planning programme has not yet achieved much success.[44]

Women's organizations in the Minangkabau, 1965–1985

During our fieldwork in Bukittinggi, we tried to get as much information as possible on the women's organizations I had already done some work on in Java. They were Perwari, Gerwani, Aisyah, Dharma Wanita and PKK. We also worked with a regional organization, the Bundo Kanduang. There are more women's groups and organizations, but the ones mentioned above, apart from Gerwani which no longer exists, are the most visible ones and they cover the whole range of independent, religious, and government-oriented women's organizations. Here I will only deal with the Bundo Kanduang and the government organization of Dharma Wanita.

Bundo Kanduang

In 1960, the Lembaga Kerapatan Adat Alam Minangkabau (LKAAM), or the Institution for Meeting on the *Adat* of the Minangkabau, was established. It was an organization of *adat* chiefs who wanted to preserve the *adat* structure of Minangkabau society. At that time one of its main goals was to oppose the PKI. Ten years later, its women's wing, the Bundo Kanduang, came into being. The organization is named after the mythical mother of Minang society.

According to Ibu Jamilah Jambek, chairwoman of the Bukittinggi branch of the Bundo Kanduang, the organization was set up at the request of women. The *adat* chiefs of the LKAAM invited some prominent Minangkabau women to a meeting in Payakumbuh where the Bundo Kanduang was officially founded. Ibu Jamilah Jambek was present too, and she delivered a speech, explaining why it was important for women to preserve the *adat* rules. In 1974, both the LKAAM and the Bundo Kanduang joined the government party, the Golkar, by which they are now controlled.

The organization has some 100 members, many of whom are *limpape* such as Jambek herself, but in principle all Minang women who support the *adat* can join. From the age of 16 the daughters can participate in its youth wing, the Puteri Bungsu (Young Daughters). Once a month members come together to listen to a lecture on the *adat*. These are mainly given by the *penghulu* of the LKAAM, such as Rasjid Manggis. Members of the Bundo Kanduang themselves also teach about the *adat*, mainly in other women's organizations, such as branches of the Dharma Wanita or the PKK. This is not easy; according to Jambek: 'It is difficult to teach the exact *adat* rules, for they used to be orally transmitted. So how can you know what is correct? Fortunately now some of the *penghulu* such as Idrus Hakimy and Rasjid Manggis have written down their knowledge. But then, this is the reason why the Bundo Kanduang is so important, to preserve our traditional ways with land, inheritance and the position of women in the Minangkabau.'

So what do the male *penghulu* teach the members of Bundo Kanduang about their position in society? The best source is a booklet by Hakimy, called Guidebook on Bundo Kanduang in Minangkabau (1978). Hakimy carries the title of *datoek rajo penghulu*, a very high *adat* title, and is the chairperson of the section on *adat* and *syarak* of the LKAAM.

Hakimy explains the meaning of the words Bundo Kanduang as the genuine woman, one who possesses the 'properties of womanhood and leadership'; she is the 'broker between the generations', who has to position herself on the regulations of *adat*, keeping in mind that the *adat* is based on the *syaria*. The position of Minangkabau women is characterized by five issues: matrilinearity, the home as a place for women, their economic importance in relation to the fields, the fishponds and their products, women's control over storing the products of the fields, and the fact that they have a voice in the councils, where they have the same rights as men do. Interestingly, Hakimy does not refer to women's political position elsewhere in his book.

He does deal with women's communal land rights. Among the duties of a genuine woman, he stresses that it is their duty to guard the totality of the *harta pusaka'* and to 'prohibit men from pawning the land for needs not sanctioned by *adat'*. How they can do that he does not explain, as women's legal means are extremely limited. He does not discuss the ambiguities inherent in trying to safeguard a regional structure which is contradictory to national law. A major part of the book is devoted to women's moral behaviour. Apparently as guardians of the *adat*, women's conduct is a crucial factor. There are long lists of what is prohibited to a genuine woman, and how she can guard her good name. Prohibited are amongs others: to destroy the unity of other families, to spread gossip and lies, to be gross, impolite and jealous, to lose one's leadership qualities, and to have the attitude of a man. There are 12 other mistakes that women must avoid (the count is only six for men, and the mistakes are not even listed). Some of these are: to sit, stand, or walk, when there is no special reason for it, in places where there are many men; to dress like a man; to carry out men's work; or in general to have social contact with men.

A good Minang woman is modest, has a sense of shame, keeps the household in order, guards Islam, attends to her husband's physical and spiritual needs, wards off the advances of other men, and teaches all this proper behaviour to other female members of the household.

If Hakimy's writings are anything to go by, the teachings of the LKAAM are mainly concerned with women's moral conduct. The women's organization has no power to legally safeguard their traditional *adat* rights. Bundo Kanduang is to Minang women what the horned ornaments on the roofs of government buildings are to Minang *nagari* democracy, an empty symbol, a cultural adornment to a hierarchical national system in which all aspects of regional identity are subordinated. Even if the leaders deplore the erosion of women's *adat* rights, they cannot defend the interests of Minang women. They are only allowed to stress the *adat* regulations in areas which are in line with government policy.

Dharma Wanita

After the coup of 1965 the Indonesian government took a right-wing turn. The women's movement which had played a vocal role in politics, especially through Gerwani, had to be restructured and its members forced to support the government. Not only was Gerwani destroyed, but eventually the programmes of all other women's organizations were affected. Before the beginning of the 1970s, there used to be women's groups consisting of female civil servants. Sometimes wives of male civil servants joined, but the main concern of the groups was defending the interests of the women actually working in the government. These groups were restructured and brought under strict government control. By 1974 they were centralized and brought together under two main umbrellas, the Dharma Wanita for all civil institutions, and the Dharma Pertiwi for the armed forces and the police. Every government department has its own Dharma Wanita Unit under its own name.

The organization no longer defends the interests of women working in the these institutions. It now organizes the wives of the men who work here, to support the government in its policies and to further the careers of their husbands. The first article of the statutes of Dharma Wanita stipulates that all wives of men working in government institutions are members. Thus their membership is obligatory, and the dues are deducted from the husbands' wages. Women working in these institutions, widows of men who have worked there or wives of retired men may also become members, but they have to submit a written request to be approved by the leadership of Dharma Wanita. The membership stops when a member dies, or when her husband is no longer employed by the government.

The structure is vertical. Wives of government ministers form the presidium which is responsible for the policies of the lower level Dharma Wanita group, which again is responsible for the next level and so on. The wife of each minister is the chairperson of the Dharma Wanita Unit of that department. Likewise the lower levels follow the structure of the male hierarchy. The president of the Indonesian Republic is the Ultimate Guide of Dharma Wanita, who decides on Dharma Wanita policy. His wife is the Ultimate Advisor.

These statutes, drawn up at the highest levels of the hierarchy, stipulate the duties of Dharma Wanita members: they must respect the government and the guidelines of the Dharma Wanita; they are not allowed to become members of a political organization not in line with the organization's policies; and they have to support their husbands in their tasks related to the development of the country.

In practice this means that members of Dharma Wanita are only allowed to be active in the government party, the Golkar. They have to help the military leaders win the elections. Also, they are present when important guests are to be received, wearing special uniforms for official occasions.

Bhayangkari, the organization of the wives of police officers, illustrates some of the issues mentioned above. Although the organization falls under the Dharma Pertiwi umbrella, its history is very like that of the member organizations of Dharma Wanita. Set up during the war of independence, Bhayangkari joined the other women's organizations after independence, in their struggle for a better marriage law and the repeal of an act which would grant all widows of a civil servant the right to a pension, thereby sanctioning polygamy. These were the demands which Bhayangkari put forward in the campaign for the 1955 elections.

As a 'logical consequence' of the changes after 1965, the wives of all armed forces were integrated and the structure of the organization was changed. In 1971 the wife of the highest police officer automatically became the head of Bhayangkari. The same year, in preparation for the 1971 elections, the organization's priorities were shifted from the demand for a more enlightened marriage law (which still had not been passed at that time) to helping Golkar win the elections. Bhayangkari had the same objectives in the 1977 elections. The demands based on women's interests had disappeared from its agenda.[45]

The Dharma Wanita women are expected to play many roles simultaneously, as dedicated wives and mothers and in all kinds of government programmes, such as family planning, nutrition and health. To solve the practical difficulties, Dharma Wanita had to give a course in how to change uniforms quickly: the Dharma Wanita uniform is different from the PKK uniform, which again is different from the Korpri uniform, and none of these can be worn on some semi-official occasions when the national dress for women, the *kain kebaya*, has to be worn.

The women are given all support necessary by the offices they belong to. Many government offices have a special Dharma

Wanita desk. Wives of important men, like mayors, may be extremely busy with these tasks. And although they may resent it very much, they had better do it all if they do not want to destroy their husbands' careers.

Reactions to Dharma Wanita vary widely among the members. Most women we spoke to abhorred the organization and everything connected with it—all the empty activities consuming time and money. Many women resented the fact that their involvement with the Dharma Wanita prevented them from taking up a paid job of their own. But some wives of senior civil servants also seemed to enjoy the power they derived from it. And younger wives who apparently had already grown used to their role as housewives, welcomed the change the meetings brought in their daily routine. Some mentioned it gave them a chance to mingle with the 'high society'. Other young women resented the fact that the older women, or at least the wives of the bosses, had all the power, while they, however competent they were, had no influence at all.

They all agreed that the nature of the organizations now under the Dharma Wanita umbrella is very much changed and that women's interests are not addressed any more. There is no forum, they said, where they could discuss problems they had in the labour force, polygamy or other issues of discrimination against them.

The organization is not only authoritarian, and set up to represent the interests of the government rather than that of its members, it is also modelled on the military leadership's ideas of kinship and women's role in the family—ideas based on the upper-class Javanese model mixed with middle-class European values, all of it alien to Minangkabau society. The matrilinear Minang *adat* classified women according to their position in the matriclans; their husbands' positions had very little to do with that. They were not appendages of their men, but members of a society which granted them important economic, social and political rights.

Conclusion

Thus neither Bundo Kanduang nor Dharma Wanita are able to defend the interests of Minang women. The leaders of Bundo

Kanduang do see the defence of *adat* rights as their objective, but are unable to effectively challenge government policies which erode those rights. Dharma Wanita members find themselves in an even more unfavourable position. Not only are they unable to define their own interests, the military leaders do that for them, but they also are mobilized to actively support policies which increase their subordination. They have thus earned the nickname of *Drama Wanita* (Women's Drama).

This situation is in strong contrast with that encountered before the Japanese invasion. As some women students from the University of Andalas, in Padang, said: 'It seems we have to start from zero, all over again.'

NOTES

1. Maxine Molyneux, 'Mobilisation without Emancipation? Women's interests, state and revolution in Nicaragua,' in: D. Slater (ed.), *New Social Movements and the State in Latin America*. Amsterdam: CEDLA, 1985.
2. Judith A. Cook, and Mary Margaret Fonow, 'Knowledge and Women's Interests: Issues of Epistemology and Methodology in Feminist Sociological Research,' in: Joyce McCarl Nielsen (ed.), *Feminist Research Methods, exemplary readings in the social sciences*. Boulder: Westview Press, 1990.
3. Anna G. Jónasdóttir, 'On the Concept of Interest, Women's Interests, and the Limitations of Interest Theory,' in: Kathleen B. Jones and Anna G. Jónasdóttir (eds.), *The Political Interests of Gender, developing theory and research with a feminist face*. London: Sage, 1988.
4. Hamka, *Islam dan adat Minangkabau*. Jakarta: Pustaka Panjimas, 1984.
5. Dt. Rajo Penghulu Idrus Hakimy, *Buku Pegangan Bundo Kanduang di Minangkabau*. Bandung: Rosda, 1975. And *Rangkaian Mustika Adat Basandi Syarak di Minangkabau*. 1978. Bandung: Rosda.
6. Dt. Radjo Panghoeloe M. Rasjid Manggis, *Sejarah ringkas Minangkabau dan adatnya*. Jakarta: Mutiara, 1982.
7. P.E. de Josselin de Jong, *Minangkabau and Negri Sembilan, socio political structure in Indonesia*. Den Haag: Nijhoff, 1980.
8. Dt. Rajo Penghulu Idrus Hakimy, 1978, op. cit. and Dt. Radjo Panghoeloe M. Rasjid Manggis, op. cit.

9. Quoted in Elisabeth E. Graves, *The Minangkabau Response to Dutch Colonial Rule in the Nineteenth Century*. Ithaca: Cornell University Press, 1981.

10. Edwin M. Loeb, *Sumatra, Its History and People*. Kuala Lumpur and Singapore: Oxford University Press, 1972.

11. Tsuyoshi Kato, *Matriliny and migration. Evolving Minangkabau traditions in Indonesia*. Ithaca: Cornell University Press, 1982.

12. Elisabeth E. Graves, op. cit.

13. Mochtar Naim, *Merantau. Pola migrasi suku Minangkabau*. Yogyakarta: Gadjah mada University Press, 1979.

14. G.D. Willinck, *Het rechtsleven bij de Miangkabausche Maleiers*. Leiden: Brill, 1909.

15. V.E. Korn, 'De vrouwelijke mama' in de Minangkabause familie,' in: *Bijdragen tot de Taal-, Land- en Volkenkunde*. 100, 1941.

16. Ibid.

17. Willinck quoted in Els Postel-Coster, *Het omheinde kweekbed, machtsverhoudingen in de Minangkabause familieroman*. Delft: Eburon, 1985. p. 49.

18. Dt. Radjo Panghoeloe M. Rasjid Manggis, op. cit.

19. Dt. Rajo Penghulu Idrus Hakimy, 1978, op. cit.

20. Edwin M. Loeb, op. cit. p. 111.

21. Elisabeth E. Graves, op. cit. p. 22.

22. Taufik Abdullah, 'Islam, history and social change in Minangkabau,' in: Lynn L. Thomas and Franz von Benda-Beckmann (eds.), *Change and Continuity in Minangkabau: local, regional and historical perspectives on West Sumatra*. Athens, Ohio: Ohio University Center for International Studies, 1985. p. 150.

23. Christine Dobbin, 'Economic change in Minangkabau as a factor in the rise of the Padri Movement, 1784 - 1830,' in: *Indonesia* 23, 1977.

24. Van Eerde quoted in Cora Vreede-de Stuers, *The Indonesian Woman, Struggles and Achievements*. Gravenhage: Mouton & Co, 1960.

25. Akira Oki, 'Economic constraints, social change and the communist uprising in West Sumatra (1926–27): a critical review of B. J. O. Schrieke's West Coast report,' in: Lynn L. Thomas and Franz von Benda-Beckmann, (eds.), op. cit.

26. Franz von and Keebet von Benda-Beckmann, 'Transformation and Change in Minangkabau,' in: Lynn L. Thomas and Franz von Benda-Beckmann, (eds.), op. cit.

27. Elisabeth E. Graves, op. cit. p. 42.

28. Akira Oki, op. cit.

29. Elisabeth E. Graves, op. cit.

30. Taufik Abdullah, *Schools and Politics: the Kaum Muda Movement in West Sumatra*. Ithaca: Cornell University Press, 1971.
31. Els Postel-Coster, op. cit, 1985. p. 47.
32. Cora Vreede-de Stuers, op. cit. p. 106.
33. Ibid. p. 104.
34. Nilakusuma, 'Sejarah Kemajuan Wanita di Sumatera Barat,' in: *Sejarah Sumatera Barat 1945–1975*. Padang: Kantor Gubernur Sumatera Barat, 1975.
35. Franz von and Keebet von Benda-Beckmann, op. cit. p. 276.
36. Joel S. Kahn, 'Tradition, matriliny and change among the Minangkabau in Indonesia,' in: *Bijdragen tot de Taal-, Land- en Volkenkunde*. 132, 1976. p. 74.
37. Susanna Gura, *Die sozialökonomische Rolle der Frauen in der ländlichen Entwicklung West-Sumatras*. Saarbrücken: Breitenbach Publ., 1983.
38. Saskia Wieringa, Dida Pattipilohi and Pamela Pattynama, *Women's Organizations in Indonesia*. The Hague: ISS, research report, 1985.
39. Interview, Agrarian Office Bukittinggi, 29 October 1984.
40. Keebet von Benda-Beckmann, 'Development, Law and Gender-skewing: an examination of the impact of development on the socio-legal position of Indonesian women, with special reference to Minangkabau.' paper presented at XIIth Congress of the IUAES, Zagreb, July 1988.
41. Susanna Gura, op. cit.
42. Keebet von Benda-Beckmann, 'Development, Law and Gender-skewing,' op. cit.
43. Mochtar Naim, 'Wanita Minangkabau dalam lapangan kerja,' in: *Kumpulan naskah simposium, 'pengaruh adat-istiadat Minangkabau terhadap kehidupan wanita, dalam mengenbangkan budaya bangsa'*. Jakarta, 7 April, 1983.
44. Kowani, Direktori Organisasi Wanita Indonesia, Jakarta, 1985.
45. Bhayangkari, *Seperempat abad Kesatuan Gerak Bhayangkari, 1952–1977*. Jakarta, 1978.